THE MELODY LINGERS ON

by

Marguerite and Terry Broadbent

The North West Player Piano Association
Wilmslow, Cheshire

By the same authors:

GREAT PIANISTS OF THE GOLDEN AGE

AN EDWARDIAN QUINTET

LEGINSKA - FORGOTTEN GENIUS OF MUSIC

Published by The North West Player Piano Association
Research Section: 49, Grange Park Avenue,
　　　　　　　　　　　Wilmslow,
　　　　　　　　　　　Cheshire, SK9 4AL.

Copyright © 1995 by Marguerite and Terry Broadbent

No part of this book may be reproduced, stored in a retrieval system, or transmitted in any form, or by any means electronic, mechanical, photocopying, recording or otherwise, without the prior permission of the copyright holders.

ISBN 0 9525101 1 1

Printed and bound by Danilo Printing Ltd.,
　　Unit C2, Enterprise Business Park,
　　Marsh Wall,
　　West India Dock,
　　London, E14 9TE.

Contents

Co-author's note and preface
Acknowledgments and picture credits

1.	Stephen Foster	1
2.	Cécile Chaminade	15
3.	Leslie Stuart	29
4.	Scott Joplin	41
5.	Jerome Kern	53
6.	Irving Berlin	73
7.	Ferdinand 'Jelly Roll' Morton	93
8.	Cole Porter	109
9.	George Gershwin	129
10.	Thomas 'Fats' Waller	145

Bibliography	166
Recordings	170
Appendices	172

Compositions of the musicians:
1.	*Stephen Foster*	172
2.	*Cécile Chaminade*	173
3.	*Leslie Stuart*	175
4.	*Scott Joplin*	176
5.	*Jerome Kern*	177
6.	*Irving Berlin*	179
7.	*'Jelly Roll' Morton*	181
8.	*Cole Porter*	182
9.	*George Gershwin*	184
10.	*'Fats' Waller*	186

Index   187

The musicians are presented in chronological order of their birthdates but the chapters are self-contained and may be read in any order.

Co-Author's Note

Marguerite and I wrote the articles on popular musicians as part of our 'Famous Musicians' series for the North West Player Piano Association. After Marguerite's sad death in April 1994 it seemed that publication of all the Famous Musicians articles, in three books with appropriate titles, would be a fitting tribute to Marguerite who had spent so much time and effort in helping to research and write them. 'The Song Is Ended - But The Melody Lingers On'. To me, this theme applies to Marguerite, as well as to the people we wrote about in this book.

Terry Broadbent

April 1995

Preface

This book tells the story of ten musicians who were the composers, and in some cases performers, of popular music. There are two song writers from a bygone era, Stephen Foster and Leslie Stuart, and other great song writers, from more recent times - the "big four" of Jerome Kern, Irving Berlin, George Gershwin and Cole Porter. Scott Joplin was the undisputed King of Ragtime. Cécile Chaminade's compositions were dismissed contemptuously by most of the critics of her day as 'salon music', but they were truly popular by virtue of the fact that the public, especially women, loved them. To complete the ten, there are two great names from the jazz era, 'Jelly Roll' Morton and 'Fats' Waller, contrasting in their styles but both immensely popular . Through their great talent these ten musicians have given pleasure to millions. The world is a richer place as a result.

Acknowledgments

Thanks are due to many friends for numerous interesting discussions about musicians, to Judith Broadbent, Susan Clews and Raymond Ince for reading the proofs of this book, and to Nigel Clews for advice on computer software. The title of the book is from a line of one of Irving Berlin's songs. His skill as a songwriter and provider of apt phrases is duly acknowledged.

Picture Credits

The picture of Stephen Foster and the photographs of Cécile Chaminade, Leslie Stuart, Scott Joplin, Jerome Kern, Irving Berlin, 'Jelly Roll' Morton, Cole Porter and George Gershwin are published by permission of the Hulton Deutsch Collection Ltd., which holds the copyright. The photograph of 'Fats' Waller was donated by EMI Ltd. and is reproduced with their permission. The help of The Hulton Deutsch Collection Ltd. and EMI Ltd. in providing suitable photographs is acknowledged.

The Melody Lingers On

Stephen Foster

Facing page 1

1. Stephen Foster

Stephen Foster lived and died long before the first phonograph needle tracked its scratchy path along a tinfoil-coated cylinder, and even longer before the first vacuum-operated player piano wheezed and creaked its way into action. Nevertheless he deserves a place in this book, for he was the first great American song writer and his best melodies live on 130 years after his death. If a good sing-song is wanted, the best songs of Stephen Foster are hard to beat.

Anyone familiar with Stephen Foster's so-called 'plantation songs' might be forgiven for thinking that he probably lived in the deep south of the United States. But it was not so. He was born and lived most of his life in Pittsburgh, Pennsylvania, the son of William Barclay Foster and his wife Eliza. William Barclay was a third generation Pennsylvanian of Irish ancestry. He married Eliza in 1807, and in 1814 bought a tract of land of 123 acres two miles north of Pittsburgh and established the town of Lawrenceville. William Barclay Foster was an entrepreneur of the true American style; his business interests were many, he dealt in real estate, canals, railways, and anything else where a profit might be made. He was also a local worthy, active in the political life of the district. At one time he was a member of the Pennsylvania State Legislature, and at various periods of his life held a number of minor public offices such as collector of canal tolls. His business success fluctuated over the years and the family were not always well off, though never poor. Everyone knew the Fosters as one of the leading families in Pittsburgh.

Ten children were born to William Barclay Foster and his wife, and they will be named here, with the year of their birth, as his family was to be important to Stephen, as we shall see later. In order of birth date the children were Ann Eliza (1808, lived six weeks), Charlotte (1809), Ann Eliza (1812, the second child to bear this name), William Barclay jr. (1814, lived four months), Henry Baldwin (1816), Henrietta (1818), Dunning (1821), Morrison (1823), Stephen Collins (1826) and James (1829, lived one and a half years). So, of the members of the family who survived infancy there were three girls and four boys, and Stephen was the youngest of the large family. The two closest in age to Stephen were Dunning and Morrison and they were also the ones nearest in companionship. In addition to all these children, a young relative of William Barclay Foster was adopted by the family around 1815 and lived as one of them. This boy, William, was older than all the Foster children so in effect became the eldest child. He was much respected by the others and later acted virtually as an extra parent, though he was always referred to as 'brother William'.

On the day that Stephen was born in 1826 there was rejoicing and dancing in the streets, bands played, and cannons fired salutes. But they were not heralding the arrival of America's great song writer. The truth of the matter was that it was American Independence Day, 4th July, and the 50th anniversary of the Declaration of Independence into the bargain. His mother decided that the child should be called Stephen Collins, after the son of one of her childhood friends, a little boy who had died just before Stephen was born. It was learned a day or so later that on the very day of Stephen's birth the second and third American Presidents had died, John Adams and Thomas Jefferson, and various people, including sister Charlotte, thought the new-born babe should be named Jefferson or Adams, or even Jefferson Adams. However, Eliza's mind was made up. Stephen Collins is what she had decided, and Stephen Collins is what his name was to be, in memory of the departed infant.

Tragedy struck the family when Stephen was three, for Charlotte died from an infectious illness at the age of 19. She was a bright, lively girl, talented at music and singing, and engaged to be married when death struck. This cast a shadow over the family for a long time. Though Stephen was too young to comprehend the tragedy, which was of a type all too familiar in those days, the music he had heard from his sister in the first three years of his life may have made a lasting impression. His childhood was unremarkable and there was little at first to indicate any particular talent. A contemporary letter speaks of how Stephen at five "has a drum and marches about whistling *Auld Lang Syne*. There remains something perfectly original about him." The family had a piano, on which Stephen no doubt experimented, but there is no account of his having had lessons. At five he attended the local infant school, and his eldest sister, Ann Eliza, also seems to have had a hand in tutoring him at home.

When Stephen was nearly seven he was taken for a trip on a river steamboat to Augusta, Kentucky, and also visited Cincinnati and Louisville, the whole trip taking six weeks. The outing provided the opportunity to see river and negro life at first hand and cannot fail to have impressed itself on Stephen's sensitive young mind. He used to hear negro music nearer home from his earliest years, for the Fosters had a negro 'bound boy' and 'bound girl', Thomas Hunter and Olivia Pine, who lived with and served the Fosters happily for many years. Olivia was a devout Christian who often took Stephen to her church, where he heard the singing and shouting which characterised negro worship. All these experiences were stored up in Stephen's mind for use later, and were re-enforced by what he saw and heard on visits to innumerable relatives.

At about eight Stephen continued his schooling, along with Morrison, at the local Allegheny academy, run by a clergyman, and seems to have done quite well there. Although he had an aversion to rigid discipline he worked hard at subjects that interested him, he was good at 'recitations' and liked nature. He seems to have been a quiet, dreamy child, usually content with his own company. Occasionally he visited his uncle John Struthers at Poland, Ohio. This uncle, then over 80, was one of the real American 'old-timers' and used to give Stephen the run of his large farm. Visits there were a delight to Stephen. Once when he was missed from the house he was found up to his neck in a pile of chaff watching the chickens and other animals, "just thinking", as he briefly explained. Uncle Struthers was always very taken with the child, and once prophesied that "Stephen will be something famous if he lives to be a man."

When Stephen was about nine the boys of local families formed a boys' theatre in a carriage house. He was regarded as a star performer. At that time minstrel shows had become all the rage in America, songs such as *Jim Crow* being particularly popular, and there were many touring companies. The boys had seen them and Stephen's imitations were so good that, child as he was, his performances were invariably greeted with uproarious applause, and he was paid a small retainer for the three-times weekly shows.

During the years of Stephen's childhood the family had moved house several times as William Barclay's business fortunes had variously waxed and waned, but all the time they lived in or around Pittsburgh. When Stephen was 13 he was sent to live with brother William, then making his way as an engineer on the railways at the town of Towanda, about 300 miles from Pittsburgh. William, a talented man, went on eventually to become Chief Engineer and Vice-President of the Pennsylvania Railroad. The purpose of sending Stephen to Towanda was to enable him to to attend the nearby Athens Academy with William *in loco parentis*. This he did, and he also attended another establishment, the Towanda Academy. In neither case were his studies particularly noteworthy. He was an attentive but unremarkable pupil, but as tuition in music was available at extra cost he may have received a little musical instruction. At any rate, various letters between relatives referred to Stephen's ability to play a variety of musical instruments including the flute and clarinet. Stephen's sojourn at these schools does not seem to have been particularly happy. Not surprisingly for one coming from so large a family he felt homesick, and the only aspects of school life which he really enjoyed were the concerts and plays, at which he excelled.

The most important fact of his stay was that he wrote a few tunes, including the *Tioga Waltz*, which was performed by three flutes on the school stage so successfully that encores were demanded. He clearly had a talent but there was no one to encourage and advise him; no one really understood what this unusual boy might best be fitted for, and he asked to come home. His mother was alone at the time except for her husband, as her large family had grown up and dispersed, and she was glad to have Stephen back, for company. So Stephen came home and at 15 (in July 1841) entered the local Jefferson College, Pittsburgh, where his father had been schooled. But this school suited him no better than the others, and in September of the same year his official schooling ended, though he may have had some private tuition. Stephen was becoming increasingly interested in music and would spend many hours improvising on the family piano. This was a concern to his parents, his father particularly, for no-one thought of music as a means of earning a living, and the problem was to find some sort of job for the drifting 'Stephy', who was happier in his room in the company of the family's tortoise-shell cat than in out-going pursuits which might lead to steady employment. An event of minor interest occurred in May 1842 when

Stephen was 15, for Charles Dickens visited Pittsburgh and Stephen's father, mayor of Allegheny (now part of Pittsburgh) at the time, took him to meet the great author, though no record remains of what was said.

At 16 Stephen was keeping a notebook of verses and melodies he had written. He had a pleasant singing voice and loved to sing and improvise on the popular ballads of the day. Stephen's father wrote that "The boy's leisure hours are all devoted to music", and Morrison told how "It was difficult to get him into any society at all. He had a great aversion to its shams and glitter and preferred the realities of his home and the quiet of his study." Stephen continued to drift and to dream, and to write songs (both words and music) for his own amusement, as well as to set to music the verses of others. His formal musical knowledge was rudimentary, and it is possible that a local music teacher, the German-born Henry Kleber, helped him to arrange his melodies.

In December 1844, when Stephen was 18, his first song was published, a setting of a poem by George P. Morris; it was *Open Thy Lattice, Love*, a sentimental ballad. It is believed that he wrote it when he was 16, and it is dedicated to Susan Pentland of Pittsburgh, who was literally the 'girl next door' to the Fosters, but romantic associations can probably be ruled out as she was five years younger than Stephen. It was published by Willig of Philadelphia, but how it came to be sent to them is not known. Stephen may have sent it, or he may have asked one of his relatives to take it to a music house on one of their journeys. Whatever the circumstances, published it was, and Stephen could now regard himself as a songwriter.

When Stephen was still 18, he and a group of young men formed themselves into 'The Knights of the Square Table', who met twice a week at the Fosters' home. Stephen wrote humorous poems about members of the group, and started to write songs for them to sing. In 1846, when he was 20, he had *There's a Good Time Coming* published, this being a musical setting of a poem he had read in *The London Daily News*. These submissions to publishers were done mainly for amusement, and no one, least of all Stephen, contemplated the prospect of his living being made by writing songs. Indeed, his interest in this pastime in preference to a search for steady employment was a sore trial to his father, who started what was in effect a "What are we going to do about Stephen?" campaign amongst his other sons. The likeable, well behaved, but apparently unmotivated youth was eventually found a job as a book-keeper with his brother Dunning, who worked for a shipping company in Cincinnati. Dunning went on to become master of a steamboat in the river trade.

But though Stephen worked conscientiously at his newly-found job, fate had other plans in store for him. In September 1847, when he was 21, he had his first great hit. *Oh! Susanna* was presented to Peters & Co. of Pittsburgh, Music Publishers, and when issued it was an immediate success. Looking at the song now this is no great surprise. With its catchy tune and its wonderfully inviting chorus of "Oh! Susanna, don't you cry for me", it is a marvellous song to sing. It caught on immediately and was soon being sung, with banjo accompaniment, all over the United States. It soon became popular in Britain and its fame spread to Europe. It was not long before stolid Germans were proclaiming "Ich komm von Alabama mit der banjo auf dem knie." *Oh! Susanna* was sung by rich and poor and became an American folk song within months of its birth through its adoption by the 'fortyniners' of the Gold Rush. It became their favourite song as they trecked, and camped around their fires at night. Stephen did not make a lot of money from this song for he had presented it to the publishers as a gift. This was not really such a naïve thing to do as it might seem, for no one had expected this offering from an unknown songwriter to achieve such a success; he had just wanted to make his presence known. But when the song did succeed the publishers made a gift of $100 to Stephen, a useful sum in those days.

Stephen followed up *Oh! Susanna* with other songs including *Lou'siana Belle,* published by Peters in 1847, and *Old Uncle Ned*, published by Millet of New York in 1848. He was now on the road to success, and from this time until the end of his life a steady stream of songs was produced, for most of which he wrote both words and music. As he wrote 188 published songs altogether only the most notable or those of interest for other reasons will be quoted.

Stephen's next big success came in February 1850 with the publication of *The Camptown Races*, another happy song set to his own words, and still sung to this day. It was first published as *Gwine to Run*

All Night, which leads us to consider the dialects used in some of Stephen's songs. It has already been mentioned that in the days of his youth, touring minstrel groups were one of the main forms of entertainment in America, so Stephen wrote 'minstrel songs' for them to sing. Consequently the words were often in negro dialect, or at least, what passed in popular entertainment for negro dialect. Stephen always wrote sympathetically with regard to negroes and never attempted to ridicule or patronise them as some song writers did.

On 22nd July 1850 Stephen, then 24, was married to Jane McDowell, daughter of the late Dr. A.N. McDowell, a former Pittsburgh physician. Information about Stephen's relationships with the young ladies of Pittsburgh is very vague, and nothing is known of the romance. Dr. McDowell had attended Charles Dickens in 1842 when the famous novelist became ill during his visit to Pittsburgh. What is known is that Stephen and his bride took a honeymoon trip to Baltimore and New York, where Stephen also took the opportunity to visit his publishers, Firth, Pond & Co., who were to publish most of his songs until 1860. Stephen's new-found success more or less coincided with the new responsibilities of marriage, so it was important that his business arrangements should be put on a sound financial footing. At the time of his marriage Stephen had taken the definite step of abandoning book-keeping for his musical career, and Jane accepted him as a musician. A daughter, Marion, was born on 18th April 1851, and was to be the Fosters' only child. Stephen and Jane lived with his parents (to whom he paid $5 per week board) at the start of their marriage, along with Henry and his wife, and Morrison.

The presence of so many of the Foster family, and the comings and goings of numerous other brothers, sisters and more distant relatives probably did little to stabilise the marriage, which does not seem to have been a particularly happy one. Both Stephen and Jane were devoted to Marion, but it seems that Jane's practical nature and Stephen's dreamy personality were not particularly compatible. Also, she probably regarded his music and writing less seriously than he did. The couple were never finally estranged, but periods of separation occurred from time to time, possibly for practical financial reasons, and Jane later found a job as a telegrapher. Jane seems to have been an efficient person, and her bustling around the house in businesslike fashion could have interrupted many a meditation of Stephen's. Marion said years later that her father hated to be interrupted when working. It seems that Stephen became more introspective and moody after his marriage. He was devoted to his parents, and to his brothers and sisters, and had been with or near them for the whole of his life; they were a close-knit family and it seems likely that 'home' to Stephen meant life with them rather than life with Jane.

Six months after the birth of Marion Foster, Stephen copyrighted his greatest and best-known song, *The Old Folks at Home*, which has become one of the world's immortal songs. Morrison Foster later told how Stephen came into his office one day and asked him if he could think of a good name for a Southern river in a verse he had just written. One or two suggestions were made which evidently proved unsuitable, so an atlas was produced and studied. After a while Stephen spotted the Suwannee river, a little river in Florida which runs into the Gulf of Mexico. "That's it - that's it exactly!" exclaimed Stephen, delighted, as he wrote the name down. He left the office, Morrison resumed his work, and shortly afterwards, 'Way Down upon de Swanee Ribber' came into the world. This song, with its sentimental, plaintive words and its simple haunting melody, was a tremendous success. Stephen received a royalty of 2 cents per copy (on a 25 cent copy) which soon made him relatively well off. The song was written to be performed by minstrel groups, the most famous of which was that of E.P. Christy, and it is an interesting quirk of the publishing system that the song as it first appeared was billed as being "Written and composed by E.P. Christy." No song-stealing was involved - all was legal and above-board. The song was allowed to be published in this way for a certain length of time until it was popularised, on payment of a cash sum to the real author, Stephen Foster, after which his name appeared as writer and composer. The arrangement was an open secret among musicians. In two years 130,000 copies had been sold, and Stephen Foster was recognised as the great song writer of the day.

Not all of Stephen Foster's songs are great ones by any means. He was not writing for posterity and would no doubt have been amazed to know that some of his songs were being sung years after his death. He was writing songs which he knew would sell in the market of the day, and one of the most popular subjects for sentimental songs in the 1850s was death. In those days death was an all too frequent intruder, and it is hardly surprising that people became preoccupied with the subject to an extent that would nowadays seem morbid. Songs about death were good sellers, and Stephen wrote many long-forgotten numbers including the following gems:

Bury Me in the Morning, Mother
Farewell, Sweet Mother
Lena Our Loved One Is Gone
Linda Has Departed
Little Ella's an Angel
Lizzie Dies Tonight
My Angel Boy, I Cannot See Thee Die
Our Willie Dear Is Dying
Under the Willow She's Sleeping
Willie's Gone To Heaven

Another favourite, *I Would Not Die in Spring Time* (1850) was so successful that Stephen followed it up with *I Would Not Die in Summer Time* (1851) and *I Would Not Die in Winter* (also 1851). Before Stephen had the chance to complete the quadrilogy, a Baltimore wag, John Hewitt, published *I Would Not Die At All* in 1852.

In February 1852 Dunning, by then master of a river steamboat, brought his ship to Pittsburgh to load for New Orleans. Stephen and Jane went to New Orleans with him, as a pleasure trip, and this enabled Stephen to see southern life at first hand once again. Further opportunity was provided by occasional visits to relatives of the Fosters at a large country house called Federal Hill at Bardstown, Kentucky. Many people believe this to be the house which inspired *My Old Kentucky Home*, published in 1853, still remembered after all these years. This was followed by *Jeanie with the Light Brown Hair* (1854), not a minstrel song but a ballad, and the nearest that Stephen ever got to writing a tender love song. He often used the names of people he knew in his songs. *Oh! Susannah* probably arose from his acquaintance with Susan Pentland, referred to earlier, and 'Jeanie' in the later song was probably his wife Jane, who did in fact have auburn hair, and was sometimes called Jeanie or Jennie. *Come Where My Love Lies Dreaming* appeared in 1855.

The years 1850-60 were the most productive in Stephen's career. Verses and tunes flowed from his pen regularly and though most are now forgotten they were popular in their day. Some, such as *Massa's in de Cold Ground* (another 'death' song) and *Old Dog Tray* were popular in the USA but never appealed to tastes in this country. Stephen was receiving regular money from royalties and his annual income over this period averaged about $1300, enough to keep himself, his wife and Marion in comfort. But he was not very good at managing his financial affairs. He often overspent and had what we might call now a cash flow problem, which could partly account for the lack of success in his marriage. Also, more ominous, from the late 1850s Stephen was drinking more than was good for him. In 1855 his mother died suddenly, and his father, who had been an invalid for four years, died later in the same year. In March 1856 Stephen's brother Dunning died in Cincinnati after a short illness, aged only 35. Stephen, Henry and Morrison brought his body back to Pittsburgh to be buried in the family plot. Later, brother William became a widower for the second time. All these events saddened Stephen, but life was not all grief and there are reports of many happy 'old time concerts' in which Stephen took part.

By 1857 Stephen's finances had reached the stage where ready cash would be more useful to him, or so he thought, than the steady income of long-term royalties. On 27th January of that year he signed an agreement with his New York publishers to sell to them for cash his entire future interest in all his songs they had published to that date. *The Old Folks at Home*, which had earned him $1647 in royalties was reckoned by Stephen to be good for another $100 and was sold for this amount. *My Old Kentucky Home*, which had earned him $1372 was also sold for $100, *Jeanie with the Light Brown Hair* (a newer song) for $350, and so on. Altogether his rights in 36 songs published by Firth, Pond & Co. were sold for a total of $2786, and in a similar agreement with another publisher his interest in a further 16 songs was sold for $461. Thus the slate was wiped clean, and Stephen started again from scratch with no royalties coming in. But new songs continued to appear and *Old Black Joe* (1860) was a great success. This song was not written in negro dialect. By then Stephen was no longer writing for minstrel bands and he could use whatever form of verse he liked. The song is said to have been inspired by an old negro of this name who had been a servant with the McDowells (Jane's family), and who drove the doctor on his rounds for many years. "Some day I'm going to put you in a song", Stephen had once told Joe, and with Stephen a promise was a promise. The old man had died before the song was eventually written, but old Joe was immortalised in the song. This turned out to be the last of Stephen's great songs, except for one, as we shall see.

In 1860 brother William died, and about that time Stephen decided to live in New York, thinking that opportunities might be better for him there than in his native Pittsburgh. It was not a good move, for Stephen was a man who needed roots and family. Those were in Pittsburgh, not New York, and his lifestyle suffered. Jane went with him but did not stay there long, though there is evidence through family letters that they kept in touch. With the move to New York, Stephen's creative fires dimmed. He continued to publish songs, but the standard degenerated, and before long he stopped writing poetry and limited himself to setting to music the verses of other people. He no longer chose to sign royalty agreements and his songs were sold to a variety of publishers for whatever cash sum they would fetch, which was generally not very much.

His drinking increased, and relatives and friends visiting New York were increasingly concerned when they observed his condition. He had become careless of his appearance and in two or three years had evidently become an unkempt, dissipated figure. He lodged in a boarding house but too much of his time was spent in bars and the excess of drink took its toll, though it is said that he was never actually drunk. A visitor described him:

"A figure slight, apparelled in clothing so well worn as to betoken a gentleman who had seen better days; his face long and closely shaven; soft brown eyes, somewhat dimmed by dissipation. His appearance was at once so youthful and so aged that it was difficult to determine at a casual glance if he were 20 years old or 50. An anxious, startled expression hovered over his face that was painful to witness. It was hard for me to force myself to believe that that poor wretched-looking object was at that moment the most popular song-composer in the world, but it was Foster indeed! He seemed as embarrassed as a child in the presence of a stranger, and this diffidence never entirely wore off. As I afterward discovered, he would walk, talk, eat and drink with you, and yet always seem distant, maintaining an awkward dignity."

Stephen Foster still had one song to offer which was capable of standing the test of time. *Beautiful Dreamer*, written in 1862 but not issued until two years later, was popular immediately upon publication and was immortalised seventy years later by the classic Bing Crosby recording. Before this song was published, or even entered for copyright, came Stephen's death, untimely and tragic. His drinking had put him in poor physical condition when, in January 1864, he was taken ill with a fever. After two or three days in bed he got up, and while washing he fainted and struck his head on a sharp object, causing a gash which bled profusely. He lay unconscious and bleeding until discovered some time later. He was then immediately taken to hospital but was so weakened by fever and loss of blood that he failed to rally, and died on 13th January 1864, aged 37. The news was telegraphed to Jane and to brothers Henry and Morrison, all of whom came immediately. His body was taken back to Pittsburgh, and the Pennsylvania Railroad Company carried the party free of charge. At his funeral the Citizens' Brass Band played *Come Where My Love Lies Dreaming* and *The Old Folks at Home* as his family and friends stood by the graveside.

So ends the story of Stephen Foster, but not of his music, for his best songs still live on. A decline in popularity of even his most famous ones occurred following his death, but gradually they inched back and soon started to be included in collections, which ensured a steady sale. In America his compositions achieved national folk-song status. *My Old Kentucky Home* became the official State Song of Kentucky, and *The Old Folks at Home* that of Florida.

Stephen's widow, Jane, started to benefit financially some years later, though she had married again by then. The original copyright of *The Old Folks at Home* ran for 28 years from 1851. Although Stephen sold out his interest for cash in 1857 the copyright was still in his name, so when it came up for renewal (for a 14 year period) in 1879 a new deal was negotiated for Jane, through the wisdom and good business sense of Morrison. Thereafter Jane (then Mrs. Wiley) received 3 cents per copy royalty on Stephen's songs for the period stated. *The Old Folks at Home* turned out to be a continuing money-spinner for it was re-popularised when the Swedish soprano Christine (Kristina) Nilsson started to include it as an encore at recitals. So did Adelina Patti, and the song became a rival to Henry Bishop's *Home Sweet Home* as the definitive 'home' song. Foster's songs also attracted the attention of classical musicians, especially Dvorak, who wrote arrangements of some of them, including *The Old Folks at Home*. Alert listeners may note other musical quotations from Foster in Dvorak's works.

It is usual for flowing tributes to be made to people after their death, but in Stephen Foster's case they were perfectly genuine for he seems to have been universally liked throughout his life. A contemporary who knew him well later wrote:

"He was just a little too inclined to be moody and thoughtful. He was very modest, too, about his achievements as a composer and writer of songs unless the subject was pressed upon him in such a manner that he could not well avoid it, and then he would drop it as quickly as he got an opportunity. He was not at all conceited, and I have often thought that his bearing amid the praise that was constantly showered upon him by his friends was something remarkable. It would have turned the head of any other man than Foster. He was always kind, never wanted for friends, and never had an enemy. Everybody who knew him liked him, and his temperament, tastes and general disposition were such that I could not imagine him writing anything else than the sweet, plaintive lines that made his name famous."

Much speculation has taken place as to what Stephen might have written had he received the benefit of a formal musical training. No one can answer this; although he would have known how to orchestrate his pieces, he might have lost some of the gift for producing the simple, uncomplicated melodies that are so appealing. The same may be said of other song writers in this book.

As a postscript, readers might like to know that Stephen's sister Henrietta died at the age of 60 in 1879 and Ann Eliza in 1891 aged 79. His brother Henry perished tragically in a fire in 1870, but Morrison, loyal friend as well as a brother, lived until 1904 and was 80 years old at his death. He published a biography of Stephen in 1896. Stephen's wife Jane (then Mrs. Wiley) died in 1903. Their daughter Marion (later Mrs. Foster Welsh) lived to the age of 84 and her later reminiscences were to provide a valuable link with the past. She died on 9th July 1935.

A list of Stephen Foster's best-known songs is given in Appendix 1.

The Melody Lingers On

Cécile Chaminade

2. Cécile Chaminade

Imagine if you will the scene in a moderately well-off French home in the 1860s. It is a Sunday evening when the family holds its weekly musical soirées. Monsieur Chaminade, in military uniform, is playing the violin; a little girl, Cécile, the youngest of the family, sits curled up at his feet, blissfully happy. Madame Chaminade sings, and Monsieur Chabrier, the composer, is playing the piano. Little Cécile loves music and loves her parents. These Sunday evenings are elegant occasions, the music is good, and they are the jewels in Cécile's life.

Imagine now the scene on Cécile's ninth birthday. She has had a happy day; her presents have included a quill pen so that she can write down her music, for already she is composing little pieces. She has also been given a little dog, a toy poodle, to replace her poodle Jean which had died. She calls this one 'Jean Deux' and she has enjoyed her day with it and with her grey cat, 'La Belle'. It is evening, and a visitor arrives whom she has not seen before. He is a short and swarthy man, bearded. He bows to Cécile. "Good evening, my little musician. I am your father's friend. Would you care to entertain me while I wait for him?" She played him the pieces she had composed, and they played the game of naming notes and chords, for she had perfect pitch. The stranger was impressed. He was Georges Bizet, the famous composer, and Monsieur Chaminade had arranged the visit, through a mutual friend, in order to get an expert assessment of Cécile's talents. The opinion of the eminent visitor was, "She has the gift, Monsieur Chaminade. If you give her every opportunity she cannot fail."

Scenes such as these reflect the background to Cécile Chaminade's childhood. Cécile Louise Stéphanie Chaminade was born on 8th August 1861 in the family home at Le Vesinet, about 11 miles west of the centre of Paris. Now a dormitory suburb of Paris, it was then a pleasant village. Cécile's father had been in the French Navy since early manhood and had done well; he now worked in the Navy Department in Paris. He was a fine violinist and the Chaminade Sunday evening soirées attracted many excellent musicians, all friends of the family, as instanced by the regular presence of Emmanuel Chabrier. There were two other children, a sister Camille and a brother

Henri, both older than Cécile by four and six years respectively. Neither was particularly musical but Cécile inherited her parents' talent for music (her mother played the piano and had a pleasant singing voice), and music was the highlight of her life. They were happy days at Le Vesinet. Cécile's compositions were often written for her pets, for example *Serenade to La Belle* for her cat and *Song to a Saucy Bird* for the family parrot. Cécile's mother gave her piano lessons and she had a good grounding in the music of the great composers. Cécile was small and dark-haired; she was very shy and sensitive - a dreamer. Her parents were her best friends. Apart from the musical evenings, she was happiest in the garden or in her little room, which she called her den, where she had an upright piano and where she spent many hours with her dog and cat. Usually the family moved to a small apartment in Paris during the winter months, when travelling was difficult for Monsieur Chaminade during the bad weather.

Cécile's idyllically happy childhood ended abruptly in September 1870 when the Germans marched into Paris at the start of the Franco-Prussian war. Cécile stayed with her mother, brother and sister, and Colette, their life-long maid, at Le Vesinet whilst M. Chaminade was in riot-torn Paris. Fortunately he escaped unharmed, as did the Chaminades' apartment, though the two adjacent houses were badly damaged in the fighting. Cécile hated all this; a gentle girl, she utterly detested war for the whole of her life. Eventually her father returned home and normal life resumed - though to Cécile things never seemed quite the same again.

At 10 Cécile started to have piano lessons at the Paris Conservatory. Monsieur Le Couppey, who auditioned her, had a passion for chocolates, and at her audition he put down an open box of chocolates in front of her. Tentatively, thinking she was being offered one, she took one. "No" - he shouted, "Those are for me!" Whereupon he proceeded to demolish them one by one as she played. As he listened his interest in the chocolates waned and his awareness of her playing increased. When she finished he smiled, told her she had done well - and gave her the last chocolate! She grew to like him and as her abilities developed the chocolates were shared more equitably. The lessons were held only once a week and Cécile used to travel to Paris for them by train with her mother, or occasionally with Colette. She never studied music full-time.

At 12 Cécile composed a short ballet, to be performed by herself (as pianist) and her friends as dancers. Following Bizet's visit to the family home on her 9th birthday he had become a family friend, and followed her musical progress closely. In turn he had become Cécile's idol; she was very fond of him and admired his music. She invited him to the performance of her ballet (held in a school room) and he came, and enjoyed the evening. At that time Bizet, recently appointed Chevalier du Légion d'Honneur, was working on the music of *Carmen*. The Chaminades, including Cécile, attended the first performance of the Opera at the Opéra Comique, at Bizet's invitation. The opera is now regarded as a classic but it was too advanced for its time. The performance was a disaster and the critics gave it poor reviews. Bizet was shattered and three months later he was dead. Cécile was devastated and it took her some time to get over the death of her idol.

As Cécile passed through her teenage years Paris was being rebuilt following the war. The house at Le Vesinet was getting quieter - Camille was now married and Henri was studying in Paris. Life for Cécile followed its quiet pattern; she was content with her own company and that of her parents, and was happiest in her den, playing her piano, or composing, with La Belle curled up in a rocking chair watching her, and Jean Deux at her feet. Every week Cécile went for her lesson at the Conservatory. Once she met César Franck, and they talked sadly together of Bizet.

When she was 17 Cécile began to study counterpoint with Emmanuel Savard at the Conservatory. She disliked working with him - she thought he was too preoccupied with the many 'rules' of music. He set her fugues to compose at home and always pulled them to pieces when she brought them back at the next lesson. Once she got so tired of this she played a joke. Searching through her father's manuscripts she found a little-known fugue of J.S. Bach. She copied it out in her own hand and thoroughly learned it, playing it again and again at home until she was note perfect and the piece bore the stamp of her own personality. At the end of the next lesson she played it to M. Savard as her own work. He criticised it and wrote a lot of changes to the manuscript. Cécile then lowered her eyes and said, "I'm terribly sorry." She smiled at him with all the innocence in the world. "I do beg your pardon but I have made a mistake. This little fugue is not one of mine - it was written by Monsieur Bach." For a long time the teacher did not speak - his face was a mask. Then, quietly and subdued, he continued the criticism. "Even the great Bach sometimes made mistakes, my child." Her next assignment was not a fugue!

During these years many well-known musicians continued to visit the Chaminade home, including Charles Lamoureux who was the conductor of L'Opéra Comique and founder of a well-known series of concerts, Chabrier, and another composer, Benjamin Godard, with whom Cécile started to have weekly lessons in composition. Sometimes Cécile met young men of her own age, sons of her father's colleagues and friends, but she was not interested in them. She lived for her music, and as most of them had no interest in music there was little in common. Cécile's mother sometimes used to say to her "There is more to life than music, Cécile", whereupon the reply was always, "Not to me, Mama."

When Cécile was 18 the family went for a holiday in the Périgord region of France; Cécile loved the beautiful countryside and the holiday marked a productive period in her musical life. The compositions she wrote there stood her in good stead, for on 15th February 1880 when she was 18 she made her public debut as a pianist at the Érard Room at the Conservatory, and two of the pieces she had written on holiday, *Song of the Gondolier* and *Hungarian March* formed part of the programme. She was terrified of going onto the stage and had to be calmed down by her mother, who said "You must share your gift with others, Cécile, otherwise you have no right to it." The magazine *L'Art Musical* said:

"She is a pianist with a delicate classic touch. She played seven selections of very remarkable talent as much because of the freshness of the melodious ideas as by the lightness and style of mood. We will often have occasion to speak of her talent."

Another reviewer remarked:

"Mlle Chaminade is a young person of good family background and an amateur, up to this time never having played in public. She showed the talent of the real artist; the pieces for piano which Mlle played with such vivacity made a great impression on us. Her playing was a great success and the entire programme was for her a long line of applause and encores."

Praise also came from the 70 year old composer Ambroise Thomas, who said:

"The girl rightfully belongs to the ranks of the great modern musicians. She is a composer, not merely a woman who composes."

Thus Cécile was launched on a long and successful public career. But she always suffered from stage-fright and never in her entire life did she face an audience without promising herself that "This will be the last time!"

Following this success, Cécile started to give a lot of concerts, featuring her own compositions as part of her programmes, and these were received with universal praise. In 1882 *L'Art Musical* said, "Mlle Chaminade, in spite of her sex and age, has taken her place today among the most recognised modern composers." Shortly afterwards she was guest of honour at a re-union of M. Le Couppey's students. He presented her with a large box of chocolates, "All for you!" In the late summer of the same year the Chaminade family again took a holiday in the Périgord region, a beautiful area full of shady forest paths, murmuring rivulets, and waterfalls. With the coming of autumn the countryside became a place of magic beauty. Cécile used to sit and gaze and dream as the sun went down, and used to put her thoughts and dreams into music. She would jot down musical phrases that occurred to her, and put them in a drawer until she went back home to Le Vesinet. Thus it was that towards the end of 1882, and following the holiday she had enjoyed so much, *L'Automne* was created. One of her best known compositions, though written when she was little more than a girl, it held its popularity during her long life and is still played today.

In 1886 Cécile started work on a symphonic ballet, *Callirhoë*, and conceived the idea of a scene where dancers pirouetted around the stage swirling gaily-coloured scarves, portraying butterflies. She worked through the summer and autumn on the ballet and completed it in 1887. But before it was presented on stage a tragic event occurred. Cécile's father collapsed and died at his desk in the Navy building. After a period of sad inactivity Cécile turned her attention to getting the ballet presented, knowing that this is what her father would have wanted, and it was staged at the Grand Theatre of Marseilles on 16th March 1888. It was well received and the *Scarf Dance* from the ballet became a well-known and popular piece in its own right, particularly in the USA. She also gained a success with *The Amazons*, a dramatic symphony for solo voices, and her other orchestral pieces were beginning to receive attention. She was fast becoming a celebrity and was being invited to play at soirées, music halls and theatres as well as at concerts. But she was always terrified; she was happiest in her composing room or in some secret hiding place of nature where, undisturbed, she could let her imagination roam.

By her 30th year Cécile had started to make winter tours of Britain and Germany. Her mother always came with her and the two were more like friends than mother and daughter, with never a cross word between them. Thus the years passed, happily, until a day came when Cécile's mother decided she was no longer young and her travelling days were over. So afterwards Cécile travelled alone but always looked forward to her mother's warm welcome on her return home to Le Vesinet. In the early 1890s Cécile played for the Sultan of Turkey in Constantinople and in June 1894 she gave a recital at the Queen's Hall in London in front of an audience of 2000 people. There was the usual panic before the performance but, as always, all was well when she started, and there was tremendous applause. Back in her hotel a huge white envelope bearing the Royal Insignia was waiting for her. It was an invitation to play for Queen Victoria. When the time came, Cécile stayed the night at the White Hart Hotel at Windsor and was collected at 1.00pm by a royal carriage. Cécile noted down afterwards what was said at the meeting. The Queen was delighted with Cécile's playing and told her, among other things, how much her daughters enjoyed her music. Three years later Cécile was invited to play at Windsor again during the Diamond Jubilee celebrations, and afterwards was awarded the Diamond Jubilee Medal. Cécile showed it to her mother with great pride when she got home. Later a picture of Queen Victoria, bearing her autograph, arrived at the Chaminade home in Le Vesinet, borne by liveried coachmen in a royal carriage.

All her life Cécile depended on the beauty of nature for her inspiration. In that respect she was similar to the American composer Edward MacDowell who was her contemporary. The different places at which she stayed all had their own form of beauty and this was reflected in her music. Like Chopin, she did her best work at dusk. In 1899 Cécile spent a month touring Germany, and met Joachim and Richard Strauss. In Berlin she played a long programme of 35 of her own compositions but the recital was not well received by the German audience nor by the critics. An American music critic who was present, Edward Perry, viewed the recital more favourably:

"She was at the piano either solo or as an accompanist for every piece, playing without notes, a true feat of memory for a three-hour concert. She is not a great pianist, as she is lacking in strength, brilliancy, speed and octave technique. Yet, regarded artistically, she is worth high consideration in spite of her limitations. Tone is small, pure but witching rather than warm, suggesting Liszt. Her songs are the best, melodious and effective, but should only be sung in French. Her *Trio*, though lacking the supposed quality of graveness, was strikingly beautiful, full of dark spirit and many novel effects. If a work of equal merit could be exhumed as a lost manuscript bearing the name of one of the old masters, the musical world would go mad with pride over it. But as it was written by a woman of modern days, and a French woman at that, the critics were unappreciative and vigorous in their censure."

Cécile was depressed by the German critics' reception. On her way home she stopped in Bonn and was allowed to play Beethoven's music on Beethoven's own piano at his birthplace, an experience she found very comforting.

In spite of the German setback she was becoming more and more popular in France, and had almost achieved cult status. Instead of calling 'Encore' after her performances people were calling "Sainte Cécile!" This tag was to stick with her to the end of her days.

In 1901 Cécile gave one of her regular concerts in Marseilles and one day, whilst browsing in a music shop in the town, she met a man who turned out to be a secret admirer of her and her music. His name was M. Louis-Mathieu Carbonel, a Marseilles music publisher. He was 20 years older than she was but the two struck up an immediate friendship; they had much in common. On 29th August 1901 Cécile and M. Carbonel were married in the village hall at Le Vesinet in front of six witnesses; both of them wanted a very quiet wedding. As she was well established in the musical life of Paris and he in that of Marseilles they decided to share their time between the two cities in preference to either giving up their home. Cécile was very happy; the marriage worked out well. She found herself enjoying the gaiety around her, the concerts and opera in Paris, the concerts and recitals in Marseilles. Her mother was pleased that Cécile, at 40, had settled into married life at last. In the same year she made half a dozen disc recordings of her own compositions for The Gramophone and Typewriter Company in London. Surprisingly for such an accomplished pianist and composer, they appear to have been the only recordings she ever made for the gramophone.

Cécile Chaminade's happiness following her marriage was soon to be tragically cut short. Only a year after the wedding Cécile's husband became ill and died within a few weeks. Cécile was heartbroken and went back to her life with mama, spending most of her time in her den with her parrot and little dogs. Slowly she picked up the threads of her life and resumed her normal work. The concerts and recitals started again, as did her stream of compositions.

In 1908 Cécile's mother died peacefully in her sleep; Cécile and Colette cried at the bedside. So now Cécile was alone as far as her family was concerned; her father, husband and mother had gone, and the only family visits were occasional ones from her sister and brother. For months after her mother's death Cécile was lonely, restless and sad, dwelling constantly on happy times that had passed. She would think of tunes but could not write anything down; she just wanted to bury her head in her hands and cry. But gradually she started once again to find joy in nature and life itself. One day she was visited by a well known American manager who renewed an invitation he had offered several times previously over the years for Cécile to visit the USA. "Do you realise," he said, "that groups of young women all over America are forming music clubs in your name, playing nothing but your music?" She didn't believe it - but he convinced her that it was true, for there were then 200 such Chaminade clubs. She had previously vowed never to go to the USA whilst her mother was alive for she did not want to leave her for months on end, but now her mother was dead she accepted the invitation with some trepidation. She and the manager persuaded two good musician friends to go with her, a mezzo soprano and a baritone, to keep her company and help share the load at the concerts.

They arrived in New York on 12th October 1908. When a reporter asked her about her music she said, "My compositions are dreams. Of flowers and moods, of spring and summer, of the songs of the birds and the deep shadows of the forests." On 24th October 1908 she played before a packed house at the Carnegie Hall. Over 1500 women were turned away, many in tears, as there was no more room. The audience gave her a triumphant reception, but the critics were lukewarm. *New York World* wrote:

"Mme Chaminade owes her world-wide fame to the charm and delicacy rather than the force and breadth of her compositions."

The Evening Post remarked:

"Carnegie Hall was crowded as it seldom is except at a Paderewski recital. Mme Chaminade's music is salon music. It has daintiness and grace but it is amazingly superficial and wanting in variety. Her pieces and songs are almost as much alike as so many eggs and no one would care to make a whole meal of eggs."

Cécile performed in 16 American cities in two months. The tour was triumphant financially in spite of the fact that many music critics condemned her compositions as well as her performance of them. *The Philadelphia Ledger* was more friendly:

"Her temperament is like that of Clara Wieck Schumann whose aim is not the exploitation of her own individuality. She dresses simply, and as she sits amid the orchestral harmonies she herself has evoked, it seems incredible that this fragile woman is the composer of music that includes in its broad range the heights and depths of heaven and this goodly frame the earth."

In Boston she played in front of 3000 people. In St. Louis, where the auditorium only held 2500, 3000 were turned away. Most of the critics' reviews continued to be hostile but *The Chicago Tribune* was perhaps nearer the truth when it said:

"Mme Chaminade's compositions are delicate, graceful creations, not pretentious, not vastly significant. They are not the largest blossoms in the tonal garden but they make it all the more attractive by their presence."

When Cécile read this she mused on the phrase "not the largest blossoms." At Le Vesinet she especially treasured the small, delicate flowers which grew in her garden.

One of the people she met and liked in America was John Philip Sousa; another was Dame Nellie Melba whom she met at a social function where she and Cécile were joint guests of honour. The social side of the tour was something of a trial to Cécile who was always quiet, retiring and shy. She went to the Chaminade clubs, but it was an effort. She liked to play there, but did not relish having to make polite conversation afterwards. She continued to play to packed enthusiastic houses at recitals, and continued to get unenthusiastic notices from the critics. This upset her. She often wondered why it was that she was so popular with the public, whilst at the same time the critics were so scathing. "What is success?" she asked her manager. "I feel such a failure." He replied, "Success is the ability to bring some sort of happiness to people by your performance. You have that ability." She was rather lonely in the USA in spite of the presence of her two friends and would sometimes cry when she thought of home - without her mother.

Back in France, with the period of mourning for her mother over, she was invited everywhere. In the street people would whisper, "There goes Sainte Cécile!" She received tremendous fan mail from the USA and elsewhere and there were endless requests for interviews from various periodicals. The walls of her den were covered in the tributes she had been given. She was good to other musicians - she loved to talk about music, and all musicians were welcome at Le Vesinet. She was a good hostess in her own home and would listen for hours to anyone who came to see her with a musical problem. The American pianist Ward Stephens wrote of her:

"She is one of the loveliest characters I have ever met. Frank, earnest in her work, with no bitter words for anyone. Her hospitality, modesty and genius left a deep impression on us all."

Society was a different matter. She went to social functions only if she had to, and when she did she sat quietly alone in a corner "like a little brown wren."

So the years passed. Inevitably she still missed her family; but she still wrote songs and other pieces. Then in 1914 war came. She grieved for the young soldiers and watched it all in horror. In the USA her music was as popular as ever. *L'Automne*, written 30 years earlier, was still selling well and sales of *Scarf Dance*, not one of her best compositions in our opinion but the favourite in the USA, had reached the five million mark. In March 1918 she was appointed to the French Légion d'Honneur.

In the early 1920s Cécile entered her 60s. Not only was she known world wide for her compositions and concert tours, her audience had been extended even further through radio. By the mid 1920s she had cut down on her tours and was living in semi-retirement at Le Vesinet, where she was content among her memories. Her home was a sanctuary for her old friends, and sometimes she was visited by her brother, now retired and living in Paris. In the USA the number of Chaminade clubs had risen to over 300, and Cécile at 65 was still as popular as ever in France and Britain. She wrote a few articles for the magazine *The Étude* on how to play her pieces, and also contributed to other French and English periodicals.

By a happy chronological chance, Cécile Chaminade's years of popularity coincided with the heyday of the player piano. Consequently a great deal of her music (at least 75 compositions of the several hundred she wrote) was recorded onto piano rolls and thereby preserved for posterity. Many different pianists recorded her work, and in addition a large number of 'standard' rolls of her compositions were cut in which the music was not necessarily recorded by a pianist's hands but by other means. During the 1920s, Cécile Chaminade recorded 11 of her own compositions in London for the Aeolian Company's Duo-Art system. It is perhaps surprising that she did not enter the piano-roll recording field earlier, for her work had already enjoyed nearly 30 years of popularity before she recorded any of her compositions on roll. These 11 piano rolls were the only ones she recorded; the last of them was issued in 1930. In the decade when these rolls were released, gramophone recording techniques had achieved an acceptable technical level. Cécile's discs dating from 1901 had long been obsolete and deleted from the catalogues, but if any efforts were made to tempt her back into the recording studio they were evidently unsuccessful.

In the late 1920s Cécile developed an incurable bone disease which put an end to her career as a pianist and restricted her movements to such an extent that by the early 1930s she was confined to bed, though she was to live for many years more. The doctors recommended that she should move to a warmer climate, so the house at Le Vesinet where she had lived all her life was sold and a house was bought at Monte Carlo. After the onset of her illness the years passed more slowly, but still fruitfully, though she gradually faded from the mainstream of musical activity. In these years of her old age she was looked after by her niece, Antoinette Lorel. As far as the public was concerned she became more or less a forgotten person, except to her particular fans. Before her 78th birthday in 1939 *The Étude* magazine came up with a nice gesture. It proposed:

"That a flood of birthday greetings be sent to dear Mme Chaminade who is now living in Monte Carlo in her 78th year. Her delightful and able compositions are masterpieces of their type. She has given joy to untold millions through their performances in concerts and over the air. Her works have become classics of the style and period they represent. She has been an invalid for years. It is now over a decade since we visited her at Tamaris on the Riviera and as long ago as that she was bedridden but she was full of smiles, sweetness and interest in life. How can you join this international birthday party? Mme Chaminade was born on 8th August 1861. Why not have the joy this year of sending her a birthday greeting?"

So the letters and cards poured in from all over the world, showing the old lady she was still remembered. She lived on for several more years, once again seeing the world in turmoil as the 1939 war came. These years were spent in semi-poverty because the Germans had liquidated her Jewish Parisian publishers, so little money was forthcoming in royalties. But still she remained happy, cheerful, and an inspiration to others. She died in Monte Carlo on 18th April 1944, at the age of 82.

After her death the obituary writers were as lukewarm as the critics had been during her life. *Time* magazine wrote:

"In Monte Carlo last week death came to the most famous woman composer who ever lived. Frail white-haired Cécile Louise Stéphanie Chaminade had been bed-ridden with a bone disease for well over a decade, and died in comparative obscurity. The era that her fragile little piano pieces represented has long since closed. Always a facile melodist, Chaminade rolled up a list of over 550 compositions which stand in the same relation to Chopin as strawberry soda to cognac."

A more gracious and fitting tribute to this sensitive musician was paid by the American music critic William Henry Humiston:

"Among the women who have composed, the one who has achieved most is Mme Cécile Chaminade, the modern St. Cecilia in fact as well as name. Not as profound or as erudite as some of her sisters, perhaps, but nevertheless uniting melodic graces with harmonic charm as few composers of either sex have done, she merits recognition as one of those whose best efforts are devoted to uplifting the standard of our noble art."

It is now half a century since Cécile Chaminade died. What is our opinion of her now? We know that she was a small, shy, dreamy, imaginative woman, who loved the beauty of nature, but who was often lonely after the death of her parents and husband. What of her as a musician? Few of her compositions, apart from *L'Automne* are ever heard nowadays on the radio or in concerts and recitals, though there are signs of two or three of them inching back into the repertoire. Much of her music was recorded on piano roll so the owners of player pianos can still enjoy it by that means. Most of her compositions were delicate and delightful. The critics condemned them contemptuously in her lifetime as *salon music*, of no great consequence and containing many repetitive phrases. But why should salon music be treated with scorn whereas chamber music is considered entirely repectable? True, her compositions did contain repetitions of various phrases, but all the great masters of the keyboard repeated whole pages of music. Her music was intended to be played by skilled amateurs and she succeeded in her aim. Hence the popularity of her music amongst ordinary pianists and singers rather than the musical élite, and hence too the springing up of the Chaminade clubs at the turn of the century. Perhaps her music was too pleasant, too easy to listen to, and too easy to play, for the critics' taste. She was not an innovator like Beethoven, Chopin or Liszt, but her best compositions are fine pieces of music which have given pleasure to thousands of people. There may yet be a revival of interest in her music. It has happened in the case of Percy Grainger's compositions. It could happen to Cécile Chaminade.

A list of Cécile Chaminade's most popular compositions is given in Appendix 2.

The Melody Lingers On

Leslie Stuart

3. Leslie Stuart

One of the unique features of popular music is the way it captures the spirit of its age. The music of the Beatles takes us back to the sixties, rock-and-roll conjures up the fifties, the Andrews Sisters the forties, and so on. If we go back to the beginning of the present century, when Britain was head of a great Empire, when hansom cabs clattered around the streets of London and the twangy tones of street pianos churned out the airs of the day, it was the music of Leslie Stuart that was heard everywhere. For a period of a dozen years, spanning the turn of the century, he was Britain's leading songwriter, and the grace and charm of his delicate melodies epitomised all that was best in that period.

Thomas Augustine Barrett (for that was Leslie Stuart's real name) was born in Southport, Lancashire, on 15th March 1864. Thomas's father worked in Liverpool, as property master at the old Amphitheatre, and when Thomas was a child he was sometimes taken to see the shows. So the theatre was in his blood from childhood, and it remained a lifelong passion. He was of an imaginative disposition and the images described in his childhood books, of scenes in far-away lands, made a deep impression on his young mind. A talent for music soon became evident and the boy learned to play the piano at an early age. Before he was very old he was also writing songs.

When Thomas was eight years old the Barrett family moved to Blossom Street, Ancoats, Manchester, where his father had set up a cabinet-making business, and Manchester was to remain Thomas's home for the next 20 years. Thomas's father, who was said to bear a striking resemblance to Buffalo Bill, was quite a character. He had been well-known in Liverpool, and when the family moved to Manchester he soon became a familiar figure there too. One of his haunts was the Slip Inn, off Market Street in Manchester. The landlord there had converted an upstairs room into a 'music hall' to bring in extra money on Saturday evenings. One night the pianist dropped dead, and Thomas was dragged out of bed to take his place. Thus, in this dramatic and macabre way, he made his public debut. On later occasions from time to time Thomas played there, and sometimes performed his songs, one of the first of which was written for performance at the Slip Inn. He had been encouraged in his song writing, for which he wrote the words and music, by an elder brother, Steve, who was a good amateur singer.

But playing the piano in a public house music hall was hardly the best way for an intelligent and talented boy to earn a living. The family were Roman Catholics, as may be surmised from Thomas's middle name, and when Thomas was 14 he applied for the post of organist at the nearby Roman Catholic Cathedral in Salford. His talents and ability to do the job were not in question, but the church authorities had heard about his exploits at the Slip Inn, and his songs, and were not very happy about either. In those days music-hall was not held in very high esteem by the church, many of the songs performed being of a rather doubtful nature. The church worthies did not wish their organist to be associated openly with the music-hall, nor did they wish to miss acquiring his services, so a compromise decision was reached. Thomas would be appointed organist provided he used another name when appearing as music-hall pianist or song writer. Thus, at the age of 14, Thomas Barrett became a cathedral organist, and at the same time a new name started to appear on song sheets, that of Lester Thomas. This name was soon replaced by a second, and final, nom de plume - Leslie Stuart. And so the young musician embarked on a dual career.

He remained organist at Salford Cathedral for seven years, until 1885, when, at the age of 21, he became organist at the Church of the Holy Name, Chorlton-on-Medlock, Manchester, a very large church a couple of hundred yards from Manchester University. There too his tenure was to last seven years, and in that time he had the opportunity to play a fine organ which still exists and continues to serve the church well, though the building is no longer a parish church. Throughout these youthful years Thomas - or Leslie - continued to compose songs, as well as to conduct and compose religious music as part of his church duties. Some people have expressed surprise that one who obviously possessed considerable musical talent and was known to be devoted to the works of Bach, Beethoven and the other great composers, could have 'lowered himself' to writing popular songs. In those days classical and popular music were regarded as incompatible, and no less a composer than Sir Arthur Sullivan had to battle against the same stigma when writing light music. But it seems nowadays perfectly natural that a youth who was steeped in the classical tradition should relax by writing popular songs. Recent examples of musicians with both classical and popular interests include Leonard Bernstein, André Previn and John Williams; there are many more. One writer on the theatre, Edward Short, has stated that the tradition of Catholic music which Thomas Barrett absorbed in his formative years was of great value to him, and showed through in his popular music.

As Thomas Barrett drew towards the close of his seven-year connection with the Church of the Holy Name, the activities of Leslie Stuart became more prominent, so that by the early 1890s, when he was 26 or 27, word of the young man had reached London, and he found a publisher there for some of his songs. Furthermore he had started to act as an impresario in Manchester, and to present concerts of classical and popular music there. His knowledge of the classical and popular scene no doubt helped him to prepare and present musical programmes that he knew would be well received by the public. In 1893 one of his songs, *The Girl on the Ran Dan Tan*, was published, and sung in the London music halls by Lottie Collins, an established music-hall star. The song was a kind of parody of *Ta-ra-ra-boom-de-ay* which had arrived from America the previous year and had spread quickly through the London music halls with Lottie Collins as its performer. This success enhanced Leslie Stuart's reputation as a composer of popular songs - he was a man to watch. But he now had more work than he could cope with and in 1893 he gave up his appointment at the Church of the Holy Name. His triple activity of impresario, organist and song writer was therefore reduced to a double one. The following year, 1894, the 30-year old Stuart sold *Lou'siana Lou* to a London publisher. It was customary in those days for successful songs to be snapped up by London agents and injected into West End shows and this is what happened to *Lou'siana Lou*, for in 1895 it was introduced into *The Shop Girl* at the Gaiety Theatre (most of the other music in the show was by Ivan Caryll and Lionel Monckton), where it was sung with much panache and conviction by Ellaline Terriss, a rising young star of the London stage. The show ran for 546 performances, then a Gaiety record. In 1895 *The Bandolero*, a ballad, was published in London, and in the same year Stuart had an even greater triumph when his latest song, *The Soldiers of the Queen*, was published. He wrote the words and the music for both these songs.

These successes signalled that a move to London was indicated and in 1895 Leslie Stuart installed himself, his wife Kitty, and their five children in a house overlooking Battersea Park, a pleasanter area then than now. Stuart started to present concerts in London, as he had done in Manchester, and used his own name, as the programmes consisted of 'popular classics' acceptable to the musical establishment. The Thomas A. Barrett concerts of classical music at St. James's Hall became famous enough to attract artists of the stature of Paderewski and Patti.

Another popular song followed in 1896. It was *The Willow Pattern Plate* which was supposed to tell the story of the traditional willow pattern picture. The song was performed by the Hawthawne Sisters, an American trio, at the Tivoli Theatre, in front of an enormous circular backdrop depicting the willow pattern scene. In the same year another Stuart song was presented at the Tivoli by Vesta Tilley. It was called *Sweetheart May* and was written by Stuart with his eldest daughter, May, in mind. Another delightful song - a typical Stuart one - appeared in 1897. This was *Little Dolly Daydream (Pride of Idaho)*. It was one of his best and is still heard occasionally. The same year saw the appearance of another new song, *The Dandy Fifth*.

The most memorable London event of 1897 was the Diamond Jubilee of Queen Victoria. It might have been a lucky chance that *The Soldiers of the Queen* happened to be written just two years before the Queen's Jubilee. But Leslie Stuart had an eye to profits, and it seems much more likely that the timing of the song's publication was arranged to be just right for the forthcoming pomp and pageantry. Whether or not this is so remains a matter for speculation, but what is indisputable is the fact that *The Soldiers of the Queen* became a kind of second National Anthem, rivalled later only by Elgar's *Land of Hope and Glory*. The theatre historian W. Macqueen-Pope described the great Jubilee Procession in detail, and, referring to Stuart's song, wrote;

"And all the bands played that famous song, that stirring, inspired song, so typical of its age, composed by the genius of Leslie Stuart. There they were - the soldiers of the Queen - the men who had always won; living up to their name by escorting their Sovereign on her Diamond Day."

It was a great day for the old Queen - and it was a great day for

Leslie Stuart. Following Queen Victoria's death in 1901, new issues of the song were published as *The Soldiers of the King*, a title which the song retained until 1952 when, following the accession of Queen Elizabeth II, it reverted to its original title.

Following his arrival in London in 1895 Leslie Stuart had become a regular visitor to the London music halls, and in 1897 an encounter occurred which significantly assisted him in his career. It was at the Oxford Theatre that he met Eugene Stratton, a 38-year old white American singer of 'coon' songs, which had been very popular for many years in the USA. Stratton had been touring Britain with an American minstrel troupe, and had stayed behind when the rest of the party went home. Sometimes he sang as his normal self, but for most of his act he appeared 'blacked up' in the manner of the day, and it was in this guise that Stuart first saw him. The song writer was immediately entranced by Stratton's act, which brought out in Stuart's vivid imagination all the romantic visions of distant lands that had impressed themselves on his young mind as a child through the books he had read. Stratton was not a great singer, he was really more of a character actor, but like Fred Astaire a generation later the lack of a fine voice was no handicap - for he knew how to put a song across. He had that indefineable charisma that sets one performer apart from and above another.

Stuart quickly reached a financial agreement with Stratton and started to write 'coon' songs for him, starting with the epic title, *Is Yer Mammie Always With Ye - Susie Susie Ann?* Others followed in rapid succession. In the following year, 1898, he wrote *The Cake Walk* (the cake walk craze was sweeping America, and Stuart, like all the other song writers, wanted to cash in). Then, also in 1898, appeared the most famous of Leslie Stuart's songs, *Lily of Laguna*. In all the songs that Leslie Stuart wrote for Eugene Stratton he wrote the words as well as the music, and paid particular attention to accommodating Stratton's unique, relaxed style. It was never the intention that Stratton should just stand up in front of an audience and sing the songs; they were in a way soliloquies, part of a story, the wistful negro dreaming of his girl. Stratton 'talked the songs through', aided by superb costume and backcloths, the effect being embellished by suitable dances.

Lily of Laguna was an immediate sensation and Stratton was soon earning £200 per week for his music hall act. Not unnaturally Stuart continued the success story by writing other coon songs for Stratton, including *The Little Octoroon*, *The Coon Drum Major* (both published in 1899) and *The Banshee* (1900). Nowadays the writing of works labelled as 'coon songs' to be performed by blacked-up singers imitating negroes would probably provoke allegations of racial prejudice and the like. But in Stuart's day the use of the word 'coon', which had come to Britain from the United States, was not intended to be denigratory. Fashions change, and what would now be frowned on was then accepted as perfectly normal entertainment. It would be a pity if Stuart's pleasant and gentle love songs were to be derided because of their 'coon' associations.

The instant success of the Stuart-Stratton collaboration had added another string to Leslie Stuart's bow, and a highly remunerative one at that. But he did not ignore his other compositions. His previous contribution to musical comedy had been the writing of individual songs to be interpolated into shows that were otherwise composed by other people, for example *Lou'siana Lou* in *The Shop Girl*. But in 1899 Stuart composed the whole score for a show that was to become a tremendous success - *Floradora*. The show was put on at the Lyric Theatre and ran for the rest of Queen Victoria's reign. After her death in 1901 it continued to run well into the reign of Edward VII, and its melodies capture the spirit of the age in just the same way as did the music of Elgar in *Land of Hope and Glory*. The story of *Floradora* was written by Owen Hall, who was a character in himself. According to W. Macqueen-Pope,

"He was a brilliant writer with many musical comedy books to his credit, and his real name was James Davis. He was originally a solicitor, but the law was too slow for him and the theatre was far more exciting. So he went to the theatre. A great character and a great bohemian, he had no idea about money and was always in debt. So he took the name of Owen Hall, because he said he was indeed owing all to everyone, and he was one of the first men to turn himself into a limited company. But there was nothing limited about his ability and wit."

Owen Hall's skills as a writer were matched by those of Leslie Stuart as a musician, and the words and music blended to form a masterpiece. The song that made the biggest hit of the show was *Tell Me Pretty Maiden, are there Any More at Home Like You*, a double sextet, with six pretty girls in long dresses, with parasols, and six top-hatted and frock-coated admirers who declared their love 'On bended knee'. Stuart's original idea was that the song should be a duet, but he was persuaded by the producer that it would have more impact if the participants were multiplied sixfold to form a double sextet, a decision that proved to be a master stroke. The show was much patronised by Royalty, and Edward, as Prince of Wales, saw it on several occasions before his mother's death. *Floradora* was also presented in New York in 1900, one of the first English musicals to appear on Broadway, and its success there mirrored that in London. It made a great impression on the youthful Jerome Kern who saw it in New York. Over the years numerous revivals were staged, and even now *Floradora* is presented occasionally by professional and amateur groups. It was reckoned that Stuart earned £35,000 in royalties from *Floradora* during his lifetime, a very considerable sum in those days.

So, by 1900, Stuart was famous. His minstrel songs were being sung in all the London music halls by Eugene Stratton, now the self-styled 'Idol of the Halls'. Stuart's tunes were being whistled throughout the land, churned out in the streets of London on barrel pianos, they were selling in vast numbers in sheet music form for home pianists, and on music rolls and discs for various types of automatic musical instruments. Not only that, Stuart had a highly successful musical comedy, *Floradora*, running in the West End. As the 19th century drew to a close and the 20th century unfolded Leslie Stuart was a rich man. In 1898 he had moved his family to Hampstead and the house became a mecca for visitors. He spent his money lavishly, and was a frequent visitor to the races. A cricket lover, he entertained visiting teams from overseas. Leslie Stuart had become a leading figure on the social scene, one of the best known and notable personalities of the day.

Songs for Stratton continued to be written at a steady rate, including *I May be Crazy* (1902), *My Little Canoo* (1903) and *My Little Black Pearl* (1904). Scores were contributed to further West End musical comedies, to succeed *Floradora*. *The Silver Slipper* was presented at the Lyric Theatre in 1901, with words again by Owen Hall. This was followed in 1903 by *The School Girl* at the Prince of Wales Theatre. This time the words were by Henry Hamilton and Paul Potter. Both these shows achieved moderate success, but never approached the tremendous popularity of *Floradora*. Then came *The Belle of Mayfair* at the Vaudeville Theatre in 1905, with words by Charles Brookfield and Cosmo Hamilton, again a moderately successful musical comedy.

Times were still good for Stuart from the financial point of view. He was earning a useful income from royalties and had bought a large house by the Thames. But clouds were gathering on the horizon. In 1905 Stuart quarrelled with Eugene Stratton at the Hurst Park racecourse, and never wrote another song for him. Also, rival composers were making their mark. He had been at the top for ten years, but now the music of Lionel Monckton, Franz Lehár and others was starting to overtake Stuart's in popularity. He was finding difficulty in holding his own in the face of their competition. Nevertheless, new stage works were presented. *Havana* at the Gaiety Theatre in 1908 was a success, but many felt that it was not as successful as it should have been, bearing in mind its good story and some excellent music. The words of this show were by George Grossmith jr., the son of the original 'patter' man in the Gilbert and Sullivan operas. In 1910 *Captain Kidd* was relatively unsuccessful and in the same year another show, for which Leslie Stuart wrote the music, flopped. This was *The Slim Princess*, which was tried out in the provinces, without success, and never got as far as a London opening.

Stuart fared better the following year with *Peggy*, presented at the Gaiety Theatre in 1911. Again George Grossmith jr. wrote the words. This show was a success - it was as sumptuously dressed and mounted as all the other Gaiety shows and benefited from the presence of the famous Gaiety Girls. The big number from the show was *Ladies, Beware* which had a violin obligato played by de Groot (who never used a Christian name), afterwards a celebrated orchestra leader at the Piccadilly Hotel. He was a virtuoso of the violin, and wore a big diamond ring, which sparkled as he played, on the little finger of his right hand. *Peggy* did well at the Gaiety, and touring companies took the show around Britain.

But *Peggy* was to be the last of Leslie Stuart's real successes. His best musical ideas were behind him and later compositions were becoming modified repetitions of his earlier successes. From 1911 his star was in decline. He lacked new ideas, his music was being subjected to increasing competition from others, and fashions in music were changing. Ragtime, imported from the United States around the turn of the century had taken hold, and jazz was just round the corner.

The British public was becoming weary of Leslie Stuart's style. Moreover, he was having financial problems, for he had grown used to the extravagent lifestyle of his affluent years, and his diminishing income was no longer sufficient to support him in the manner to which he was accustomed. After *Peggy*, little was heard of Stuart's music until the Great War started in 1914, by which time he was bankrupt.

On the outbreak of war, most of the stage 'stars' of the day embarked on the task of raising the country's spirits by plying their trade, and the 50-year old composer joined their ranks, appearing on the stage for the first time since his boyhood days of 40 years previously. Leslie and Kitty's daughter, May, to whom *Sweetheart May* had been dedicated, was a fine singer, and in 1915 Leslie and May began a series of appearances on the variety stage, Leslie accompanying on the piano as his daughter sang medleys of his famous songs. Their fee was £125 per week, not a lot by comparison with what he had earned a few years earlier, but still handsome by most standards. In the same year *Floradora* was revived at the Lyric Theatre, to be followed by the last of Stuart's shows, *Midnight Frolic*, which was presented in London in 1917 but failed to achieve a significant impact.

In 1920 a new production of *Floradora* was staged in New York. Stuart went to New York with the show, and took with him the score of an opera, *Nina*, on which he had been working in secret for several years. This was Stuart's most ambitious project. An American producer agreed to stage the opera, and Stuart stayed in New York to put the final touches to the score. The opera was to contain a dancing part (a tango) for the rising young star Rudolph Valentino, whom Stuart had met in New York. But nothing came of the whole project, for Stuart quarrelled with his American producer, and took *Nina* back to England before rehearsals had begun. That was in 1921, and no one in Britain was interested in the opera, which remains unpublished to this day.

On his return to England from America, Stuart and his daughter May returned to the variety stage and for the next four or five years, to ever-declining remuneration, they eked out a modest income. In 1922 Stuart contributed a few numbers to *The Lady of the Rose*. This marked the end of his association with British musical comedy. Fashions in music had changed completely from the days of the leisurely, melodic music of the late Victorian and Edwardian eras that marked Stuart's most productive period. Ragtime had come and all but gone, jazz was firmly on the scene, and the new extravagant dances of the 1920s were a far cry from Stuart's pre-war era. He was unable to adapt his music to the changing times - and indeed there was no particular reason why he should, for in his own relatively limited sphere he had for a time been supreme; in a different realm it was best to leave the work of composing to others - it would have been foolish to try to imitate them.

By 1926 Stuart was a forgotten man, a name from the past to the younger generation, a 'golden oldie'. But in that year a revue was staged at the London Palladium, and one of those engaged was Leslie Stuart. W. Macqueen-Pope described the scene in which, just before the interval, the curtain rose on an elderly, silver-haired, sad-looking man, sitting alone at a grand piano:

"His strong mouth was closed in a firm line, his eyes gazed far away as if oblivious to his surroundings. Then, quite softly, he began to play. The audience grew still, and listened, as from his skilful fingers came the strains of songs he had given the world - songs that audiences had known and remembered since childhood. Many of them had never seen him before, but they knew his songs. He wove a spell around them, and that great audience began to nod and move in time to the music. And then it began to sing. The man at the piano played on and on, seemingly unconscious of the ever-growing excitement around him as one well-beloved melody followed on another. Leslie Stuart, as he sat there playing, must have seen his whole life pass in review before him, as the vast crowd began to cheer and acclaim him."

Only two years later Leslie Stuart was dead. He died, at his home in Richmond, Surrey, on 27th March 1928, aged 64.

For thirty years after Stuart's death, many of his minstrel songs were kept alive by G.H. Elliott, 'The Chocolate-Coloured Coon', who, following the death of Eugene Stratton in 1918 had taken over the mantle of Britain's greatest dark-faced singer just as surely as Elijah handed his mantle to Elisha. Elliott had been performing since the end of the Victorian era but refused during Stratton's lifetime to sing the songs that he regarded as Stratton's territory. But after Stratton's death he felt free to sing them. Elliott was born in Rochdale but had studied minstrel troupes at first hand in the USA as a young man. His recording career extended from 1904 to 1960. He topped the bill in the music halls well into the 1950s and was active almost up to the time of his death in 1962. The gentle, innocent love songs of Leslie Stuart always formed the core of his repertoire. At the age of 66 he toured in the 'Thanks for the Memory' show of 1948. The highlight of his act was *Lily of Laguna,* sung to a back-cloth of a cotton plantation and subdued lighting, accompanied by a little shuffling dance. The beauty of this song, as in many of Stuart's best ones, is that it does not consist, as do many songs, of a nondescript verse followed by a rousing chorus. The verse itself is an excellent and memorable tune, full of pleasant little melodic accompaniments as the story is told.

There are parallels between the life of Leslie Stuart and that of the great American songwriter, Stephen Foster. Both rose to fame rapidly soon after their first song was published. Each of them wrote minstrel songs and both prospered financially for a period, as their compositions enjoyed a few years of popularity. Both suffered a decline, marked by financial hardship. Each of the two composers is now remembered only for a small number of songs. It is an interesting fact that Leslie Stuart was born (as Thomas Barrett) just two months after Stephen Foster died. In music, as in life generally, the closing of one door is often followed by the opening of another.

Since G.H. Elliott's departure from the music-hall scene, Stuart's melodies have been heard only rarely. Occasionally during ceremonial parades a military band plays *The Soldiers of the Queen* and sometimes we hear a chorus or two of *Lily of Laguna* in old-time music-hall shows. But his melodies still have a characteristic grace and charm which, to a lot of people, are infinitely preferable to the more strident offerings of the present day. When Leslie Stuart died, the obituary notice in *The Manchester Guardian* recalled that to hear Stuart's best melodies "Is to find an oasis in a desert of percussion and syncopation." The same apt comment applies today, and we can remember Stuart's contribution to the world of light music with gratitude.

A selected list of Leslie Stuart's compositions is given in Appendix 3.

The Melody Lingers On

Scott Joplin

4. Scott Joplin

Scott Joplin was a musician whose ragtime compositions achieved a modest success in his lifetime. After his death in 1917 his work became almost, but not entirely, forgotten for nearly 50 years until a gradual revival of interest occurred. This culminated in the anachronistic but effective use of his music in a film released in 1973, *The Sting*, (set in the 1920s), as a result of which his compositions at last came to the forefront of popularity. Scott Joplin said towards the end of his relatively short life that it would take 50 years for his music to be appreciated, and he was not far wrong.

In the 1860s slavery was of recent memory in America and Scott Joplin's father, Jiles Joplin (sometimes spelt Giles) was born and reared a slave, achieving his freedom from bondage only five years before Scott was born on 24th November 1868, in Texarkana, Texas. Jiles, a railroad labourer who had come to Texarkana from North Carolina, played the violin and had performed in a plantation band in his slave days. Scott's mother, Florence Givens Joplin, who was freeborn and came from Kentucky, had musical talents as a singer and banjo player. Scott was one of a large family, for there was one elder brother, two younger, and two sisters.

The Joplins, like most black families in Texarkana, had little money, but music was in their blood and Scott was given every encouragement at home to indulge in musical recreations. He soon learned to play the family guitar, and he played the bugle in the local band. He started to play the piano at a friend's house and his talent in this direction was so obvious that his parents scraped together enough money to buy an old piano. On this dilapidated instrument his skills blossomed, and he so impressed a local music teacher that he gave him free lessons. By the age of 11 Scott was an able pianist and was familiar not only with the 'plantation' music of Stephen Foster and other American composers, but also with the music of the great European masters. He attended the local Baptist church and heard a lot of lively and emotional music there.

From an early age Scott wanted to make his living from music and this led to a quarrel with his father, who, in spite of having some musical talent himself, thought that the boy should look for some less uncertain form of employment. Scott left home as a result of the dispute, resolving to achieve fame and fortune as a musician. He was then about 14 years old, which was not a particularly early age for young black boys to leave home. He had been attentive at school, and being intelligent, he was ready for the world. His intention to make his living was immediately realised, though at a lowly level. In the regions of Texas and Louisiana near his home he was able to scrape together a living by playing in gambling halls, cafés, brothels and travelling shows. Such was the manner in which he and many other young men acquired their pianistic skills. Whatever the ethics, he learned popular music the hard way, and the experience was of great value to him in his composing for years to come.

In 1885, when 17, Scott arrived in St. Louis, where there were abundant opportunities for young pianists. They would gather at "Honest John's" Silver Dollar Saloon, which acted as a kind of clearing house for such as Joplin, and would there await requests from whatever establishments needed their temporary services - all seedy places alive with the sound of honky-tonk pianos. In this atmosphere he continued to absorb the music of the day, much of it consisting of syncopated rhythms having their origins in banjo playing, but not yet developed into what became known as ragtime. Scott made St. Louis his temporary base, living in the most respectable boarding house he could find or afford. Most of his engagements were in St. Louis itself, but some took him to neighbouring towns like Sedalia and occasionally as far afield as Cincinnati. This life continued for several years - it became the normal established pattern of his existence.

In 1893 Chicago held a World's Fair, a major event by any standard, and along with the industrial and trade aspects, pianists and entertainers were attracted from all over the USA. Scott formed and led a small orchestra there, playing the piano and cornet. Afterwards he stayed on in Chicago for a while, supplying musical entertainment wherever he could get an engagement. After a few months he moved on to Sedalia, where he took a job as second cornet in the Queen City Concert Band, and also sang in choirs and quartets, as well as continuing his itinerant work as a pianist. By this stage of his career he was composing a variety of pieces, such as cosy sentimental songs, piano pieces, marches, and waltzes for local performance, none of which were published and none of which bore much resemblance to his later ragtime compositions. Again his travels took him to St. Louis where he stayed for a short time before moving on once more to Sedalia.

Sedalia, 189 miles west of St. Louis, was less of a ghetto town than St. Louis or New York. Music flourished there and Scott found himself employment, playing nightly, at one of the many taverns. His talents were beginning to put him ahead of the many other popular pianists. He played better than they did and his compositions were beginning to be heard. Scott took lessons for a while at the George R. Smith College for Coloured People in Sedalia, and was taught how to write down his music correctly. He formed an octet in which two of his brothers sang whilst he played, and he wrote music for the group. They sang plantation songs and, more importantly, the new songs "written by Scott Joplin Esq."

In 1895, when Scott was 27, the group got as far as Syracuse, New York, where he sold his first two works to music publishers. *A Picture of Her Face* and *Please Say You Will* were both sentimental ballads offering no hint of the genius to come. Continuing their travels the group reached Temple, Texas, in 1897, where Scott managed to get his first piano piece published, another indifferent morsel. Soon afterwards the group disbanded and Scott went back to Sedalia, working again in what we would call the red light district. In that year he became resident pianist at the Maple Leaf Club, and wrote *Maple Leaf Rag* which, although written near the beginning of his career, has remained his most famous composition. It was clear even then that he wanted to write down 'classic' ragtime, music written and set down according to proper musical principles. He was pleased with *Maple Leaf Rag* and told his young black pianist friend Arthur Marshall, "One day it will make me King of Ragtime composers."

In that year (1897) ragtime was just coming into vogue. Arising from Negro plantation music, its syncopated, hesitant rhythm owed its origins to the plucking irregularities of the banjo, which formed the basis of negro music. The origin of the word 'ragtime' is uncertain, for there are differing views on how the expression came about, but the obvious explanation, which is generally believed to be the true one, is that it described syncopated or 'ragged time' music. The first published ragtime piece for piano was *Mississippi Rag* by William H. Krell which appeared in January 1897. Joplin's *Maple Leaf Rag* was not far behind, but at first he could not find a publisher. He offered it to the Sedalia music publisher, A.W. Perry, who turned it down. He wrote more ragtime pieces, and had *Original Rags* (a single piece despite its plural title) published in 1898 by Carl Hoffman of Kansas City. Joplin could now call himself a ragtime composer. But *Maple Leaf Rag* was still unpublished.

Back in Sedalia, the other local music publisher, John Stark, whose firm published mainly sentimental ballads, heard Joplin play *Maple Leaf Rag*. On enquiring whether it was Joplin's own work, and being told that it was, Stark asked Joplin to bring it round to his publishing office the next day. Joplin did, with his music in one hand, and a small black boy (no doubt recruited for the occasion) held by the other. While Joplin played his rag, the boy danced, demonstrating the 'danceability' of the music. Stark liked the piece and took the plunge. He paid Joplin a $50 advance plus 1% royalty on all sales. Though this sounds a meagre reward, Stark was in fact taking a gamble, as few black composers had had their work published. The presses set to work and *Maple Leaf Rag* appeared on sale towards the end of 1899. Reports of its initial sales differ. One authority says it was an immediate sell-out not only in Sedalia but in the surrounding towns, and in six months sold 75,000 copies; another report says it got off to a slow start and sold only 4,000 copies during its first year of publication. There is no doubt, however, that by the end of 1900, sales had really taken off. Ragtime was fast becoming a national craze; *Maple Leaf Rag* was the best ragtime piece on the market, and soon became immensely popular. So popular in fact that the Stark Publishing Company dropped all other work. The presses were set to roll off *Maple Leaf Rag* and nothing else, and its composer soon became famous.

On the strength of the success of this one piece Stark moved his premises to St. Louis and bought new printing presses. Stark was 59 when this bolt from the blue occurred; Joplin was 31. Not many years elapsed before one million copies were sold, and the piece continued to sell in small numbers long afterwards when most ragtime pieces were almost forgotten. It has been played and recorded more than any other ragtime piece, and in every possible style. It changed Joplin's fortunes and provided him with the opportunity to give up the lifestyle which circumstances had for years dictated. A quiet, reserved and dignified man, he welcomed the new-found independence that would enable him to compose the sort of music that interested him.

Soon after *Maple Leaf Rag* became such a hit, Joplin married Belle Heyden, who was a widow and sister-in-law of a fellow pianist and Joplin pupil, Scott Heyden. They set up home in St. Louis, where Joplin composed and established himself as a respected music teacher, an occupation he seems to have enjoyed. There is no doubt that Joplin wanted to be regarded as a serious musician and not as a bar-room pianist and composer of trifling pieces. Sometimes he went back to Sedalia, but it was no longer to work; instead it was as a celebrated visitor who might be persuaded to sit down and play his famous composition for the delight of the local people.

With *Maple Leaf Rag* so successful, Stark was hungry for more piano rags and Joplin duly obliged with *Swipesey* (1900), *Peacherine King* and *Sunflower Slow Drag* (both 1901). But the relationship between Stark and Joplin was an uneasy one. Not surprisingly, the hard-headed publisher wanted to publish only things he thought would be successful commercially. Joplin had ideas for a ragtime ballet (*The Ragtime Dance*) which all Stark's instincts told him, no doubt correctly, would stand no chance of achieving commercial success. Joplin spent a lot of time between about 1899 and 1902 writing the work, and Stark steadfastly refused to publish it. This dispute soured the relationship between the two and as a consequence Joplin had much of his work in the next few years issued by a variety of publishers though from time to time the rift was patched up and Joplin returned temporarily to the Stark fold. Stark and Joplin, for all their differences, were well aware that each owed a lot to the other, for the success of *Maple Leaf Rag* had 'made' both of them. *Rag Time Dance* was never published in its original form as a ballet, but Stark somewhat grudgingly published a piano version of it in 1906; it was not very successful. Meanwhile Joplin had continued to issue his piano rags under the imprint of various publishers with *Easy Winners* (1901), *Elite Syncopations, The Strenuous Life* and *The Entertainer* (all 1902) and *Weeping Willow* (1903).

In 1903 Joplin bought a large house in one of St. Louis's better neighbourhoods. Stark thought Joplin should continue to write piano rags, which he was very good at, and should abandon ideas to shine in spheres 'above his station', but Joplin had other plans. About 1902 Stark's heart sank when he heard reports that Joplin was writing a ragtime opera, *A Guest of Honor*, and that several numbers were already composed. Joplin's interest in having the opera published and performed became a fixation and was bitterly opposed by Stark, who declined to publish it. Nor could Joplin find another publisher. The opera, dated 1903, was never published, and the music is now lost. Rumour has it that the only manuscript was in a travelling trunk which Joplin lost or had stolen in Pittsburgh in 1907, but there is no firm evidence. Some of the numbers may have been published later as separate pieces, but again that is speculation.

With *A Guest of Honor* not getting off the ground, a further temporary healing of the Stark/Joplin breach occurred and Stark published *The Cascades* and *The Chrysanthemum* in 1904. That year was the year of the St. Louis Fair, at which 100 automobiles were featured, one of which had actually been driven all the way from New York. Another feature of the fair was a great cascade of waterfalls, which Joplin had in mind when writing *The Cascades*. A further rag issued that year was *The Favorite*, published by A.W. Perry of Sedalia, who had turned down the original version of *Maple Leaf Rag* a few years earlier. Perry's decision to reject *Maple Leaf Rag* when Joplin offered it might seem inept in retrospect, but Joplin had revised and improved the piece after it was offered to Perry, and the version he took to Stark was better than the one which Perry had turned down. In 1905 *Leola* was published, and also *Bethena*, a concert waltz, which is a very charming piece. On the first page of *Leola* Joplin issued the following advice which was to be repeated in some form or other on all but one of his subsequent piano rags:

"Notice! Don't play this piece fast. It is never right to play rag-time fast. Author."

The hyphening of rag-time hints that Joplin still regarded the term as a colloquialism. Joplin had strong feelings on the question of tempo. It had been the custom for pianists in bars and similar places to see who could play ragtime pieces the fastest. Such ragtime pyrotechnics were abhorrent to Joplin. He thought, rightly, that to treat his compositions in this way was as objectionable as it would be to apply similar treatment to a Beethoven sonata.

Though Joplin's music at this time was very successful, things were not going well in his personal life. His marriage was breaking up, due in part to the fact that his wife had no interest in music. A baby girl had been born, their only child, but died a few months later, and this may have hastened the end of the marriage. Scott Joplin and his wife parted early in 1906. She was not in good health at the time and, sadly, she died a couple of years afterwards. Soon after parting from Belle, Joplin moved to New York and lived there for the rest of his life. He met a lady called Lottie Stokes there and the two were married in 1909. The second marriage proved more successful than the first. What Joplin yearned for was quiet respectability and companionship, and this Lottie was able to provide. The stable and serene atmosphere they enjoyed together enabled Joplin to devote all his attention to composing and teaching. The days when he was forced by circumstances to play for his living in bars and gambling halls were long past. Joplin was an established figure, looked up to and respected by young and old musicians.

Piano rags continued to be produced from Joplin's pen at a steady rate and in the years 1906 to 1910 there appeared, under various publishers, *Eugenia, The Ragtime Dance* (arranged for piano), *The Nonpareil, Gladiolus Rag, Search Light Rag, Rose Leaf Rag, Fig Leaf Rag, Pineapple Rag, Sugar Cane, Paragon Rag, Wall Street Rag, Solace - A Mexican Serenade, Euphonic Sounds,* and *Stoptime Rag*, most of which sold well. Joplin was by no means the only ragtime composer around, but he was isolated from the others by superior talent. Then, as now, his rags were regarded as the best, and are almost certainly the best-structured musically. The two composers who most nearly approached Joplin's title of 'King of Ragtime', by which he had been universally known since about 1904, were James Scott and the white composer Joseph Lamb, both a few years younger than Joplin.

In 1908 Joplin published at his own expense a booklet containing six piano exercises on the 'correct' way to play ragtime. It was called *The School of Ragtime* and was priced at 50 cents. In the 'Remarks' at the beginning of the book he says:

"What is scurrilously called ragtime is an invention that is here to stay . . . . That all publications masquerading under the name ragtime are not the genuine article will be better known when these exercises are studied. That real ragtime of the higher class is rather difficult to play is a painful truth which most pianists have discovered. Syncopations are no indications of light or trashy music. To assist amateur players in giving the 'Joplin Rags' that weird and intoxicating effect intended by the composer is the object of this work."

The years 1900 to 1910, when Joplin wrote so many of his piano rags, mark the peak of his career. He was accepted as a composer whose music was taken seriously; he was not a purveyor of trash. His music was well thought out and constructed, and if financial success had been his only goal he would have no doubt continued to work in similar vein. But once again Joplin had thoughts on what to him were higher things, as had happened when he put so much time and effort into the unsuccessful ragtime opera *A Guest of Honor*. Again he set his sights on creating an opera, writing the words as well as the music. This one, to be called *Treemonisha*, was to be more ambitious than before, and from about 1907 when he started to draft out the first numbers for the new work it demanded an increasing amount of time. His interest in writing ordinary ragtime pieces dwindled and all his energies went into his plans for the opera. *A Guest of Honor* had been a preoccupation but the new opera, *Treemonisha*, became an obsession. By about 1910 the piano draft was finished, and a search began for ways and means of getting the opera into production. No one could be found who was prepared to publish the work, least of all John Stark, for the nightmare of *A Guest of Honor* was still fresh in his memory and his acute commercial sense told him the opera stood no chance of financial success. But Joplin was not to be dissuaded, and in spite of the fact that his health seemed to be deteriorating, more and more of his time was spent on revising the opera. In the continued absence of a prospective publisher Joplin finally published it at his own expense under his own name, 'Scott Joplin Music Publishing Co., New York City, N.Y.' in May 1911.

The story of the opera, which is a negro folk opera rather than a ragtime opera, is simple. The scene is set on a southern plantation in the years 1866 to 1884. Ned and his wife Monisha had no children and had always longed for a child to brighten their home. They had dreams of educating the child so that when it grew up it could teach the people about something better and higher than superstition and conjuring, which abounded locally. One morning Monisha found a two-day old baby girl under a tree that grew in front of their cabin. The couple adopted it as their own and called it Monisha, but later it became known as Treemonisha because it grew so fond of playing under the tree where it was found. In due course the child grew up, was educated, and started a career as a teacher and leader. The opera then deals with subsequent events.

Now that *Treemonisha* was published (though not yet performed) its score was available for anyone to study, and a single review of it appeared in *The American Musician*. The report was a lengthy one and the following is an extract:

"Scott Joplin, well known writer of music and especially of what a certain musician classified as 'ragtime', has just published an opera in three acts, entitled *Treemonisha*. The achievement is noteworthy for two reasons. First, it is composed by a negro, and second, the subject deals with an important phase of negro life. A remarkable point about the work is its evident desire to serve the negro race by exposing two of the great evils which have held this people in its grasp, as well as to point to higher and nobler ideals. Scott Joplin has proved himself a teacher as well as a scholar and an optimist with a mission which he has splendidly performed. Moreover he has created an entirely new phase of musical art and has produced a thoroughly American opera, dealing with a typically American subject, yet free from all extraneous influence. He has discovered something new because he has confidence in himself and his mission."

The review continued at length in laudatory vein and this spurred Joplin on in his efforts to have the opera presented.

The fact that only one periodical bothered to review the work might have served as a warning, but it did not. All other work was dropped and as Joplin's health deteriorated further, all was sacrificed to *Treemonisha*. The publication of the opera had seriously reduced his finances and the couple moved to cheaper premises, where Lottie took in boarders to help make ends meet. He took on an assistant to help copy out parts and this impoverished him further. The two would work far into the night, drafting out orchestral parts. Somehow, while all this was going on, two rags found their way to the publishers; they had probably been sketched out earlier and were presented now to bring in a little welcome money. These were *Scott Joplin's New Rag* (1912) and *Magnetic Rag*, a delightful piece which appeared in 1914. It turned out to be the last of Joplin's piano rags to be published in his lifetime.

By 1915, when Joplin was much reduced in health and circumstances, the opera was ready for presentation. Joplin hired the Lincoln Theatre in Harlem and collected together a group of singers and dancers for the performance. A contemporary report said Joplin "worked like a dog" rehearsing the cast. There was no money for scenery, costumes or musicians and the single performance of the opera went ahead with Joplin at the piano, improvising all the orchestral parts himself. The performance was a flop. Even if it had been possible to present a full production of the opera it would probably not have succeeded, for America was not yet ready for its subject matter. Southern plantations and black superstitions were too much part of the recent past of many black New York citizens. They wanted to forget it, not remember it. They viewed the subject objectively, but were not yet ready to see this period of their history raised to the level of art.

The public lack of interest in *Treemonisha* finished Joplin. Dispirited and ill, his emotions and senses were dulled. His piano-playing skills left him, and the few piano rolls he recorded at that time were said to be disorganised and amateurish; his earlier ones had been much better. Unfinished manuscripts littered his desk for he had lost the drive to write any more music. He was suffering from the terminal stages of syphilis, a disease which had carried off greater composers than Joplin. From late 1916 onwards he became mentally feeble, and lucid periods became rare. He was taken into Manhattan State Hospital on 5th February 1917 and died there on 1st April of that year, a date which Joplin in a cynical moment might have thought fitting for the death of a poor southern-born black man who aspired to write high class music and opera. He was only 48. After a modest funeral he was buried in a common grave in St. Michael's cemetery on Long Island. He had asked, years before, that *Maple Leaf Rag* should be played at his funeral. When the time came, his wife, Lottie, decided it was not appropriate to do so, though later she wished she had allowed it. Eight months after Joplin's death his old publisher John Stark issued *Reflection Rag - Syncopated Musings*, probably compiled from previously unpublished pieces that Stark kept in his files. Some experts think it is not genuine Joplin; if it is, it was the last Joplin Rag.

What of Joplin as a composer? He never wished to be a musical rebel. On the contrary, he wished above all to be regarded as an orthodox, serious composer, albeit in a particular sphere. It is interesting to note that in 1914, at a time when the classically-trained Percy Grainger was writing instructions such as "Play it Thumpingly" at the head of his compositions, Scott Joplin was writing "Allegretto Ma

Non Troppo" at the head of *Magnetic Rag*. No one would pretend he was a great composer, but he deserves an honourable place in the world of music. His output was small in quantity and restricted in variety, but within his limited sphere he was to ragtime what Mozart was to late 18th century music. Though he only wrote just over thirty piano rags they are models of their type and set a standard for all other composers who attempted to write music of similar form.

After Joplin's death, ragtime gradually went out of fashion; indeed, it had been declining in popularity for some years beforehand, and by the 1920s it was a thing of the past. For many years the only Scott Joplin rag that could be bought as sheet music in Britain was *Maple Leaf Rag*. Then, in the 1940s, 50s and 60s there came a gradual revival, culminating in the issue in the early 70s of three long-playing recordings by the American pianist Joshua Rifkin of 24 of Joplin's piano rags correctly played in classical style, and the subsequent use of some of Joplin's music in the film *The Sting* referred to earlier. Suddenly, more than 50 years after his death, Joplin was a national figure in his own country, and a new discovery to many people in Britain. Joplin would probably have been surprised, if he were looking down from above, to see his piano rags being played in classical style in front of a concert audience by a man dressed in an evening suit seated at a grand piano. But he would have approved.

In October 1974, as a belated tribute to Joplin, the American Society of Composers, Authors and Publishers held a brief service at the site of Joplin's grave. On the rough patch of ground a bronze marker was placed. It read, "Scott Joplin, American Composer" and gave his birth and death dates. At long last, Scott Joplin's talents had been acknowledged. As the dignitaries stood in silence a slight breeze wafted across the graveyard. As if ironically, the brightly coloured leaves of a nearby maple tree rustled gently.

Footnote: John Stark died in 1927, aged 86. Joplin's wife, Lottie, died in 1953, aged about 79. *Treemonisha* was performed on Broadway in 1975.

A list of Scott Joplin's compositions is given in Appendix 4.

The Melody Lingers On

Jerome Kern

5. Jerome Kern

Who was the greatest popular song writer of the century? The question is subjective and has no definite answer, but the name of Jerome Kern must be high among the possible contenders. Along with his fellow Americans (Irving Berlin, George Gershwin, Cole Porter and a handful of others), he composed a string of melodies that have become immortal. His 40-year career began in the early years of the century, and lasted until the end of the Second World War. With his great gift for creating bright and easily remembered tunes, it is not surprising that he established a niche for himself in songwriting's hall of fame. Today we can still enjoy songs like *A Fine Romance, Look For The Silver Lining, Smoke Gets In Your Eyes,* and a host of other Kern melodies.

Like so many other geniuses of western music, Jerome Kern was of European Jewish ancestry. His father, Henry Kern, was born in Germany in 1842 and had come to New York around 1857. His mother, Fannie Kakeles, whose parents had emigrated from the Prague neighbourhood in the late 1840s, was born in New York in 1852. A skilful pianist by her teens, she even considered the possibility of becoming a professional musician. In later life she was active in charitable work for immigrants. After Henry and Fannie's marriage they took an apartment on New York's East 49th Street. Seven children were born to the couple, all boys, but as was so often the case in those days several failed to survive. The first two (Joseph, 1875 and Edwin, 1877) did live, but then followed three others (Milton, Irving and Charles) who all died in infancy. The sixth boy, Jerome David Kern, was born on 27th January 1885. With the date of her confinement near, Henry Kern had taken his wife to see the races at nearby Jerome Park; on the way home Fannie's labour pains began and the baby was born as soon as the couple reached home. Whether or not the child was named after the racecourse is open to speculation, but Jerome he definitely was, though he soon became 'Jerry' to his family and friends. The last of Henry and Fannie's sons, Bertram, died in infancy, so Jerry was, in effect, the youngest of three.

Jerome Kern's story is not one of 'Rags to Riches' for his father, like so many other Jewish immigrants, had a good head for business and had built up for himself a comfortable financial position. An entrepreneur, he headed a street-sprinkling contracting business to which the local residents contributed a fee; without sprinkling the primitive city roads of those days would have become a dust bowl. It was said that the sprinkling machines were turned off when passing the premises of payment-defaulters! In addition to this business, he had an interest in a local store, Wolff's, and became a partner.

Jerry's early schooling was unremarkable but he learned to play the piano and soon proved to be good at it, having probably inherited his musical talents from his mother. When Jerry was 10 he was taken to see a Broadway show as a birthday present. He loved it - he thought the show was marvellous, and from that day he was hooked on popular music. When he was 12 his parents moved to nearby Newark, New Jersey, a predominantly German-Jewish area, and Jerry was transferred to Newark High School. There he used to play the piano for assembly and, more significantly, he started to write music. In 1901 he contributed to a minstrel show presented by the school. The song *My Angeline* was billed as "written by Mr. J.D. Kern for the occasion". The school magazine wrote in glowing terms about the 16-year-old Kern: "Mr. Kern's superior ability as a pianist is too well known among the scholars of the high school to require further comment". Another report referred to "Selections by Mr. J.D. Kern on the piano". A teacher told him, "Jerome - you're an all-round whizz!" At about the same time he wrote the score for a musical satire, a spoof on 'Uncle Tom's Cabin' given by the Newark Yacht Club, which despite its rather upper-class name, was really just an ordinary social club. *The Newark Evening News* said: "Mr. Kern's music was made the basis of many congratulatory speeches to the young composer last night", whilst *The Daily Advertiser* observed: "Mr. Kern has shown great ability as a composer".

Soon after this (late in 1901) Jerry left school and was fortunate enough to spend the first few months of 1902 in Germany, in and around Heidelberg. In those pre-World War I days it was commonplace for wealthy Americans of German extraction to send their sons to 'the home country' in order to absorb the atmosphere. Whilst there Jerry may have taken part in musical activities but there is no evidence of his undertaking any formal musical instruction.

Back in the USA in the summer of 1902, Jerry at 17 wanted above all else to become a composer, but his father had other ideas for him. Joseph, Jerry's eldest brother, was already in trade and Edwin was in the legal profession, so Henry Kern decided he wanted Jerry in the family firm. Consequently he was employed on a trial basis and was promptly given an assignment, to attend an auction. Jerry dozed off, nodded in the wrong place, and D. Wolff & Co. became the proud owner of several crates of prunes, requiring two horse-drawn drays to remove them. But worse was to follow. Wolff's store had a small music department, and Henry decided to send Jerry to a piano wholesaler to buy two pianos. Jerry went to the wholesaler's, started to play the pianos, was plied with drink by the wholesaler, and signed an order for two hundred pianos! The deal was evidently irreversible and Henry's jaw dropped when the pianos started to arrive. So, for a while, Mr. Kern senior had to hire extra premises and become a piano dealer. From Jerry's point of view everything had worked out for the best, as his father decided that enough was enough. Business was clearly not Jerry's forte. He would never do well in trade and might as well become a composer after all.

In the autumn of 1902 when Jerry was still 17 he got his first job in music, as an odd-job boy with the Lyceum Music Company, run by Edward B. Marks. He had already sent numerous songs to a variety of publishers, only to see them all rejected, but very shortly after joining Lyceum they published one of his songs, *At the Casino*, the first published song with the name of Jerome D. Kern on the cover. Initially his job was merely clerical, but Marks soon recognised his musical ability and he became a song plugger for the firm at a salary of seven dollars a week. He was sent to Wanamaker's store where his job was to 'plug' (i.e. demonstrate and sell) Lyceum's songs. There were other song pluggers doing the same work who were much more eminent at that time than Jerry. One was Jean Schwartz who later was to write *Rockabye Your Baby with a Dixie Melody* and *Chinatown, My Chinatown* for Al Jolson. Another was Ernest Ball, who wrote *Mother Machree, When Irish Eyes Are Smiling,* and *Let the Rest of the World Go By*. Schwartz used to do the first session, then Jerry took over, and Ball ended, but as Schwartz often left early and Ball arrived late Jerry was usually in great demand and got plenty of practice. After leaving school Jerry had enrolled for night school classes at the New York College of Music, where he studied composition, counterpoint, and the other essentials of his trade. In May 1903 Lyceum published another of Jerry's songs, *In a Shady Bungalow*, a piece far in advance of the first from a musical point of view. Jerry was making progress.

Jerry stayed with Lyceum for about a year and then moved to another music publisher, T.B. Harms & Co., run by Max Dreyfus. His salary shot up from $7/week to $12; apparently when Dreyfus asked Jerry what he was earning, and Jerry replied $7, Dreyfus thought he had said $11, and offered him one more. Jerry's career prospered with Dreyfus; at the end of 1903 he was asked to write music to go into the English show *An English Daisy* which had transferred from London to Broadway. British shows were often put on in New York, but they had to be 'Americanised'. He didn't write the whole of the score for this show or subsequent ones at that period, but wrote songs to be substituted for ones considered unsuitable. This in turn led to an extra source of income, for Max Dreyfus arranged for Jerry to act as a rehearsal pianist for the shows into which the songs were interpolated. This practice was to continue for many years and provided invaluable experience, for Jerry was able to take an active part in the preparation of the shows all the way through to final rehearsal. Late in 1903 his financial situation became even more secure when he purchased an interest in the firm which employed him (probably with the aid of an inheritance from his grandfather who had died earlier in the year) and thus became a partner.

With Jerry established as a successful songwriter, let us look briefly at the way his songs were written. Unlike Irving Berlin, who wrote the words and the music for his songs, Kern wrote only the music. Usually his songs were intended for shows; he knew what kind of music was required at a particular point in the plot and would write a tune. He would then suggest a 'dummy verse' (e.g. dum-di-dah-dah) to indicate the required vocal stresses and then give it to a professional wordsmith who would produce a verse. Over the years he worked with many different lyricists, unlike George Gershwin who collaborated mainly with his brother.

About the end of 1903 Jerry made the first of innumerable trips to

Britain. He took a temporary job with Charles Frohman, an American impresario with an office in London, at £2/week. In London Jerry sold a few songs, all now long forgotten, but more importantly, he met many of the leading figures in the London theatre, including George Grossmith jr. who wrote lyrics for London shows. In 1904 he went back to New York as Max Dreyfus's personal assistant, and 'Americanised' another British show, *Mr. Wix of Wickham*, which drew good reviews from the critics, notably Alan Dale of *The American*. By now, Jerry was not only modifying British shows for the United States market, but he was also producing songs to pep up substandard American shows. He was a kind of musical first-aid man. When a song proved wanting in vitality, Jerry as 'Mr. Fixit' would produce a substitute, and when asked who wrote it he would say, "Oh, it's a little number I wrote myself."

In 1905 the 20-year old composer had his first big hit with *How'd You Like To Spoon with Me?* a minstrel number for the show *The Earl and the Girl* with lyrics by Edward Laska. This song and the others he had written for a variety of shows were bringing in a steady income, so he could indulge himself by travelling to London as and when he wanted. In 1906 he met P.G. Wodehouse at the Aldwych Theatre and collaborated with him in the song *Mr. Chamberlain* for the West End show *The Beauty of Bath*. It was sung by Seymour Hicks and earned 10 encores on the first night. From then on, for many years to come, Jerry had an interest in shows running on both sides of the Atlantic, and he shuttled to and fro regularly. Already an Anglophile, he liked to look English and to pretend by all means possible (in the presence of Americans) to *be* English.

Back in the USA in 1906 Kern wrote songs for Frohman's Broadway show *The Little Cherub* and for a series of other shows. But the following couple of years were sad ones, for his mother died of cancer on the last day of 1907 and his father died of pernicious anaemia in August 1908. Jerry and his two elder brothers naturally attended both funerals and it is interesting to note that the local press, listing those present, singled out "Mr. Jerome D. Kern, the well-known songwriter."

In 1908-9 Jerry fell in love with Edie Kelly, a star in one of the musicals he wrote, but at the end of 1909 the romance ended and she married someone else. More shows followed, and in 1910 Jerry was back in England, partly to write musicals, and partly on holiday. Whilst on holiday he and a couple of friends went boating on the Thames, and one night they stayed at the Swan Hotel, Walton-on-Thames. It was there that he met the landlord's 18-year old daughter Eva, and promptly fell in love. He soon had to go back to New York to fulfil commitments but he wrote to Eva regularly, and before many weeks had elapsed the couple were engaged. They married at St. Mary's Church, Walton-on-Thames, on 25th October 1910. Eva sailed back to New York with him.

Eva didn't like New York to begin with; this was hardly surprising as it was a far cry from Walton-on-Thames. It seems to have been an odd sort of marriage; Jerry was not one to hide his light under a bushel and considered himself very much his wife's intellectual superior. According to Guy Bolton, who later was to write librettos for Kern's scores and who stayed at the Kerns' home while doing so, Jerry was not averse to belittling Eva in front of other people. If, for instance she proffered an opinion that Jerry thought was stupid, he would clench his fists and move his arms slowly in and out in front of himself as she talked, as his way of indicating what to his mind were her pint-pulling origins. Later on, when telephones came into fashion, Eva was apprehensive of using the 'new-fangled' instrument, but Jerry made her do so, to her public embarrassment, even when he could have spared her the ordeal by answering it himself. Nevertheless the marriage survived, and lasted until his death many years later. In their own way Jerry and Eva were fond of each other, though there were difficult times, especially in the 1920s when she had a nervous breakdown. In short, she learned how to handle him. As she settled into New York life she became more confident, and became as ardent a lover of America as he was an Anglophile.

Jerry and Eva set up home in Manhattan, New York, and he continued to write music for shows. In 1914 one of his songs for the show *The Girl from Utah* was a tremendous success and put Kern right into the front rank of songwriters. The song was *They Didn't Believe Me*. In a year of many famous songs by other composers, such as *It's a Long Way To Tipperary* and *When You Wore a Tulip*, Kern's song more than held its own. Moreover it has a timeless quality. Whereas *Tipperary* and many of the other First World War songs epitomise their era, *They Didn't Believe Me* still sounds fresh today when arranged with modern orchestrations.

In the following year, 1915, Jerry had a lucky escape from death. He was booked to sail for Europe with the impresario Charles Frohman; Frohman sailed, but Jerry overslept and missed the boat. The ship in question was the *Lusitania*, torpedoed a few days later by a German U-boat off Ireland. Frohman perished, along with more than a thousand others. Jerry remained, thanking his good fortune. During the years of the Great War he poured his energies into writing songs for shows. Countless numbers of songs were produced for dozens of shows on both sides of the Atlantic. The shows and songs are listed by Kern's biographers but, it has to be admitted, they were written purely in order to keep a show going for a few weeks or months, with no thought of enduring quality. It would be pointless to catalogue hundreds of long-forgotten songs in long-forgotten shows. Like all popular songwriters, Jerome Kern is remembered by his best efforts. The vast majority of his output has sunk into oblivion and will remain there.

In 1916 Jerry wrote *Till the Clouds Roll By* for the show *Oh, Boy!* and that song has lasted. About the same time, he wrote *Bill* (words by P.G. Wodehouse) for *Oh, Lady, Lady!* but the song was discarded as being unsuitable for the show on the grounds that its words and sentiments were out of context. It was therefore put on one side, to reappear years later as one of the hits of *Show Boat*. Like most songwriters, Jerry was loth to waste any material that he thought had potential, so songs were often 'lifted' out of one show and put in another, and tunes acquired a new set of words.

In 1918, after eight years of marriage, a daughter was born to Eva and Jerry. Elizabeth Jane (Betty) was to be the Kerns' only child. Jerry doted on her and was to lavish on her all that money could buy. And money there was in plenty. As *The New York Times* wrote in 1918,

"At 33 Kern finds himself today one of the most successful and sought after composers of the world."

There had been five new Kern shows in 1917 and six in 1918. Said *The New York Times*:

"If the Kern scale of mathematical progression continues, there will be seven new Kern shows on Broadway next season and eight the year after. If he lives to be 70, there is no telling what may happen."

Certain it was that Jerry judged himself to be the best songwriter in America. After himself he considered Irving Berlin the best songwriter, that Vincent Youmans wrote the best melodies, and George Gershwin created the best rhythms. Hardly a modest man, Kern could at times be distinctly prickly. He once invited the young George Gershwin, just starting off on his musical career, to come to him for help when he got a major assignment. When the time came, one of Gershwin's friends who knew Jerry well advised George not to go to Kern but to sort things out himself, saying, "You're quite capable", which in fact he was. So George didn't go to Kern. When Jerry realised that George had spurned his offer of help, and achieved success nevertheless, he was furious and wouldn't speak to George for a while. Eventually relationships became reasonably cordial but some of Jerry's friends felt he never completely forgave George.

As the First World War drew to its close and the twenties approached, Jerry was involved in numerous 'run of the mill' shows such as *Oh, Lady, Lady!* and *Zip Goes a Million* (resurrected in London in the 1950s with George Formby in the lead). All had shallow plots and bright jingling melodies but few if any are remembered today. But in 1920 Kern wrote the music for *Sally*, which turned out to be one of the biggest hits on the New York stage for years and the biggest ever Broadway musical success up to that time. Presented by Ziegfeld from a book by Guy Bolton with lyrics by P.G. Wodehouse, the hit tune was *Look for the Silver Lining*, a song which remained one of Jerry's favourites of his own compositions. The show ran in New York from November 1920 almost until the end of 1923, with Marilyn Miller in the lead role of Sally in over 1500 performances. In 1921 the show came to London and equalled its New York success, with Dorothy Dickson in the lead. She was apprehensive on the first night as to whether she was capable of playing Sally as the heart-rending waif she was supposed to be, and was terrified lest Kern, present for the occasion, would make disparaging remarks, for he was a stickler for perfection. At the end of the second act she had to sing Sally's saddest song. Immediately afterwards Jerry came into her dressing room and pointed to his cheek, showing Miss Dickson a tear. He told her Marilyn Miller had never achieved that. Dorothy Dickson's day was made!

Kern was pernickety about his music; everything always had to be just right and to his liking. Actors and singers dreaded his presence at rehearsal for he was a martinet who found fault continuously. He often dropped in at rehearsals for new shows, and with several Broadway shows featuring Kern's music often running concurrently he was kept pretty busy. Various theatres were used for rehearsal other than the one where the show was actually appearing. On one occasion Jerry breezed into the theatre to observe a rehearsal and was horrified to see a bevy of high-kicking girls on the stage. "Hey there", stormed Jerry. "Stop! That's not how I want it!" "Just take it easy, Mr. Kern", suggested the director gently, leading him to a seat. It soon dawned on Jerry that it wasn't one of his shows; he had come to the wrong theatre. Somewhat deflated, he quietly departed.

Not only was he fussy about his music, he insisted on a large share of the takings. Guy Bolton, P.G. Wodehouse and he collaborated in many shows and on one occasion Bolton and Wodehouse suggested to Kern that between them they should insist on receiving 30% of the profits, i.e. 10% each. "Oh, No", said Jerry, "There's no point, they wouldn't give us that." Bolton and Wodehouse *did* see the management, however, and discovered Kern was already getting 10% whilst they were getting 7½% each. As Bolton and Wodehouse had assumed they had all been getting the same they were *not* amused. There were many squabbles about who got credit for what (though Kern once said "I don't care about the credit so long as my name's on the cheque"), which star was to sing which song, there were arguments with conductors and producers, and Jerry had a reputation for being as tetchy as anyone. But his co-writers humoured him and together they formed one of Broadway's most successful teams. He was one of the New York theatre's most familiar figures. About 5ft 6in tall, of Jewish appearance, dapper, with thick glasses, he favoured bright trousers (usually green) and flashy ties. When Jerome Kern was in the theatre everyone knew it.

Throughout the 1920s Jerry continued his transatlantic shuttle, usually with Eva and Betty. When in London they generally stayed at Claridges. By now he had become a collector of rare books after having bought his first one some years earlier for $40. One of his main pleasures was to wander round the bookshops of the Charing Cross Road. He was knowledgeable and had an eye for a bargain. No dealer could ever take advantage of the fact that he was awash with money; Jerry never paid a penny more for a book than it was worth.

The Melody Lingers On

After *Sally* in 1920, Jerry had written the scores for dozens of other musicals, all less distinguished than *Sally* but still good enough to run for several months and bring him a steady (and large) income. His next really big success was *Sunny*, presented in 1925 by Charles Dillingham, with words by Oscar Hammerstein II (then only 30) and the German-born Otto Harbach. *Sunny* ran for 517 performances at the New Amsterdam Theatre on Broadway with Marilyn Miller as 'Sunny', followed by a tour. It also crossed the Atlantic, Jack Buchanan and Binnie Hale starring in the London production. The big hit song of the show was *Who?*, a number which to this day epitomises the 1920s.

After *Sunny*, Jerry didn't have to wait long for another big success. He had read Edna Furber's novel, *Show Boat*, the story of a steam boat ('Cotton Blossom') that chugged up and down the Mississippi staging melodramas and comedies for the benefit of passengers. Edna Furber had done her homework; knowing that such boats existed but were unchronicled, she found a real-life one in North Carolina. For a while she lived with the company, sat in the box office, watched the shows, and absorbed the atmosphere. All this came out faithfully in her book. Jerry was excited by the book and bought the theatrical rights. Having invited Oscar Hammerstein II to write the script, he then had to persuade the impresario Ziegfeld to put the show on. When Hammerstein asked Jerry, "Is Ziegfeld enthusiastic?" Jerry replied, "He doesn't know anything about it yet!" Ziegfeld soon found out about Jerry's ideas, for Jerry bombarded him with them. It didn't take the astute impresario long to realise he was on to a money-making winner, and he promised to put the show on, but only when the run of his current show, *Rio Rita*, had finished. *Rio Rita* ran longer than had been expected and it was not until the end of 1927 that *Show Boat* opened in New York.

Show Boat was an immediate sensation; not surprising with a string of numbers like *Why Do I Love You?*, *Bill*, *Ol' Man River*[*], *Can't Help Lovin' Dat Man*, and *Only Make Believe*. As we have already seen, *Bill* was written by Kern and Wodehouse years earlier for another show but not used. Kern decided it would fit beautifully into *Show Boat*, so with

---

[*] In the original programme of *Show Boat* the song appeared as *Old Man River* and also as *Ol' Man River*. There were many similar inconsistencies in Kern's song titles.

Wodehouse's blessing (plus appropriate royalties) it was interpolated into Kern and Hammerstein's show and was one of its big hits. It is interesting to note that although *Ol' Man River* is inextricably linked with the name of Paul Robeson, and does not sound right when sung by anyone else, he was not in the original production. Kern was aware of his existence and wanted him, but Robeson had other commitments and could not be in the show at the start. Initially *Ol' Man River* was sung by Jules Bledsoe. In March 1928 *Show Boat* was presented at the Drury Lane Theatre in London (with Robeson in the part of Old Joe) and was to be as successful there as in New York.

There are several factors that contributed to the success of the show. For one thing, it had a good story, with all shades of emotion from joyful exuberance to the melancholy plight of the negro worker. Moreover, unlike most of Kern's shows, which he dashed off in days purely as a matter of expediency in order to keep a theatre going for a few weeks, he and Hammerstein took their time in writing *Show Boat*. They visited the deep south, took in the atmosphere of the river, worked and re-worked their songs and did a thoroughly professional job. So professional, in fact, that Kern was accused of using a traditional negro melody for *Ol' Man River*. Kern claimed it was original, and so it must have been, for a search through the archives of negro music by many experts failed to reveal any tune resembling it. *Show Boat* had a lengthy run on both sides of the Atlantic and to this day there are frequent revivals. Two major film versions have been made, the first in 1936 and the second in 1951. For the 1936 film, starring Paul Robeson, Kern wrote an additional song, *I Still Suits Me*, so that Robeson would have more than one song to sing.

In 1929 Jerry sold his vast collection of rare books. He had decided they were becoming too much of an obsession; they were possessing him rather than he them. All were sold at auction except the first and last he had collected, and any that had been given to him as gifts. The sale fetched $1,729,462; nearly double the estimate. He invested the proceeds but with the Wall Street Crash nine months later lost much of the money. However, he was still a very rich man. He bought a yacht which he christened *Show Boat* and spent money lavishly in other ways, enjoying night clubs and good food. One day, having discovered Eva had borrowed his car, he walked to the showroom down the road and bought another. For many years Betty had an English governess as he wanted her to be brought up in the manner of an English lady.

More London and Broadway shows followed *Show Boat*. *The Cat and the Fiddle*, with words by Otto Harbach, was a big hit and included the song *She Didn't Say Yes*. *Music In the Air* followed, which featured another hit song, *I've Told Every Little Star*. The way the tune came to be written is interesting. When Jerry and Eva were staying in Nantucket he heard an unusual bird call outside his window. Later he wished he had written it down. Fortunately the bird duly obliged again the next day, and this time Jerry noted down the tune. Returning home he played it to a friend who was a wildlife expert; he identified it as the song of 'Melospiza Melodia', popularly known as the Cape Cod Sparrow. Jerry prompty turned the bird song into the tune of *I've Told Every Little Star*.

In the early 1930s Jerry wanted to do a musical based on *Porgy* but discovered that George and Ira Gershwin were writing *Porgy and Bess*, a negro opera, so the idea was scrapped. A new stage show came in 1932, *Roberta*, which included the classic number *Smoke Gets in Your Eyes,* the words of which were by Otto Harbach. One of the stars of the show was a young comedian named Bob Hope. Another show, *Three Sisters*, which Kern scored for the Drury Lane Theatre in London, contained *I Won't Dance*, later made famous by Fred Astaire. With the increasing success of the talkies, RKO bought the rights of *Roberta* for Fred Astaire and Ginger Rogers. This was the prelude to an increasing move on Kern's part away from the Broadway Musical and into films. After all, this was the mid thirties; it was the era of the depression and the general public could no longer afford to go to stage shows, but they could afford the cheaper cinema seats. Astaire and Rogers had become stars and it was only natural that Jerry would want to cash in on the act.

In 1934 Jerry was in London again for the British version of *Three Sisters* at the Drury Lane Theatre, and an amusing incident occurred during rehearsals. An old horse was required for the plot, and the management had procured an elderly animal that they said Binnie Hale had ridden hundreds of times in the stage run of *Sunny* eight years earlier. Somewhat sceptical when he saw the geriatric creature, Jerry walked to the piano and started to play the circus music from *Sunny*, whereupon the aged animal pricked up its ears and went through its

Sunny routine to perfection.

On 27th January 1935 Jerry celebrated his 50th birthday. A radio channel presented a special programme to mark the event; a kind of precursor of *This Is Your Life*. Eva and Betty, sworn to secrecy, had to ensure he was in the house at the appropriate time (no mean feat) with the radio on. The programme started, with Kern's music playing, and the announcer said words to the effect, "If you're listening, Jerry, go and open the front door." He did, and there was Irving Berlin with a large bouquet of flowers. There was an emotional greeting, and the two great songwriters sat down in the lounge with Jerry's family to enjoy the tributes that followed. As Jerry said, "Isn't it wonderful to be eulogised whilst you're still alive to hear and enjoy it."

Jerry was now spending nearly all his working time writing musical scores for Hollywood films, so Broadway had to take a back seat for the time being. Compared with Broadway, the work was relatively easy. Whereas he had always taken an active part in the weeks of preparation necessary for a stage show, strutting around the rehearsal hall shouting out orders, he soon found Hollywood's method was to leave all the details of the film's preparation to the director. All Jerry had to do was compose the music for the songs. Consequently he had more time to revise and modify his songs than had usually been the case in the past, so they became high quality finished products. He and Eva took temporary accommodation in Hollywood; in spite of the attention he paid to his songs the work took so little of his time that he had plenty of opportunity for leisure, especially, in his case, pitch and putt, and playing cards with his cronies late into the night. He was a confirmed gambler.

In rapid succession came a stream of films containing a mixture of new and old songs. The films included 20th Century Fox's *Music in the Air* (a film version of his 1932 show, for which he wrote a new title song), MGM's *Reckless,* and RKO's *Roberta* with Astaire and Rogers. For this film he resurrected *I Won't Dance* and the film included *Smoke Gets in Your Eyes*. Warner Brothers made *Sweet Adeline* and then came the new film version of *Show Boat* with Paul Robeson in the cast. *Swing Time* with Astaire and Rogers included *A Fine Romance, Never Gonna Dance, Pick Yourself Up* and *The Way You Look Tonight*. This last song won him his first Oscar. One of the reasons *Swing Time* did so well was the perfectionism of both Kern and Astaire. After a take of *A Fine Romance*, Kern mentioned to Astaire that his pronunciation of the word 'arctic' could possibly be misinterpreted as 'artic'. No-one else had noticed nor were they likely to, but Astaire insisted on doing the song again; if anything he was even more of a perfectionist than Kern. Apparently Jerry had difficulty writing the music for *Bojangles of Harlem*, as that type of music was not his usual style. Fred Astaire came round to Jerry and Eva's home and Astaire went through a lengthy dancing routine, dancing from room to room, to suggest ideas to Kern, after which Jerry completed his work brilliantly.

In 1935 and 1936 Jerry and Eva were spending so much time in Hollywood, and seemed likely to continue to do so, that they decided to sell their Bronxville home and move to California. The move occurred early in 1937 and was accompanied by an event that nearly killed Jerry. He owned two pianos, a Steinway and a Blüthner, but the Blüthner was his favourite. He asked the Steinway Company to crate both pianos, and when the removal men came to unpack the Blüthner in Los Angeles they found the piano impaled to its container; one of the long screws used for assembling the crate had penetrated the Blüthner's soundboard. Jerry was incensed; "white with rage" was how one observer put it, and very shortly afterwards he suffered a massive heart attack which left him unconscious. This in turn was followed by a minor stroke which left his left side paralysed. Gradually he recovered, but his piano playing was never the same again according to his friends - although *he* blamed the piano! He didn't like illnesses or anything to do with them, nor did he like hearing anything unpleasant. During his convalescence his family kept from him the news of George Gershwin's illness and death. He only learned of Gershwin's death when listening to a radio programme about the composer's music, and noticed that Gershwin was referred to in the past tense. Gershwin's untimely death upset him and, combined with his own condition, caused him to go through a period of profound depression lasting several months. Eva knew he was finally getting better when, one day, she heard him on the telephone placing a bet with a bookie.

In 1937 Kern and Oscar Hammerstein II wrote the music and words for Paramount's *High, Wide and Handsome* starring Dorothy Lamour, a film that contained *Can I Forget You?* and *The Folks Who Live On the*

Hill. By now Jerry was spending much of his leisure time on his passions for collecting. Another book collection had built up and he also collected coins, silverware, furniture and paintings. In 1939 Betty married Dick Green, younger brother of John Green who wrote the music of *Body and Soul*. However, the marriage did not last long and Jerry's attention, like everyone else's, turned to the war in Europe.

After the German invasion of France in 1940 Oscar Hammerstein wrote a poem, 'When I Last Saw Paris', a nostalgic piece recalling the delights of Paris before its fall to Hitler. Oscar's son Bill changed the words to *The Last Time I Saw Paris*, and Oscar asked Jerry to set it to music. This was against Jerry's custom, for he never normally wrote without a show or film in mind, nor did he compose music to words. However, he agreed to do it on this occasion and the song became a great hit in the early years of the war. Indeed, it makes one wonder what Jerry might have achieved had he set words to music more often. MGM put the song into the film *Lady Be Good* (without Astaire and Rogers but starring Eleanor Powell and Robert Young instead), most of the music of which was by Gershwin. Kern and Hammerstein won an Oscar for the song, but both maintained that Johnny Mercer and Harold Arlen should have won it for *That Old Black Magic*, on the grounds that Mercer and Arlen's song was written for a film, whereas *The Last Time I Saw Paris* was not, and therefore should not have been considered.

An RKO version of *Sunny* followed, starring Anna Neagle and Ray Bolger, and in 1941 Kern was asked to make a concert arrangement of his *Show Boat* songs to be played in the New York Philharmonic Orchestra's 1941 season. The work proved very difficult and Kern wrote to the organisers pointing out that after a lifetime of writing music for the theatre, and latterly for films, he was "not equipped" to undertake the work. However, he made a 'skeleton sketch' of what he thought was required and the musical arrangements were completed by Russell Bennett, who excelled in such work. Entitled *Scenario for Orchestra on Themes from Show Boat*, it was performed in Carnegie Hall on 23rd October 1941. More arrangements followed, with a transcription for string quartet of *All the Things You Are, The Way You Look Tonight, Smoke Gets in Your Eyes* and *Yesterdays*. But Kern was happier writing popular music and these concert arrangements were merely a brief interlude in his busy film schedule. In 1942 the film *You*

Were Never Lovelier was released, starring Fred Astaire and Rita Hayworth, and featuring another new Kern song, *Dearly Beloved*.

After the breakdown of Betty's marriage to Dick Green she had married the bandleader Artie Shaw in 1941, and in 1943 a son was born, Steven Kern Shaw. He was the only grandchild to be born in Jerry's lifetime and he doted on the child almost as much as he had doted on Betty years earlier.

In 1941 Oscar Hammerstein had asked Jerry to work with him on a new show, *Green Grow the Lilies*, which was to be a Western. Jerry declined - he didn't like Westerns. This decision cost him dearly. It coincided with the break up of the partnership of Lorenz Hart and Richard Rodgers, and as a result Hammerstein took Richard Rodgers into partnership to write the music. The show was re-titled *Oklahoma* and, after the première in 1943, it became one of the musical hits of the century. Whether it would have done so well had Jerry written the music is impossible to know, but he was very jealous of its success and bitterly regretted his decision. Nevertheless there was still plenty for him to do. Tiring of Hollywood, as others had before him, and mindful of the success of *Oklahoma*, he started to write songs for stage shows again. *Wild Rose* was presented in London (it was a kind of wartime version of *Sally*) with Jessie Matthews singing *Look For the Silver Lining* in the starring role. But Kern had not abandoned his film work completely. In 1943 he collaborated with Ira Gershwin, with whom he had not worked previously, in *Cover Girl*, a film starring Rita Hayworth and produced by Arthur Schwartz, himself a well-known composer. After playing one new song through to Schwartz and noting Schwartz's lukewarm reaction, Jerry wrote ADL on the manuscript and discarded it. Asked by someone what ADL meant, Jerry explained, "Arthur doesn't like." By next day he had come up with something else to replace it - the tune of *Long Ago and Far Away*, which became a big hit. In the film it was sung by Gene Kelly, then young and unknown. In the recording session for the song, which Kelly sang in a soundproof studio, Kern sat at the other side of the glass panel looking stern and inscrutable. Kelly apologised to Kern when he came out, feeling his performance hadn't done the song justice and suggested he should do more 'takes'. But Jerry told him to relax, for what he had just heard was fine. Afterwards Jerry sent him a signed photograph bearing the additional caption: "GK is OK with JK."

During the war film biographies were very popular, so shortly after the release of *Cover Girl* MGM came up with the idea of an idealised film version of Kern's life story to be called *Till the Clouds Roll By*, after one of his early songs. Jerry liked to keep his private life to himself but said he wouldn't mind the film being made provided that its story bore little resemblance to reality. This condition naturally presented no problem to Hollywood. With a script by Guy Bolton it contained a lot of Kern songs, starting with *How'd You Like To Spoon With Me?* and culminating with a youthful Frank Sinatra singing *Ol' Man River*.

With the end of the war in 1945, and Kern, now aged 60, still able to produce songs of the quality of *Long Ago and Far Away*, he was invited to New York for a revival of *Show Boat* and to write a new Broadway show. Following the success of Rodgers and Hammerstein's two shows, *Oklahoma*, and, more recently, *Carousel*, the new show would be based on the legend of Annie Oakley, with the story written by Dorothy Fields. In the late autumn of 1945 Jerry and Eva took the long train journey from Los Angeles to Manhattan and checked in at the St. Regis Hotel. On 4th November he had a quiet lunch with his old friend and collaborator Guy Bolton whilst Eva was lunching elsewhere with Dorothy Fields. Afterwards Jerry set out alone on foot to do a bit of shopping for Betty at a local store. As he reached the junction of 57th Street and Park Avenue he stopped - then collapsed, and lay unconscious on the pavement. Passers by who saw him fall called an ambulance and he was rushed to the nearest hospital, the City Hospital on 56th Street, ironically within sight of the house where he was born 60 years earlier. He carried no papers to indicate his identity, but the doctors found in his pocket his ASCAP (Musicians' Union) card with a membership number. They phoned ASCAP, who asked the doctors to describe their patient, and it became instantly clear that the unconscious man was Jerome Kern. Eva was sent for, and Betty came from California. Over the next few days there was barely a flicker of consciousness. Most of the patients in the ward were down-and-outs; the doctors asked them to keep quiet for the benefit of their famous co-patient.

Although the hospital was doing all that could be done and he was

The Melody Lingers On

being attended by his own physician, his family had him moved to the more impressive Doctors' Hospital on 5th Avenue. But it was to no avail; he had had a massive stroke and was beyond medical help. Family and close friends took turns by his bedside and at 1pm on Sunday, 11th November 1945 with Eva, Betty and Oscar Hammerstein by his side he died, having never recovered consciousness.

So ended the life of one of America's greatest songwriters. The show he was to have written with Oscar Hammerstein was put into the capable hands of Jerry's old friend Irving Berlin, who wrote the score of *Annie Get Your Gun* with brilliant results. But Jerome Kern lives on in his songs.

A list of Jerome Kern's shows, films and songs is given in Appendix 5.

The Melody Lingers On

Irving Berlin

6. Irving Berlin

Strictly speaking Irving Berlin was not a musician at all, for he never learned to read or write music and the intricacies of musical theory were a closed book to him. Nor was he particularly adept as a pianist for, strange as it may seem, he could only play effectively on the black notes. Key changes had to be accomplished by a transposing lever under the keyboard of his purpose-built piano. When he had an idea for a song he would sing it to a 'musical secretary' who took it down in musical notation. Whereas a businessman would ask his secretary to "take a letter", Irving Berlin dictated his songs, and the arrangement and orchestration were done later by others.

In spite of these limitations, however, Irving Berlin was a genius, for he possessed that rare commodity, inventiveness. His ability to create catchy tunes with words to match (he wrote the words as well as the music for nearly all his songs) has never been surpassed. Berlin's songs have the common touch; they appeal to all classes of society, rich and poor. He is probably the greatest writer of popular songs the world has produced, with an immensely long list of 'hits' to his credit. True, he probably wrote more 'flops' than anyone else, but that is only because he wrote more songs than any other songwriter. A creative artist must surely be judged by the number and quality of his best efforts. On that basis Irving Berlin stands supreme.

To have been born in Russia, and a remote part of Siberia at that, hardly seems the right background for a man destined to become America's greatest songwriter, but such was the case. Moses Baline, his wife Leah and their eight children lived in Temun, Siberia. The family were poor and Moses's work as cantor in the town's synagogue hardly earned enough to provide food and shelter for the Jewish family. Israel Baline, the youngest of the family, who was later to achieve fame as a songwriter, was born on 11th May 1888. Jewish persecution is not new, it was rife in those days in Russia, and Israel Baline was only four years old when in 1892 he and the rest of his family watched helplessly as their house was burned down by a group of marauding Cossacks, an event that remained indelibly ingrained in his memory. To Moses and Leah this was the final straw in a chain of outrages, and they decided to join Moses's cousin in the USA. Thus the family (all except the eldest son who stayed in Russia) embarked on the trail travelled by many other Jews before and since, making the long trek through the Jewish Pale of Settlement, then through Latvia and Lithuania to the Baltic coast. There, weary and penniless, they and a shipload of other emigrants boarded a steamer for the promised land - America. After a month-long voyage they sailed into New York Harbour, past the Statue of Liberty, and disembarked on Ellis Island (then the transit point for immigrants) where they satisfied the authorities and were granted immigrant status.

In New York the family were met by Moses's cousin who had emigrated a few years earlier. He had procured accommodation for them though it was only three small, smelly, windowless rooms in a New York slum. All the buildings were ugly, dirty and black, quite unlike the fine domed buildings the family had been used to seeing in Russia. Moses had to find employment, and quickly, to support his large tribe; no easy task in a city with many other unemployed immigrants. One son who had been trained as a tailor in Russia found a job in a 'sweatshop' but for Moses himself it was more difficult - there was little demand for synagogue cantors. Eventually he found a job as a shomer - supervising the ritual slaughter of cattle according to the Jewish laws. Later he found extra work as a deputy cantor in a synagogue and also earned a few extra cents teaching Hebrew to the children of other Jewish immigrants. Meanwhile Israel (nicknamed Izzy) quickly learned the English language. At seven he started school but had a reputation for laziness. "He dreams and sings to himself" his teacher said - and he liked all the American songs he heard.

In 1896, only four years after bringing his family to New York, Moses Baline died. Not only was this a family tragedy, it was also an economic calamity. Izzy, then eight, promptly decided to leave school in order to become a breadwinner. He got a casual job as a newspaper seller for *The New York Evening Journal*, the proceeds of which gave him a sense of independence. After he had sold his papers (and most of the money went to his mother) he used to walk to the Bowery, a sleazy district near the family's home, and there he would listen to the music emanating from the saloons and taverns that abounded in the district. He rapidly picked up the songs and would sing them on street corners where passers by threw coins to him. His ambition at that time was to be a 'singing waiter' who sang as he walked around with trays of food and drink, all calculated to out-do rival establishments in entertainment value and therefore custom.

Between the ages of eight and fourteen young Izzy lived on his wits, making money from casual work and by singing where and when he could; on street corners, in saloons, as assistant to 'Blind Sol' (a busker) and so on. One night someone heard him sing and arranged for him to go to the offices of Harry von Tilzer, the composer and publisher, who hired him as a song plugger. In those days, before radio, an artist would sing a song on stage in a music hall or tavern and a 'member of the audience' would then stand up and start to sing the same song, apparently spontaneously, thereby indicating what a wonderful song it was. He was the song plugger. (Song plugging took many different forms). The spotlight would find its way onto this man who so fortuitously happened to be there and to know the words of the song. All, of course, designed to imprint the song into the minds of those present.

Izzy received the then princely sum of $5/week for doing this at Tony Pastor's Music Hall on 14th Street. He had a pleasant, fairly high but clear voice, and he was doing what he wanted to do - singing. He got to know many show-biz people there including 'The Three Keatons'; mum, dad, and their sad-eyed little boy, Buster.

After a while Izzy decided to go back to busking, which he found quite profitable, and then found a regular job as a singing waiter with 'Nigger' Mike Salter at his beer hall (Pelham's) in Chinatown, New York. That was in 1906 when Izzy was 18. 'Nigger' Mike Salter was a white man (another ex-Russian Jew) who acquired his nickname because of his swarthy appearance. Izzy served food and drink and sang the popular hits of the day, such as *Yankie Doodle Dandy*, for $7 a week plus tips. One visitor to the establishment was Prince Louis of Battenburg, German-born cousin of King George V. Later he was to become Britain's First Sea Lord. It used to be the custom for celebrities to tour the less salubrious districts of New York to see what city life there was really like - hence his visit. The reporters were there and it resulted in Izzy's first press notice in *The New York World* by a man rejoicing in the name of Herbert Bayard Swope.

At Pelham's Izzy taught himself to pound out a tune on the piano (the black notes seemed to come to him easily) and he also started to make up his own tunes. He said later, "Once you start singing, you start thinking of writing songs - it's as simple as that." Izzy, ambitious young man that he was, thought he could write songs as good as or better than some of the ones he was singing. There were thousands of expatriate Italians as well as Russians in New York, and the pianist at Callaghan's, which was a rival establishment to Pelham's, had written an Italian dialect song that had been very popular, *My Mariuccia Take a Steamboat*. Nick Nicholson, who was the resident pianist at Pelham's, and Izzy decided they could do better; Nick supplied the music and Izzy the words for *Marie from Sunny Italy* which Izzy sang in May 1907 on the day it was written. Two days later it was published. The music cover contained a printer's error; it said "Words by I. Berlin, Music by N. Nicholson." That didn't matter. Izzy decided that 'Berlin' rolled off the tongue more easily than 'Baline', so from then on he became Berlin. The name change became a double one in the following year. 'Israel' had too much of an Old-Testament ring for a writer of popular songs, so Izzy decided to call himself 'Irving' on the grounds that it sounded more classy. So, in 1908, Izzy Baline became Irving Berlin, the songwriter.

Marie from Sunny Italy earned only 37 cents in royalties for Irving, but it boosted his morale and fired his ambitions. Soon afterwards he lost his job at Pelham's for sleeping on duty, but found himself a better position at Jimmy Kelly's, a classier bar. More songs followed; *Dorando* was based on an event that occurred in the 1908 Olympic Games when an Italian waiter of that name 'won' the marathon but was disqualified when the judges ruled he had been pushed towards the line. The story was in all the papers and Irving capitalised on the topicality of the event in his song, which he took to Tin Pan Alley (the street where all the music publishers were located) himself. It earned him royalties of $4000, a lot of money in those days, and a job with Snyder, the music publisher. As staff composer with the firm for the sum of $25 a week he wrote the words and Snyder the tunes for *Christmas Time Seems Years and Years Away, I Didn't Go Home at All,* and *I Wish You Was My Girl, Molly,* now all long forgotten by everyone but the most fervent Berlin disciples. He was essentially a wordsmith at that time;

other people generally provided the tunes, but he did put together some of the melodies himself. *That Mesmerising Mendelssohn Tune,* a rag consisting of a parody of *Spring Song*, was one of them and it sold 500,000 copies. By the middle of 1909 he had become a man-about-town with his own apartment and smart new clothes.

One day a fellow song writer came to see Irving and said, "Let's go to the theatre. My wife's gone to the country." Said Irving, "We're not going to the theatre - we've got ourselves a song!" and sat down and wrote *My Wife's Gone To the Country - Hooray, Hooray!* Snyder helped him with the melody and the song sold 300,000 copies. An unfortunate sequel was that Irving's friend's wife left him for good shortly afterwards, when she heard the story.

On the proceeds of the sale of his songs, Irving moved his mother out of the slums and into a pleasant apartment; success was now gathering pace. *The New York Journal* paid him to write 100 new verses for *My Wife's Gone To the Country*, and by 1910 Berlin's songs were being performed on Broadway in the show *Up and Down Broadway*. Not only were they presented there, but Irving himself sang them in the show. Columbia signed him up to record some of his songs but he wasn't really a great singer and got no further than *Oh, How That German Could Love*. Surely a collector's item!

Irving was now writing his own tunes. Though he couldn't play the piano properly he could play reasonably effectively, better on the black keys than the white. He discovered that 100 years earlier the firm of Norris & Hyde in London had manufactured a piano with a transposing lever so that it could change key even though the pianist continued to play the same notes. Enquires indicated that the Weser Co. in the USA could make a similar instrument for him for $100. He ordered one and used it, and later one made by Buick working on the same principle, for the rest of his composing days. This enabled him to change key at will as he composed. The refinements of the process, i.e. writing down the resulting music, was left to others. At about this time, Ted Snyder, Henry Waterson and he formed a new Company; Waterson, Berlin and Snyder. From then on he was his own publisher - a remarkable achievement for a man of 22.

Irving was soon to have the really big 'hit' he had been hoping for. In 1910 he worked out the tune of *Alexander's Ragtime Band* and got one of the firm's arrangers to write it down. At that time the music had no words. Irving himself played it in public on a number of occasions and the tune was also taken up by others. The orchestra played it on the opening night of The Follies Bergères' *International Revue*, but the response was lukewarm. Then, in 1911, Irving took the tune out of moth balls and wrote words for it. Its first few public airings excited little attention, and it seemed destined soon to disappear into oblivion. But the fate of many a song is determined not only by the quality of the song but by the charisma of the singer. Later that year it was taken up by Emma Carus, a large, deep-voiced lady. From a stage in Chicago she didn't so much sing it, she belted it out. At the same time Al Jolson, just making a name for himself as a top-class entertainer, took it up, and it spread like wildfire in vaudeville. And so, *Come On and Hear, Come On and Hear, Alexander's Ragtime Band* burst upon the world. Three weeks after its Chicago debut it had sold a million copies of sheet music and by the end of 1911, two million. It was a sensation. The country was 'rag crazy' and the song thrust the 23-year old Irving Berlin into the forefront of song writers of the day. He hadn't invented ragtime, it had been 'in' for a long time, but he had capitalised on it. Many people have said the song isn't really proper ragtime, but it made no difference. George Gershwin, then a youngster of 13, was greatly taken by the new song and was reported to have said: "This is American music. This is the way an American should write. This is the kind of music I want to write."

Irving was not one to let the grass grow under his feet. Before the end of the same year he had written *Everybody's Doin' It*, which enjoyed nearly as much success as *Alexander's Ragtime Band*, and *Ragtime Violin* which Eddie Cantor sang. Berlin was now being dubbed 'The Ragtime King'. But he had not become a ragtime specialist; there was also the Jewish and Italian market to cater for, and such musical gems as *Yiddisher Nightingale, Yiddle On Your Fiddle, Goodbye Becky Cohen, When You Kiss That Italian Girl, Antonia You'd Better Come Home, My Sweet Italian Man*, and *Dat's - a - My Gal* were soon resounding through America.

On the proceeds of $100,000 royalties from his songs Irving bought a car and set up his mother in a house in the Bronx (an area popular amongst well-off Jewish families) with two servants. People wondered how this little Russian Jew (he was only 5ft 5in tall) managed to do it. The answer was innate genius.

In 1912 Irving, 24, fell in love with Dorothy Goetz, 20, the sister of one of his closest friends, Ray Goetz, and they were married in the same year. Tin Pan Alley showered its congratulations, and his mother's only regret was that Dorothy was not a Jewish girl. The couple honeymooned in Cuba and then moved to an apartment on Riverside Drive in New York, overlooking the Hudson River. But disaster struck. There had been an outbreak of typhoid whilst the couple were in Cuba and after their return to New York Dorothy developed the disease and died, only five months after their marriage. Irving's joy turned to black despair.

For weeks Irving did nothing but brood, in abject misery. Then Dorothy's brother, Ray, took him to Europe and he gradually started to pick up the pieces of his life. His songwriting always reflected his moods; when he was happy he wrote cheerful songs, when he was sad, sombre ones. The first song he wrote after Dorothy's death was *When I Lost You*, which sold a million copies in a week. Some people felt he was making money out of his wife's death, but Ray had encouraged him to get his thoughts out of his system in the only way he knew how, in a song. It helped him to face life again.

In 1913 came another success, *When the Midnight Choo-Choo Leaves for Alabam'*. In the same year there followed *Ragtime Sextet* and, for Al Jolson, *I Want To Be in Dixie*. Then came an offer to sing and play his own songs at the London Hippodrome; he took his musical secretary with him and dictated *The International Rag*. The *Daily Express* enthused about him. Remarking that Berlin made £20,000 a year from ragtime, it described him as "A genius who dictates his syncopated melodies." Berlin, for his part, said, "I don't know anything about harmony but I can make tunes."

Throughout his composing career Berlin preferred to work at night. An insomniac, he chain-smoked and got nervous indigestion when brewing up a new song, which he would sometimes sing into a dictaphone during the night for his musical secretary to write down later.

On his return from London he put together his first score for Broadway, *Watch Your Step*, and wrote *Play a Simple Melody*, a clever counterpointed song. By now (1914) he was a great friend of Al Jolson whom he regarded as one of the finest interpreters of his songs, and would often phone Jolson to ask his comments on technical details. He also met Fred and Adele Astaire who were then still in their middle teens. They bought a new Berlin tune, *I'd Love To Quarrel With You*, which they used in their act on vaudeville. Another Broadway score followed in 1916, *Stop! Look! Listen!* at the Globe Theatre. It contained various new Berlin numbers including *The Girl On the Magazine Cover, I Love a Piano,* and *Smile and Show Your Dimple.* This last number flopped, but Berlin, like all other composers, kept a file (mental and physical) of discarded pieces for possible future use if he thought the music had potential. *Smile and Show Your Dimple* was in this category. Irving resurrected the tune 17 years later, put new words to it, and it was reincarnated as the highly successful *Easter Parade.*

All Berlin's successes made the publishing firm of Waterson, Berlin and Snyder famous, and amongst the many applicants for jobs was another Jewish boy of immigrant ancestry, George Gershwin. He applied for the post of arranger and musical secretary to Irving Berlin. Irving offered George the job but told him not to take it; "You've got more talent than an arranger needs," he said. George heeded Irving's unselfish advice and found a job at Remick's music publishers instead. Soon afterwards he hit the headlines with *Swanee*.

When America entered the war in 1917 Irving was drafted into the army, which caused one newspaper to perpetrate the headline 'United States Takes Berlin'. He had to report to Camp Upton at Fort Yaphank on Long Island, New York. He thought he would be able spend his time playing tunes to the other conscripts but the tough sergeant-majors would have none of it. They treated the weedy little songwriter to the same rigorous routine of chores, early rising and square-bashing as the other conscripts and told him, "The only tunes you'll hear will be bugle calls." He hated the régime but took the punishment manfully like the rest. Then, without warning, he was promoted to sergeant, told the camp needed a new community hall, and instructed to organise a concert to raise the necessary funds.

The show he created was *Yip, Yip, Yaphank* which opened on Broadway on 19th August 1918. Irving wrote the whole show, including the song *Oh, How I Hate To Get Up in the Morning*, the tune of which was based on bugle calls. Unlike previous army shows, *Yip, Yip, Yaphank* was slick and very professional though all the cast were serving soldiers. The army needed $35,000 to build the new community house; Berlin raised $83,000 for them.

One of the keys to Irving Berlin's success as a song writer was that he knew exactly what the public wanted; his finger was firmly on the nation's pulse when it came to understanding their thoughts and needs. His tunes were bright and clever, his words witty and to the point. Though born in far-away Russia he had a wonderful grasp of American speech, especially the vernacular. When the war ended he wrote another great success that was taken up by Al Jolson, *I've Got My Captain Working for Me Now*, knowing that it reflected the secret thoughts of many an ex-serviceman. Not only did Irving Berlin know how to write popular songs, but he also knew how to capitalise on them financially. He withdrew from the publishing firm of Waterson, Berlin and Snyder and set up his own publishing company, Irving Berlin Inc. From then on he received not only the royalties for both the words and the music, but all the publishing royalties as well. Astute businessman that he was, he bought up the copyright of as many of his old songs as he could lay his hands on, so was then able to scoop the whole takings. He was the king of Tin Pan Alley.

In 1919 he was invited to write virtually the whole score of the *Ziegfeld Follies Revue*, which included his latest song, *A Pretty Girl Is Like a Melody*. He also took into employment Walter Donaldson as an assistant in his company; it was Donaldson who had written *My Mammy, Carolina in the Morning* (a Jolson hit) and Eddie Cantor's post-war song *How Ya Gonna Keep 'Em Down On the Farm?* In the following year Irving wrote *After You Get What You Want, You Don't Want It*, a song that made little impact at the time and remained in Berlin's filing cabinet until the 1950s when Marilyn Monroe took it into the charts. A less memorable Berlin gem from 1919 was *Since Katy The Waitress Became an Aviatress*.

In the early 1920s the production of music rolls for player pianos was a significant part of the overall sales picture for Irving Berlin and he could count on a song that sold a million records selling over 100,000 music rolls. Over the years a vast number of rolls of Irving

Berlin's music were manufactured. The Ampico Company alone issued over 100 different Berlin rolls and their main rivals, the Aeolian Company, also featured Berlin's music prominently in their Duo-Art lists. Another Company, Meloto, issued a large number of rolls of his music including many of his lesser known songs that would probably now be forgotten but for the piano roll, and his music was also very well represented on all the lists of the other manufacturers of standard rolls. In short, Irving Berlin was a godsend to the player piano industry - and still is - for many of his rolls are still available from present-day roll-manufacturing companies.

In 1921 Irving's mother died and was buried in a Brooklyn cemetery. Now into his thirties, Irving was taking stock. His next ambition was to set up his own theatre, so in partnership with Sam H. Harris, a legendary Broadway figure, he opened 'The Music Box' theatre on 22nd September 1921. He wrote *Say It with Music*, another hit, for the opening. Year by year came successive *Music Box Revues*, the second in 1922, and so on. Irving engaged the principals and selected all the chorus members for the show.

In the early 1920s Irving enlisted the help of 24 other songwriters and composers including Victor Herbert and J.P. Sousa in demanding royalties for songs performed on the radio. Up to that time they had not received a penny. This was not the last time he appeared in court to give evidence; throughout his career he kept a close watch on any infringements of copyright of his songs, and he objected to any of them being parodied, except, on occasions, by himself.

In 1924 Irving met and fell in love with Ellin Mackay who was nearly 21 and the daughter of Clarence Mackay, a communications cables millionaire and also a Director of the Metropolitan Opera. Mr. Mackay disapproved of Irving, not so much because he himself was a Catholic and Irving a Jew, but mainly because he was a snob and objected on principle to his daughter falling for a songwriter. Later in the same year he took his daughter to Europe, "To make you forget that man", but predictably the ploy did not work. People said that Irving's big hit of 1924, *All Alone*, the lyrics of which referred to sitting alone by a telephone, were an expression of his feelings at the time. They said the same about *What'll I Do?* written in the same year, and about *Remember*, but in each case he denied it. But it was obvious what was on his mind. Clarence Mackay was adamant - he refused to approve the marriage. "The day you marry my daughter, I'll disinherit her", said Mackay. "The day I marry your daughter, I'll settle $2M on her", said Irving. "I'm worth $4M and that's enough for Clarence Mackay's daughter or any other woman to live on."

The couple responded in the only way they could, or knew how to; they eloped. That was on 4th January 1926. They went by subway to the New York Municipal Building (they would have been recognised had they gone by car) and were married in front of three witnesses. On the marriage forms Ellin declined to fill in her father's name and left the space blank. When Clarence Mackay heard about the marriage he was furious, and issued a statement to the press: "The marriage was performed without my knowledge or approval." The couple went on to Atlantic City and booked into the Ritz Carlton Hotel. Irving had written a song especially as a wedding present for Ellin; it was *Always*. It wasn't just a romantic gesture; he assigned all its royalties to Ellin and altogether it made over half a million dollars for her. On 8th January 1927 the couple sailed to Europe on the *Leviathan* and continued their honeymoon at the Carlton Hotel in London. Someone asked Joshua Low, Irving's London agent, why Berlin hadn't written a Bridal March. Low, who knew the songwriter better than most, said, "He hasn't written a Bridal March for the simple reason that there is no money in Bridal Marches."

Ellin at that time was caught up in the 'Charleston Fever' that was raging, but she was no dumb flapper; she was an intelligent woman who had a gift for writing. One of her plays was performed shortly after their honeymoon and she went on to write a string of novels.

Irving's big hit of 1927 was *Blue Skies*, recorded by Jolson and later by Bing Crosby and a host of other singers. Jolson sang it to his aged screen mother in the 1927 film *The Jazz Singer*, which at a stroke sounded the death knell of the silent film. After *Blue Skies* came *The Song Is Ended*. Perhaps the title was indicative of the fact that Berlin at the time was going through one of his periodic bouts of depression, when inspiration failed him and he felt "all washed up". He knew as well as anyone that a songwriter is only as good as his last song. As soon as the first flush of success of any new number was over, the public was clamouring for the next song. It was a relentless treadmill.

Radio made matters worse. Whereas in the pre-radio days a song lasted two or three years before fading away, the exposure on radio made a song's rise and decline far more rapid. Irving could write a new hit every year but he couldn't write one every month.

Nevertheless one event made him very happy, the birth of an 8lb daughter, Mary Ellin, in October 1927. There were to be two more girls, Linda Louise (1932) and Elizabeth Iris (1936) as well as a son, Irving jr., who died of a heart defect on Christmas Day 1928 aged only 25 days. Clarence Mackay's continuing refusal to see or have anything to do with his daughter was a worry, upsetting to Irving and even more to Ellin, and they brooded about it. Ironically, Clarence Mackay, the multimillionaire who looked down with contempt on Irving Berlin's profession, lost practically all his fortune in the Wall Street Crash of 1929. He had earlier sold out of his Company and had, unwisely as it turned out, taken nearly all his resulting fortune in company shares that became worthless when the crash came. He also had to meet a huge tax bill from the US government and was obliged to sell his paintings, silver plate and gold and to move into the porter's lodge of his former home. Irving also lost money on Wall Street, but he was not a man to bear a grudge and he helped Clarence Mackay financially. In 1931 Ellin helped her father to fight and win a difficult lawsuit case; indeed, her evidence proved decisive. After that the family were at last reconciled, much to Irving and Ellin's relief. Clarence Mackay died in 1936.

Meanwhile Irving's depression had abated to some extent and he had come up with more hits, including *Shaking the Blues Away*, brilliantly sung at the time by Ruth Etting, and *Let Me Sing and I'm Happy* which appeared in Al Jolson's film *Mammy* and became a kind of theme song for Jolson; he sang it as the cast list unfolded in *The Jolson Story* nearly 20 years later. *Say It Isn't So* was made into a hit by Rudy Vallee and *How Deep Is the Ocean*, memorably recorded by Bing Crosby, helped Irving to restore his confidence in himself. The title of *How Deep Is the Ocean* was a line that appeared in the middle of one of his earlier songs, *To My Mammy*, that was not commercially successful. He thought the phrase deserved greater exploitation and is another example of how Berlin's meticulous filing system often brought forth harvest eventually.

With the 1930s in full swing came the song *Easter Parade*, another filing cabinet success rescued from *Smile and Show Your Dimple*. Then came a new venture - films. Although his songs had already been used in films, writing a film score was new to him. Irving was invited to write the score for a Hollywood musical, *Top Hat*, starring Fred Astaire and Ginger Rogers. The film became a classic; it could hardly be otherwise with numbers like *Top Hat, Cheek to Cheek,* and *Isn't This a Lovely Day To Be Caught in the Rain,* and enriched by the dancing of Astaire and Rogers. The film showed that Irving was as good at writing for film musicals as he was for Broadway shows, though he preferred the immediate response of a live audience. It was followed up in 1936 by another Astaire - Rogers film, *Follow the Fleet.* The songs he wrote for this included *Follow the Fleet, I'm Putting All My Eggs in One Basket, Let's Face the Music and Dance, Let Yourself Go,* and *We Saw the Sea*. Again the skill and artistry of the great perfectionist, Fred Astaire, backed up by the vivaciousness of Ginger Rogers, enhanced the songs and ensured the success of the film.

On 31st January 1936, 150 of the USA's foremost songwriters gave Irving and Ellin a testimonial dinner to celebrate his "leadership in our ranks." The event marked 25 years since *Alexander's Ragtime Band* hit America. Irving was generous in his attitude towards his fellow songwriters, including the great names of that era; George Gershwin, Jerome Kern and Cole Porter. He was a particular admirer of Porter and thought *Night and Day* was one of the best popular songs ever written. But he hated the new rage, 'Swing'. According to Berlin, "Ragtime is on the beat, Jazz off the beat, and Swing has no beat at all." Meanwhile Irving himself continued to write 'hits' and the mid thirties saw *I've Got My Love To Keep Me Warm* become one of the leading songs of the day.

In 1938 Irving was in London as Chamberlain flew back from Munich, waved his piece of paper and proclaimed "Peace in our Time". A wave of patriotism followed in America, inducing Irving to try to write a patriotic song. After several abortive attempts he raided his filing cabinet and pulled out a song he had originally written for *Yip, Yip, Yaphank* in 1918 but had omitted from the show because he didn't think it fitted. It was *God Bless America*. He made a few minor changes and gave it to Kate Smith who sang it on the radio. It soon became a second National Anthem. With a range of only eight notes it was easy for anyone to sing, unlike *The Star Spangled Banner* with its much larger range and difficult jumps. Irving didn't capitalise financially on the success of the song, for he assigned all the proceeds "To the youth of America", more specifically, to the boy and girl scout movement.

As we all know, Europe was soon plunged into war once again, though America didn't enter until Pearl Harbor was attacked in 1941. One day the British film producer Alexander Korda was with Irving in a taxi in New York and said to him, "Why don't you write a war song?" By the end of the taxi ride Irving had sketched out *It's a Lovely Day Tomorrow* which became a firm favourite in Britain as well as the USA. That was in 1940, but an even bigger success was round the corner. Berlin had been asked to write the songs for a new Paramount picture, *Holiday Inn*, starring Fred Astaire and Bing Crosby. It was set in a mountain resort at Christmas, and Paramount asked for a Christmas song for Bing to sing. Irving responded with *White Christmas*, which became one of the most popular songs of all time. When the film was released in 1942, *White Christmas* became a 'nostalgia song' for the thousands of servicemen abroad and since then its popularity has never flagged.

When America entered the war Irving was 53 years old, much too old to be enlisted, but as in the First World War he was asked to write a show, this time to raise money for service charities. Some professional singers and dancers were loaned from the Armed Forces to take part. The result was *This Is the Army,* the hit theme song of which was *This Is the Army, Mr. Jones* and which cleverly incorporated some of his songs from his First World War army show. It opened on Broadway on 4th July 1942, ran for 112 performances (to 26th September), then toured for the rest of the war. Kate Smith always brought the house down with *God Bless America*, introduced to produce the necessary emotional patriotism. The show also came to Britain; Edwina Mountbatten helped in the organisational arrangements for its performances in London and its subsequent tour of Britain, and Irving himself toured with the show and sang some of his own songs on stage. He met the King and Queen and the two Princesses, and also met Mr. Churchill. In Manchester he was given a Civic Reception by the Lord Mayor after the show had been staged at the Palace Theatre. He wrote

My British Buddy specifically for the British tour. The royalties of this song went to British service charities and raised £90,000. Altogether the show raised $7M in the USA and $120,000 for British charities. Its final performance on stage was in Honolulu on 22nd October 1945. It was also made into a film by Warner Brothers, starring the original cast.

Berlin's popularity was strengthened by a series of films which had thin story lines but were really vehicles for his songs. The mid-thirties classic films such as *Top Hat* and *Follow the Fleet* contained a lot of new songs, but the later films were made up mainly of old favourites with a sprinkling of new material. One of the earliest films in this category had been *Alexander's Ragtime Band* made by 20th Century Fox in 1938; it contained no fewer than 28 of Berlin's greatest hits. After the war Paramount's *Blue Skies* was also a compendium of old songs though it included two new ones, *A Couple of Song and Dance Men* written for the film's stars, Astaire and Crosby, and *You Keep Coming Back Like a Song*. Later films of this type included MGM's *Easter Parade* starring Fred Astaire (who had half-heartedly "retired" at the time but eagerly stepped in because Gene Kelly had broken his ankle) and Judy Garland. It included *We're a Couple of Swells*, written earlier but resurrected for the film. In 1954 Paramount's *White Christmas* starring Bing Crosby capitalised on the stunning success of the song of the same name dating from 1942.

By the end of the Second World War Irving Berlin was nearing the end of his active career as a songwriter, but he had one more remarkable success still to come. Jerome Kern had been invited by Rodgers and Hammerstein to write the songs for *Annie Get Your Gun* but he had died suddenly before starting work on the show. Irving was invited to take over in his place, but viewed the assignment with some trepidation. "I've never written music for a Western", he said, "It's hill-billy stuff." But after reading the book and writing a couple of trial songs that delighted Rodgers and Hammerstein who were putting the show on, he was persuaded to take on the job. The result was a brilliant musical, full of hit tunes, that displayed Irving's marvellous talents at their best. Nearly every song was a show stopper: *They Say It's Wonderful, You Can't Get a Man With a Gun, Anything You Can Do I Can Do Better, The Girl That I Marry, I'm an Indian Too, My Defences Are Down, Doin' What Comes Natur'lly, I Got the Sun in the Morning and the Moon at Night*, and *There's No Business Like Show Business* (this last song was written years earlier). Ethel Merman, loud and brash, was an ideal choice as Annie Oakley. She belted out Berlin's songs to such effect that they soon reverberated around the world. Berlin's snappy, witty words, backed up by his catchy tunes, were just what the post-war public wanted. Later the show was made into a picture by MGM but the project was beset by problems. Ethel Merman, who had done so well in the stage production, was unavailable. Judy Garland was enrolled as Annie Oakley, a part she had longed to play, and recorded the songs. But during filming Judy was befuddled by narcotics and was well below her brilliant best. After many problems on the set she was eventually sacked, to her utter dismay. Betty Hutton took over the part, performed creditably, and the film was finally released in 1950.

The success of *Annie Get Your Gun* demonstrates Irving Berlin's intuitive sense of what would appeal to the public. At his best (and his best lasted about 40 years) he knew instinctively whether a certain phrase, verbal or musical, sounded "right". Sometimes when he was 'dictating' a tune his assistant would venture to suggest an improvement, based on sound musical principles. Berlin would listen to what he had to say and the conversation would then often proceed thus: Berlin: "O.K., Play it your way." (listens carefully). "Now play it my way." (listens). "Now play it your way." (listens). "Now play it my way." (listens). "Now play it your way". (listens). Then came the verdict: "Leave it the way I wrote it."

When the 1950s came Irving Berlin was over 60 years old and was starting to take things easy. He played golf and went fishing, but was not very happy. The only activity he really enjoyed was writing songs. As he himself said, "I never had a hobby. Writing songs was my hobby." But the truth of the matter, not unexpectedly, was that his inspiration was starting to dry up. It could hardly be otherwise for a man who had been writing songs for over 40 years and had written more hits than anyone else. He couldn't go on for ever. Moreover, musical tastes were changing. 'Rock and Roll' was just around the corner and Berlin's style of song would soon be yesterday's music. Nevertheless he wrote the songs for a new show, *Miss Liberty* (about the Statue of Liberty) but it was a flop, to his bitter disappointment.

Call Me Madam in the early 1950s did much better. It included a new song, *It's a Lovely Day Today* and the clever counterpoint number *You're Just in Love,* which Ethel Merman and her partner exploited brilliantly. The success of the show restored some of Berlin's self-confidence.

From then on Irving Berlin continued to write songs for a while though few were published and most remained locked away in his filing cabinet. Rosemary Clooney recorded a new song, *You Can't Lose the Blues with Colours* in 1957 but there were to be no more big hits, and 1958 was the first year since 1907 that no new Irving Berlin songs were published. In 1962, at the age of 74, he wrote the songs for a new show, *Mr. President*, but the show made little impact and *The Daily Herald* wrote "Should he have stayed in retirement? Has America's Mr. Music lost the magic touch?" It had to be admitted, he had. Over the next few years, in his seventies and eighties, he still wrote a few songs, but they were for members of his family to celebrate events, birthdays, and so on. It was many years before he formally announced that he had "retired" and said, sadly, "I don't write songs any more now." As though to confim this he donated his two transposing pianos, by now old and battered, to the Smithsonian Institute who proudly put them on display. Life became a succession of the award of university degrees, the conferment of honours, and celebrations of past glories; the 25th anniversary of this, the 50th anniversary of that, and so on. Not least amongst these events was the celebration of his and Ellin's Golden Wedding in 1976.

And so the great songwriter gradually bowed out of his profession. But what a vast legacy of songs he has left us, and what other songwriter can compare with him? Irving Berlin in retirement was not a forgotten man for although he did not allow a film of his life to be made, the many re-issues of films like *Top Hat, Follow the Fleet, Blue Skies, Easter Parade* and so on, together with modern arrangements of his many songs, kept the royalties rolling in. Though the days of his songwriting were over he kept an eagle eye on any perceived infringement of the copyright of his material.

As Irving Berlin passed quietly though his eighties and nineties he became reclusive, like many old people, and shunned any appearance in public. Not unreasonably, he did not want his increasing frailty to be

The Melody Lingers On

put on public display. But he remained mentally alert and was most upset, at the age of 98, when the copyright of *Alexander's Ragtime Band* finally ran out and the song entered the public domain. It had been his first big hit and he had always regarded it as his theme song. In 1988 the centenary of his birth was marked by world-wide celebrations and the performance of many of his songs and films in special programmes on radio and television. On his 100th birthday an enthusiastic group sang *Happy Birthday* and *Always* outside his house. The curtains twitched, but he was too old and infirm to appear at the window.

Three months after Irving's 100th birthday, Ellin Berlin died, aged 85 and on 22nd September 1989, death finally came to the old songwriter himself at the great age of 101. He will be long remembered as the creator of a wealth of popular song. It is doubtful whether his prodigious output will ever be surpassed.

A list of Irving Berlin's shows, films and songs is given in Appendix 6.

'Jelly Roll' Morton

7. Ferdinand 'Jelly Roll' Morton

'Jelly Roll' Morton was a rather different type of person from most of the musicians in this book. He was eccentric and idiosyncratic, with vices enough for ten ordinary mortals. He was a gambler, card sharp, a shark at the pool table, a high-liver, improvident, a pimp, a braggart, self-centred and arrogant. Yet there was a much more sensitive, caring side to his nature. The reason he is featured here is that he was a brilliant pianist in his own field - jazz - and an outstanding leader of jazz groups. Moreover he was an innovator who was responsible, perhaps more than anyone else, for moving popular music forward from the ragtime era to the jazz age. Indeed, Morton claimed to have invented jazz. That may be going a little too far, but it is doubtful whether any single figure contributed more to the development of jazz than he did, and the 1920s recordings of Jelly Roll Morton and his Red Hot Peppers have become jazz classics.

Ferdinand Joseph La Menthe, later to become famous as Jelly Roll Morton, was born in New Orleans, Louisiana, of creole French-speaking forbears. His great-grandfather, Pierre Pechet, was a cigar manufacturer in the Southern States; his great-grandmother, Felicie, lived to the age of about 100, long enough to see Ferdinand grown up. Ferdinand's grandmother, Laura, married a French settler named Monette in New Orleans. They had four sons; Henri, Gus, Neville and Nelusco, and three daughters; Louise, Viola and Margaret. Louise, the eldest girl, married F. P. La Menthe, who was also of French extraction and was a building and demolition contractor. Their son Ferdinand, the subject of our story, was born on 20th October, 1890.* It is said that he was named after Ferdinand, King of Spain and husband of Isabella.

It was Ferdinand's godmother, Eulalie Echo, who persuaded his parents to name him Ferdinand, and she played a large part in his upbringing for he spent a lot of time with her. She was well off and wore ostentatious clothes. She used to let the young child wear her jewellery, and she dabbled in the occult. It is no surprise that Ferdinand grew up to be a flashy dresser from his early years and was

---

*There is much doubt about his birthdate which various sources give as 1885, 1886 and 1890. It cannot be verified as the church where records were kept was destroyed by fire. For the purpose of placing this chapter in its correct chronological sequence the year 1890 is assumed.

superstitious for the whole of his life.

Ferdinand's musical talents soon became manifest. Like all children his first essay into music was banging things, tin pans and so on, but it was not long before he progressed to the musical instruments in the house, of which there were many, for his father liked music and was a proficient trombonist. Ferdinand started with the harmonica, which he didn't like, but soon mastered the jew's harp, drums, piano and trombone. At six his godmother paid for him to have guitar lessons from a local Spanish gentleman. By seven he was a competent guitarist and sometimes played in the string bands that were common at the time; little three-piece combinations of bass, mandolin and guitar, which used to play late at night at friends' homes. So, from his earliest years Ferdinand was playing all the popular favourites of the day such as *Bird in a Gilded Cage, Hot Time in the Old Town Tonight*, as well as the current blues and ragtime numbers.

A visit to the New Orleans French Opera House where a man with long hair (then considered rather ostentatious and 'artistic') played a selection on the piano inspired Ferdinand to want to excel at the instrument, but because the piano was thought of in his circle as a lady's instrument he was afraid of being called 'cissy'. However, soon afterwards he heard a short-haired man playing good ragtime and from then on he had no qualms. He was about 10 years old at the time. Even at that age he was one of the best guitarists in the district, but after hearing Bud Scott, a guitar virtuoso, he decided to give up the guitar and concentrate on the piano.

Several teachers were tried but none proved very satisfactory until Ferdinand had lessons from Professor Nickerson, a black piano teacher at St. Joseph's, a Catholic college in New Orleans. Under him he learned the rudiments of efficient playing and was taught to read music. These lessons seem to have been the only formal musical training Ferdinand ever had, and his rapid development into an outstanding player of popular music can only be put down to his own innate talent. At this stage of his life, ten or eleven years old, the only language he could speak was French.

Music was beginning to play an ever-increasing role in his young life. New Orleans was full of what Ferdinand called clubs - they were really youth gangs which had their own bands, and used to parade the streets. Relations with neighbouring clubs were far from cordial; other gangs' territories were entered at great risk to life and limb, and the streetwise boy learned to look after himself in this rough-and-tumble environment. The fact that he had an outstanding talent for music figured largely in the clubs' activities, and his godmother's constant showering of jewels and other gifts onto him enabled him to dress in a very showy manner even as a child and young teenager. The clubs' bands often played at wakes where liquor flowed freely.

When Ferdinand was still young his father left home and his mother married a man named Morton; two half-sisters were born, Amède and Mimi. At 11 Ferdinand got his first job, washing dishes after school for 75 cents/week. At 14 his mother died and his favourite uncle became his guardian. He was a barber and gave Ferdinand a job at 25 cents/week plus tips. Soon he moved to the local cooperage to be apprenticed to a barrel-maker. For this he was paid $3/week. His piano-playing had developed dramatically and by his mid teens he was one of the best pianists in New Orleans and was starting to be in demand for evening engagements. His lack of musical training did not prove to be much of a handicap. Some children seem to have the inborn ability to just sit down at the piano and play; he was one of them.

New Orleans had its seamy side, its 'red-light' district known as Storyville*, or as Ferdinand called it, the tenderloin. All the bordellos there had musical entertainment as part of their 'attractions' and it is hardly surprising that the young pianist was drawn in, for his undoubted pianistic talent enabled him to make easy money, far more than he was able to make in his day job at the cooperage. Sometimes he made as much as $20/hour in tips. He kept this side of his evening activities secret from his family, but eventually, and inevitably, his grandmother guessed where the money was coming from and virtually disowned him, telling him he was unworthy of the family name.

From the time of his grandmother's disownment Ferdinand was on his own, his father having recently died, but fortunately he could turn to his godmother for somewhere to live. Earning money was not a

---

* In 1896 a New Orleans Alderman, Sidney Story, promulgated a city law which restricted prostitution to a 38-block district adjoining Canal Street. Much to the dismay of the Alderman someone nicknamed the area 'Storyville' and the name stuck. It retained the name until 1917 when the Navy, mindful of the effect of the area on sailors' health and morals, closed it down.

problem. As one of the best pianists in the Southern States, there was an ever-open door at any of the bordellos where he chose to play the piano. There was plenty of drink, pool-playing and gambling apart from the prostitution, so Ferdinand knew all the big-time and small-time gamblers, murderers, criminals and 'tough guys' who dropped into New Orleans. Each of the 'mansions' as they were called in New Orleans had its own resident pianist (traditionally called "The Professor"); the town was full of good ragtime and blues musicians and Ferdinand was steeped in the music of the day, for which New Orleans at that time, the early 1900s, was famous. He knew all the pianists and other musicians who lived in New Orleans or visited, and the recollections he set down nearly 40 years afterwards (of which more will be said later) are an encyclopaedia of ragtime, early jazz history and the musical personalities of that era. By the early years of the century the only pianist who rivalled (and some say surpassed) Ferdinand in his particular field was Tony Jackson, later to write the song *Pretty Baby*.

Ferdinand's working life was spent in these bordellos and he made no pretensions of standing aloof from what went on there. He became a very good pool player and card sharp, always ready to win by whatever means were available. One of his favourite tricks in both games was to 'play stupid' if he was playing newcomers to New Orleans. In pool he would sometimes play left-handed, losing a lot of money in the process, then in the final game when *all* the money was at stake he would suddenly switch to his his natural right-handed game and clean up. He does not seem to have had any conscience about this; it was the sort of thing everyone did if they thought they could get away with it. In cards, he and his associates were up to all the tricks in the book to make a killing. Naturally he made enemies, which meant that then (in New Orleans) and in the future, wherever he happened to be, he often had to 'leave town' in a hurry to avoid retribution. At about 15 years old he left for Biloxi (on the coast) where his godmother had a summer residence and then went on to Meridian (200 miles inland), but he caught typhoid and had to be taken back to Biloxi on a stretcher where his godmother nursed him back to health. Soon he was back in New Orleans where for a while he was resident pianist at 'The Frenchman's'.

Jazz music at that time was in its infancy. It originated, according to Ferdinand and others, in New Orleans. He described it in these terms:

"Ragtime is a certain type of syncopation and only certain tunes can be played in that idea. Jazz music is to be played sweet and soft, plenty rhythm."

On the development from ragtime to jazz he said:

"Most of these ragtime guys, especially those that couldn't play very well, would have the inspiration that they were doing OK if they kept increasing the tempo during a piece. I decided that was a mistake and I must have been right, because everybody grabbed my style. I thought that accurate tempo would be the right tempo for any tune. So I found that the slow tunes, especially the medium-slow tunes, did more for the development of jazz than any other type, due to the fact that you could only hit it once, which gave it a very good flavour."

"About harmony, my theory is never to discard the melody. Always have a melody going some kind of way against a background of perfect harmony with plenty of riffs*. A riff is something that gives an orchestra a great background and is the main idea of playing jazz. No jazz player can play really good jazz unless they try to give an imitation of a band, that is by providing a basis of riffs. Now the riff is what we call a foundation, like something you walk on. It's standard. But without breaks†, and without clean breaks and beautiful ideas in breaks, you don't even need to think about doing anything else, you haven't got a jazz band and you can't play jazz. Even if a tune hasn't got a break in it, it's always necessary to arrange some kind of spot to make a break. A break, itself, is like a musical surprise, which didn't come in until I originated the idea in jazz. We New Orleans musicians were always looking for novelty effects to attract the public, and many of the most important things in jazz originated in some crazy guy's idea that we tried for a laugh or just to surprise the folks."

The pattern of Ferdinand's life as jazz musician, gambler, entertainer and man-about-town (counting 'town' as the seedier part of wherever he happened to be) was established before he was 20. At the bordellos where he was pianist much of his income came from tips from the girls' clients, so it paid to be on good terms with the resident prostitutes. It was a short step from this to becoming a pimp, which he did, and never made any secret of the fact. This, together with his gambling, brought him the bulk of his income for several years. His piano-playing became just a side-line, a passport into a world of bordellos and gaming houses.

***Riff:** In jazz the 'riff' is the general background accompaniment. It is often of a repetitive nature, but with variations, and in a band may be produced by several instruments.

†**Break:** In jazz, the 'break' is a brief solo passage, usually one or two bars long, occurring during an interruption in the accompaniment, but maintaining the underlying momentum of the piece. The break is one of the features that distinguish jazz from ragtime. It is analogous to the cadenza in classical music. It was Jelly Roll who introduced the break into jazz, an innovative feature which lends some credence to his claim of having invented jazz, for its use soon became universal.

Nevertheless, as a musician there was no-one to surpass or even to equal him.

At this point in the story let us explain how Ferdinand Joseph La Menthe became 'Jelly Roll' Morton. He took his stepfather's name of Morton as soon as he started earning his own living, for he didn't want a French-sounding name. "Jelly Roll" came about one day when he was on stage doing an ad-lib comedy turn (which was rare for him) with a colleague. During the act his comedian friend said "You don't know who you're talking to." Ferdinand said, "I don't care." After pretending to have an argument, Ferdinand finally asked who he was. He said he was Sweet Papa Cream Puff, right out of the bakery shop. This produced a laugh, so in answer to the question of who he was, Ferdinand told him he was Sweet Papa Jelly Roll. This too got a laugh and the name stuck. So from that time Ferdinand became "Jelly Roll" Morton and everyone referred to him by that name.

Jelly Roll Morton didn't just play jazz; as we have indicated, he helped to formulate it, to lay down its principles, and he soon became a major composer in the genre. One of his first successes was *Tiger Rag*, the authorship of which has been disputed, but Jelly Roll claimed it was his composition, or at any rate his arrangement of an old French quadrille. The tiger's growl was produced by running his left forearm along the piano keys. In the early 1900s he wrote *King Porter Stomp* (not copyrighted until 1924) in honour of a musician he respected, Porter King, masking the identity slightly by reversing the order of the names. Many years later Benny Goodman and his band used the piece as a theme tune. *Alabama Bound* was written at about the same time when Morton was still in his teens.

Few of his musical compositions of this period were copyrighted. He just didn't bother, for he knew there were plenty more where they came from, the product of his fertile musical imagination. Another reason why he didn't copyright them was that publishers at that time paid only very small sums ($15 or $20) for each composition. This seemed a trivial amount compared with the money he made from engagements at which he played his own music. He kept his compositions for his own personal use as far as possible. His jazz compositions were becoming well known throughout the Southern States and beyond, and everyone knew who had written them.

It was said earlier that Jelly Roll was a flashy dresser. In some ways he was a pre-cursor of Liberace in that respect; diamonds in particular formed decorations to his everyday wear and he had a large diamond set into a front tooth - a not uncommon practice amongst the well-to-do who wanted to be seen as such. He owned dozens of suits, the number eventually running into about 150 at any one time.

As a teenager Jelly Roll had discovered that the ability to play the piano opened doors into a white world. Although his colour was light, he was categorised as black by the race-conscious establishment. He thought of himself as white (and he sometimes referred to negroes in disparaging terms) but no-one else did. But because of his talent he was able to go more or less where he wanted, though he always had something of a chip on his shoulder about his colour. In musical terms he was unabashed by the 'hot' playing of the black American bands. He worked on his technique and his playing became better than ever. A fellow musician said years later: "Jelly Roll played piano all night and practised all day." He wasn't just a pianist; he often led scratch bands when need arose in order to play in clubs. A typical 7-piece band would consist of bass horn, trombone, trumpet, alto horn, possibly a baritone horn, bass and snare drums.

After the age of about 20 Jelly Roll never stayed in one place for very long. At first he returned from time to time to New Orleans, but links with his home town became more tenuous as the years rolled on. In the first few years of his wandering life he worked in Biloxi, Meridian, Gulfport, and various other small towns up and down the Gulf coast. From there he moved to Chicago, Houston (Texas), California and Oklahoma before returning to New Orleans. His outstanding ability as a pianist always opened doors to 'high-class sporting houses' of any town he entered, and enabled him to earn considerable sums as card-sharp, pool player (he was exceptionally good at the game, able to beat all but the very best in the land) and con-man. He carried a gun, regarded himself as a bit of a 'tough-guy', and had frequent brushes with the police. But any attempt to 'make it into the big time' in this world was doomed to failure, for his adventures were a litany of disaster; partners who double-crossed him, women who were unfaithful, and villains who robbed and attacked him. He really didn't have the character to be an effective 'baddie'.

Fundamentally he was decent; his misguided efforts to do well in a crooks' world were born of a fruitless attempt to show that he was someone big. He needn't have bothered, for as a pianist and jazz composer he *was* someone big; he stood head and shoulders above his rivals.

In 1912 or thereabouts, Jelly Roll started to write down his musical arrangements, something that most ragtime or jazz pianists of that era didn't have the knowledge or the desire to do. He knew all the 'rags' of Scott Joplin, James Scott, Louis Chauvin and countless others. He had the musical perception to differentiate one style from another, and he could imitate the playing styles of all the pianists of that era. (When he demonstrated this, many years later, a comparison with their piano rolls showed how accurate his memory was.) It was a short step from imitating their styles to extending them; to develop ragtime and to move it forward into the early jazz era.

Soon afterwards Jelly Roll returned to Chicago, a city he liked, for he could go anywhere regardless of colour or creed. His *Jelly Roll Blues* was so popular there that he re-named it *Chicago Blues*. It was published there under that name, and soon became a success all over America. Brass bands took it up throughout the land. In Chicago he formed one of his early jazz groups, billed as "Jelly Roll Morton and his Incomparables", with Jelly Roll on piano and other instrumentalists on drums, trombone, clarinet and trumpet. It soon earned a reputation as "The hottest thing in Chicago". An offer came to tour Europe with Vernon and Irene Castle, the dancers, but he turned it down in favour of a cabaret spot at the 'Elite' club in Chicago. However, even though he didn't go to Europe his music did, for *Jelly Roll Blues* (alias *Chicago Blues)* was well known throughout the European continent.

By the year 1917 Jelly Roll was tiring of Chicago and on receiving an offer to play at the Cadillac Café in Los Angeles he packed his things and departed for California. There he wrote *Cadillac Rag.* Soon he got a different job out of town. Such was his popularity that his clientèle (mainly the Hollywood stars) followed him, so the Cadillac's business went down and it closed. But then he secured a financial interest in the Cadillac (in fact half the business) and re-opened it. All the movie stars came back!

When America entered the Great War in 1917 the authorities asked

Jelly Roll to enlist as an officer. But he resisted, saying he would be "No better off as a dead officer than a dead private." He kept out of the forces by playing in a lot of fund-raising benefits; eventually he was drafted, but only as the armistice was about to be signed, so was soon demobbed.

In Los Angeles Jelly Roll lived with Anita Gonzales, a good-looking wealthy woman he had known for years. He described her as his wife but in fact they were not married. She owned an hotel, 'The Anita', in Los Angeles and Jelly Roll bought a gaming club next door to it. He put Zack Williams (reputedly the first man to play Tarzan in films) in to run it. Together Jelly Roll and Anita set up a variety of business ventures. Anita bought a restaurant in Arizona and he went there with her, but the restaurant didn't last long. In San Francisco they together ran the 'Jupiter Club'; he provided the entertainment with a 10-piece band whilst she operated the bar with a team of 10 waitresses. But they ran into trouble with the police, who threatened to close the place down if they allowed dancing. Jelly Roll thought the police didn't like the club because it was open to everyone, white and coloured alike. When prohibition was introduced in 1920 there was even more trouble with the police.

Because of the problems in San Francisco, Jelly Roll and Anita went to Seattle, then on to Vancouver, and eventually travelled to Alaska before returning via a circuitous route to California. Jelly Roll was based on the West Coast of America from 1917 to 1922, but travelled extensively. During this time he won and lost a lot of money in gambling. In Washington, where he was living at the 'Regent' hotel he lost $2,000 in one night then went on to win $11,000. Little stakes were not for him! In Denver, Colorado, he lost $20,000 and ended up 'broke'. At Tia Juano on the Mexican border he got a job at the Kansas City Bar and wrote *Kansas City Stomp* and *The Pearls*, dedicated to a pretty waitress there. Other compositions of this period were *Someday, Sweetheart* and *Wolverine Blues*. Towards the end of the period the relationship with Anita became increasingly strained and eventually they parted company.

1922 saw Jelly Roll back in Chicago, and then began the most productive years of his life from the musical point of view, due in no small measure to the fact that at last he pushed his gambling into the sidelines (it was not proving profitable) in order to concentrate on music. In the next decade he composed or arranged 100 original works of jazz in clear musical notation. He was also at his peak as a pianist.

When Jelly Roll got to Chicago he made himself known to Melrose Brothers, a music store which was then plugging *Wolverine Blues*. Lester Melrose recalled:

" A fellow walked into our store with a big bandana around his neck and a 10-gallon cowboy hat on his head and hollered - "Listen, everybody, I'm Jelly Roll Morton from New Orleans, the originator of jazz." He talked for an hour without stopping about how good he was, and then he sat down at the piano and proved he was every bit as good as he claimed, and better."

It was a propitious day for Jelly Roll. To him the Melrose Brothers were a couple of nice young fellows from Kentucky who needed a break. But he was beginning to realise it was more profitable to publish and own music than it was to compose or play it. The *big* money was to be had from gramophone records, sheet music and band-booking. As music publishers the Melrose brothers were only small fry, but as it turned out, they and Jelly Roll were good for each other and it was to be a profitable collaboration. In particular, minor publishers though they were, the Melroses had connections with The Victor Record Company and it was through an introduction by the Melroses that Victor offered Jelly Roll a recording contract.

He had in fact made a few records previously, for a Californian company in 1918 and some for Paramount and for Gennett (a subsidiary of the Starr Piano Company) in 1923-24. He had also recorded for Autograph and Vocalion in 1924, and earlier had made a few piano rolls for QRS, American and Imperial. But none of these recordings were the money-making winners that the Victor records proved to be.

The exclusive recording contract with Victor, signed in 1926, secured Jelly Roll's place as one of the great figures of jazz. Apart from his excellent piano solos, the records on which his fame is based are some 50 or so tracks made between 1926 and 1930 under the title "Jelly Roll Morton and his Red Hot Peppers". Victor billed the group as the 'Number One Hot Band'. The composition of the band varied in personnel and instruments but the basis of it was Jelly Roll on piano assisted by trombone, cornet, clarinet and drums, supplemented as required according to the piece being recorded. Sometimes the recordings were made by smaller groups, for example trios, as well as

Ferdinand 'Jelly Roll' Morton

Jelly Roll's own piano solos. There seems little doubt that Jelly Roll Morton was the most original and creative figure in jazz of the period. With his Red Hot Peppers he produced the finest recordings of New Orleans music ever made.

The success of the recordings was due to the quality of the playing, which in turn came about through meticulous preparation. We hear a lot about the 'jam sessions' of the early jazz bands where the players were allowed to 'do their own thing', but Jelly Roll believed in careful groundwork prior to the recording. Omer Simeon, creole clarinetist, worked for Morton in the Red Hot Peppers band and recalled:

"Those people at Victor treated Jelly like he was somebody special, which he was, being the best in the country at that time in his style, and they paid us boys a good deal over scale to work with him.... See, Jelly Roll was mighty particular about his music, and if the musicians couldn't play real New Orleans, he'd get someone else. I'll tell you how he was rehearsing a band. He was exact with us. Very jolly, full of life all the time, but serious. We used to spend maybe three hours rehearsing four sides and in that time he'd give us the effects he wanted, like the background behind a solo - he would run that over on the piano with one finger and the guys would get together and harmonise it. The solos, they were ad lib. We played according to how we felt. Of course, Jelly had his ideas and sometimes we'd listen to them and sometimes, together with our own, we'd make something better. For me, I'd do whatever he wanted. In other words, I just co-operated with him, where a lot of the fellows wouldn't. It was my first big break."

So, as we see, some ad-libbing was allowed, but basically the secret of Morton's success on record was the carefully prepared musical text. He used to tell his band: "You'll please me if you'd just play those little black dots - just play those little black dots that I put down there. If you play them, you'll please me. You don't have to make a lot of noise and ad lib. All I want you to play is what's written. That's all I ask."

In 1927 Jelly Roll met Mabel Bertrand, a night-club dancer, at the Plantation club in Chicago. Born in New York and raised in a convent, her father was French and her mother an American Indian from Oklahoma. She had toured Europe years earlier and had appeared before royalty at Buckingham Palace. Jelly Roll was immediately attracted to Mabel. For a long time she rejected all the overtures of this ostentatious man with his big car and diamond-studded tooth, believing he was just another undesirable follower. However, when she realised that he really cared for her and wanted to marry her she accepted, and the couple were married before a Justice of the Peace in Gary, Indiana.

The Melody Lingers On

The wedding was in November 1928 and for the next two years she was 'on the road' with Jelly Roll and his band. They were one of the best-paid bands in the USA. The band travelled in a luxurious bus with the words JELLY ROLL MORTON AND HIS RED HOT PEPPERS emblazoned on the side, but Jelly Roll and Mabel travelled in his Lincoln car. Jelly Roll used to arrange all the band's bookings himself. An average pay for the band was about $1,500 or $1,600 a night. On stage they were immaculate; the band wore white tuxedos, but Jelly Roll wore a wine-red jacket and tie to match, white trousers and white shoes. They never carried a singer, but Jelly Roll had a pleasant voice and used to do the 'vocals' himself when necessary, on stage and on some of his records. They were the top jazz band at that time. Duke Ellington and Count Basie came later. Jelly Roll was known as 'The Diamond King' because of the number of these jewels adorning his person. Apart from the half-carat diamond in his tooth he had diamonds set into his ring, tie-pin, watch, locket and sock-supports, and wore a gold belt-buckle studded with diamonds. He, Mabel and the band stayed at the best hotels and ate the most expensive food.

Though he did not know it, Jelly Roll's fortunes were about to take a tumble. He had dominated the jazz world of the 1920s, but times were changing. The era of the big band was dawning, and swing was beginning to edge its way in to supplant the kind of jazz that Jelly Roll had developed. Moreover, Jelly roll was never the easiest man to get on with. Always argumentative and often abrasive, he was beginning to have trouble with his band. Various players got drunk at inopportune times, which did nothing for Jelly Roll's reputation. These factors contributed to his loss of the title of Number One Hot Band. Suddenly his music seemed old-fashioned, and when RCA took over Victor in 1930 they did not renew his recording contract. Louis Armstrong was already making the Hot Five records that set jazz in a different direction, and at the same time the Depression was making its presence felt. Consequently the sales of Jelly Roll's records slumped dramatically, and as he was no longer a current recording star, he could not now command high fees for performances by himself and his band. So, from about 1930, his career steadily declined, as did his income. He had always had an 'easy come, easy go' attitude to money, but as he had always been in demand as a pianist he had been able to go out and

Ferdinand 'Jelly Roll' Morton

earn money when he needed it. Now things were different; Jelly Roll Morton was a 'has-been', so for the first time for many years he was not well off.

The Red Hot Peppers became a thing of the past, but Jelly Roll appeared with scratch bands whenever opportunity arose. In the 1930s he was no more than a small-time operator, down (as he saw it) on his luck. Relations with Mabel were not all sweetness and light and the couple separated for a couple of years. But they seem to have had a good basic relationship in spite of their problems and the marriage survived. By 1936 or 1937, Jelly Roll at 50 was resorting to finding what work he could in low-class night spots and even tried his hand as a fight promoter.

Jelly Roll had an outsize chip on his shoulder, feeling that the established music world was against him. The best jobs were now reserved for the Music Corporation of America members and he couldn't get membership. Neither would the American Society of Composers, Authors and Publishers allow him to be a full member; he had long-running disputes with both organisations. For years he had grandiose plans to sue them, but they came to nothing. He also attributed some of his 'bad luck' to voodoo.

In 1938 Jelly Roll was working in a sordid back-street night-spot in Washington; he was little more than a pianist/odd-job man and had to help out at the bar as part of his job. It was then that an interesting turn to his career occurred. Alan Lomax, who was Curator of the Library of Congress in Washington, knew about Jelly Roll Morton, and discovered he was working in the city. Realising that Jelly Roll's career went back to the beginning of the century, Lomax thought he would have an interesting tale to tell if he could be persuaded to come to the Library of Congress and tell his life story.

At first Jelly Roll did not appreciate being regarded as an historical monument, but he accepted Lomax's invitation and on a May day in 1938 he turned up in the chamber-music auditorium of the Library of congress where the busts of great composers disturbed him not at all, for he was at home with great men. Lomax remembers:

"Years of poverty and neglect had neither dimmed his brilliance at the keyboard nor diminished his self esteem. He came to the Library of Congress to put himself forever on record, to carve his proper niche in the hall of history. There was something tremendously appealing about the old jazzman with his

Southern-gentleman manners and his sporting-life lingo. I decided to find out how much of old New Orleans lived in his mind. So, with the microphone near the piano of the Coolidge Chamber Music Auditorium I set out to make a few records of Jelly Roll, little knowing that I had encountered a creole Benvenuto Cellini. The amplifier was hot. The needle was tracing a quiet spiral on the spinning acetate. "Mister Morton", I said, "How about the beginning? Tell me about where you were born and how you got started and why . . . . and maybe keep playing piano while you talk."

The afternoon's recording sessions extended to a month and a lengthy series of musical piano performances was recorded, together with his recollections. He showed himself to be a charming raconteur and an encyclopaedic authority on jazz and its personalities. In all, 116 sides were recorded, creating an historical document second to none. The records were eventually issued in 12 volumes, some in 1948 and the remainder in 1957.

Jelly Roll's attendances at the Library of Congress were reported and some of his records were again played on the radio. A generation to whom Jelly Roll was no more than a name from the past was now beginning to take notice, and to realise that here was a man of outstanding talent. Once again he was in demand to play in clubs and gigs, and he appeared on Long Island with scratch bands in 1939. The French critics discovered him; suddenly it became fashionable to collect records of early Morton. RCA-Victor re-issued some of his old Red Hot Peppers records, and a small company issued selected titles from his Library of Congress recordings. In September 1939 RCA-Victor invited him to re-record some of the best tunes he had recorded for the Library of Congress. These were the last records he made.

This mini-boom in Jelly Roll's fortunes certainly did not make him a rich man, but at least it took him away from abject poverty. Unfortunately his health was not good. In 1938 he had been stabbed in the head and chest during a fracas at the Jungle Inn in Washington, an injury which seemed to trigger heart trouble and asthma. In 1939 he spent three months in hospital and the doctors told him to stop playing. Needless to say, he didn't. In November 1940 Jelly Roll heard that his godmother had died in California. He was worried about his godfather who was blind, and feared (with good reason as it turned out) that someone would step in and take advantage of the old man. In spite of the protests of Mabel and the local catholic priest, Jelly Roll insisted on

Ferdinand 'Jelly Roll' Morton

going to California to sort matters out. He dumped his belongings in his Cadillac, chained the car to the rear of his Lincoln, and set off for California in the Lincoln with the Cadillac in tow. Why he chose to travel by road, and to take two cars at that, is a mystery.

It proved to be a nightmare journey. That year the winter was particularly bad, and as Jelly Roll made the long journey from the east coast of the United States to the west, he met storms and snow in almost every State he passed through. He slid off the road in Wyoming and damaged one of his cars. In Idaho he had to leave one car behind because of the weather, and on a mountain in Oregon the police had to pull his car out of deep snow. Eventually he reached his destination, but the long journey had worn him out and he became ill. Anita Gonzales, who was living in Los Angeles at the time, nursed and financed him. Over the next few weeks Mabel, back home in Washington, received a series of sad letters, indicating that he was unwell and had little money. The last communication, dated 26th April 1941, was written on a Post Office Money Order application form and said only, "Will write soon. Still sick."

Jelly Roll died in Los Angeles on 10th July 1941, aged about 50 or possibly a little older. He was buried there in Calvary Cemetery after a solemn high requiem mass at St. Patrick's Church. Only one white man was present among the approximately 150 people who attended the church service and accompanied the cortège to the cemetery. He was Dave Stuart of the Jazz Man record shop. Four of Jelly Roll's Red Hot Peppers band were among the pall bearers. They were Kid Ory (trombone), Papa Mutt Carey (cornet), Fred Washington (piano) and Ed Garland (bass). Two other members of the band were also present.

Jelly Roll Morton was the greatest exponent of New Orleans jazz, a brilliant pianist, and an important link between ragtime with its associated miscellany of Spanish creole and New Orleans traditions, and mainstream jazz of the 1930s. His work is immortalised in his musical compositions, about 175 gramophone recordings, and a handful of piano rolls. He was a pioneer, who did as much if not more than anyone else to formulate and develop jazz.

A list of Jelly Roll Morton's compositions is given in Appendix 7.

The Melody Lingers On

Cole Porter

8. Cole Porter

Cole Porter deserves a place in any book on popular musicians, for he was one of the 'Big Four' writers of popular song who dominated the scene in the first half of the present century, along with Irving Berlin, George Gershwin and Jerome Kern. Like Irving Berlin he wrote his own words as well as his music, and his lyrics were renowned for their slick wit, or 'sophistication' as many call it. As a songwriter he was one of the giants of the century. Yet as a man he was not very appealing. Selfish, snobbish, and vain are some of the adjectives that can fairly be used to describe him. For the whole of his adult life he was a practising homosexual who employed the services of male prostitutes through procurers. But it is primarily the artistic aspects of his life that we are to examine here, for his impact on the musical scene was enormous.

To say that Cole Porter had private means would be an understatement. He had enough income handed out to him to enable him to live in opulent luxury for most of his life. It is to his credit that he worked at his trade and became one of the leading songwriters of the age when he had absolutely no financial need ever to put pen to paper. Let us look briefly at Cole's family background, to see how it came about that he was the recipient of such great worldly wealth, quite apart from the equally vast amount of money he was to make as a songwriter.

Cole's forbears on his mother's side hailed from Peru. But it was not the Peru in South America. This Peru was a small town in Indiana, about 65 miles north of Indianapolis. It was Cole's maternal grandfather, James Omar Cole (always known as J.O.) who was the source of the family fortune. An entrepreneur in the true American pioneering style, he made $700 in the Californian Gold Rush, operated a general store and built a water conduit from Maryland to Sacramento which made $30,000 for him. Then he ran a brewery, an ice and cold store in his home town of Peru, a sawmill in Cincinnati, and had forestry interests in Indiana, Illinois, Ohio, Kentucky and West Virginia. In short, he was a financial wizard, a self-made millionaire, and a dominant force in Peru. Down to earth and practical, he had no time for the arts or the refinements of life, but he knew a lot about making money.

In 1860 J.O. married Rachel Henton. Two children were born, Kate (1862) and Louis (1865). J.O. lavished attention and money on his wife and daughter, whilst Louis was left somewhat on the sidelines. Kate was sent to school in Connecticut and New York, the recipient of the best education that J.O.'s money could buy.

On 9th April 1884, Kate Cole married Samuel Fenwick Porter, a shy pharmacist of limited financial means. Of unprepossessing appearance, fond of poetry and literature, Kate's choice was a bitter disappointment to the self-made magnate, J.O. Nevertheless, like many fathers before and since, he had to make the best of matters and the wedding took place quietly in J.O.'s house in the presence of only a few guests. Samuel was amiable and well-meaning; he built up his pharmacist's business in a small way, but he was no J.O. It was J.O. who remained the dominant figure in Kate's life. Kate and Sam's house was built at J.O.'s expense on J.O.'s land, and Kate depended, and continued to depend, on J.O.'s largesse in keeping her in the style to which she was accustomed.

A son, Louis, was born to Kate and Sam in 1888 but died soon after birth, and a daughter, Rachel, died at the age of two in 1890. These sad events followed the common pattern of those days, but the couple had better luck with their third offspring. Cole Porter was born at his parents' home on 9th June 1891, and was to be the only child of the family to survive infancy.

Cole resembled Kate and she spoiled him excessively, perhaps not surprising after the deaths of the two previous children. He was a small, thin, lithe child, and no expense was spared in his upbringing. He had his own Shetland pony at an early age as well as private tutors for French and dancing. At six he started to learn the violin and piano. The violin was not to his liking and he preferred the piano. The violin teacher lived in Marion, Indiana, 30 miles from Peru, so Cole had to be taken to and fro for his lessons. Later he played in the Marion Student Orchestra and even made a debut as a violin soloist. A local paper reported: "Master Cole completely charmed his audience with sweet music and the gracefulness of rendition."

But Cole was by no means a prodigy, nor could it be said he was mad about music. One thing he did enjoy though was writing songs. At the age of 10 (in 1901) he wrote *Song of the Birds*, dedicated to his mother. The following year his *Bobolink Waltz* so pleased Kate that she had 100 copies of it published at her own expense and distributed them to her friends.

Once he reached the age of 10 Kate used to take Cole to Chicago for two weeks every winter in order to visit the theatre and opera. Cole enjoyed these trips very much and there is little doubt they kindled his interest in the theatre. His childhood in Peru was both normal (by the standards of a rich family) and unremarkable. At the age of 14 he was sent away to school at Worcester Academy, Worcester, Massachusetts, a school noted for its emphasis on the classics. Just as Kate had received a good education, J.O. saw to it that Cole had nothing but the best, including a generous monthly allowance and his own piano in his room at school. Cole was enrolled there in September 1905, but for some reason his age appeared throughout his school records as two years younger than he was, possibly through Kate's wish to make people think he was exceptionally precocious. He soon became popular at school because of his ready wit and sparkling personality. Though competent at his school work it was in the extra-curricular activities that Cole really made a hit. He belonged to the debating and dramatic societies, and also the mandolin and glee clubs. At 17 he gave up the violin. Academically he did well at school, but more importantly he wrote songs. His headmaster, Dr. Abercrombie, gave him a good grounding in the classics, from which Cole learned the importance of metre in verse - very important in songwriting. Dr. Abercrombie took an enlightened view of Cole's activities and encouraged his musical talents. Cole's success at school can be gauged by the fact that he was selected as Valedictorian of his graduating class; i.e. the speaker of the college valedictory address.

From the time Cole was sent away to school at the age of 14, Peru was really just a place for occasional visits. J.O.'s graduation present to Cole was a trip to France - which broadened his horizons. A visit to France became virtually an annual event for the remainder of his life.

In 1909, 18-year old Cole was sent to study English, History and Languages at Yale University. At least, that was the intention, but 'study' would hardly be the correct word to describe Cole's lifestyle at Yale. He arrived there with his piano amongst his luggage and immediately launched himself into a whirl of extra-curricular activity.

Whereas he had done reasonably well academically at Worcester, it was a different story at Yale. He was in most of the Yale clubs and was a leading light in everything he took part in. He was a football cheerleader, an actor, a singer, a pianist and was conductor of the glee club. But it was as a lyricist and composer that he really shone, and much of his time at Yale was spent in putting together the Yale musical shows. Though it didn't help him to pass his examinations, the experience he gained in all aspects of presenting a show was to be invaluable to him. Cole wrote the shows, performed in them, collected the actors together and supervised rehearsals, advised on costumes and lighting, conducted the performance, and saw the whole event through from beginning to end. In short, he learned his trade. In his years at Yale he turned out the scores and lyrics for four shows, *Cora, And the Villain Pursued Her, The Pot of Gold*, and *The Kaleidoscope*. He became a college celebrity and was invited to the richest homes in the area. Already he was a heavy smoker and drinker, and it is probably at this stage of his life that his active homosexuality began.

Fortunately for Cole the College Authorities took a sympathetic view of his life at Yale and gave him credit for his non-academic contribution to the community. Thus he graduated in the spring of 1913, the beneficiary of an academic system which recognised that examinations were not everything. Similarly, it used to be said that the best way to be sure of graduating from Oxford or Cambridge was to be awarded a 'blue' at cricket. At Yale he had become a 'big man in music' on the campus and had managed to get a song published by the Tin Pan Alley company, Remick's. It was called *Bridget* and it established his credentials as a songwriter. He was good at putting across his songs himself. Like Irving Berlin and Jerome Kern he was small (5ft 6in) and had a high tenor voice; he was not a great pianist but his personality was enough to make people sit up and take notice when he performed. After graduating from Yale, J.O.'s present to him was a trip to England, to complement the earlier one to France.

After Yale, Cole was sent in the spring of 1913 to Harvard's Graduate Law School, J.O.'s intention being that he should become a lawyer. He was a dutiful student there for a couple of months but it was manifestly obvious to anyone who knew Cole that he would never make a lawyer. After the first few weeks of his course all pretence disappeared, and thereafter he did no academic work at all. Instead he continued as he had done at Yale, putting on shows, many of them for Yale, where his heart evidently still resided. For the whole of his time at Yale and Harvard Cole received a generous monthly allowance from J.O. Cole's father seems to have taken no part in financing him or in making decisions regarding his future. J.O. had no time for Cole's musical philanderings; he thought he ought to be getting on with some good solid work. Cole used to tell his mother all about what he was doing, but discretion had to be exercised in what was passed on to J.O. So Cole continued to get his monthly allowance from J.O., with no questions asked.

In the 1914-15 session, on the advice of the Dean, Cole switched from the Law School at Harvard to the Graduate School of Arts and Sciences, but he still didn't apply himself, and enrolled for only two courses - musical appreciation and basic harmonies. He was in great demand at parties, where his ebulliance and wit set him apart from the others. He was 'a personality' at Harvard. It was at one of the parties that he met Elizabeth (Bessie) Marbury, who knew all the society élite and who also worked as a theatrical producer and agent. Through her Cole met many of the Broadway professionals, including Jerome Kern and Sigmund Romberg. It was Bessie Marbury who helped to get a Cole Porter song, *Esmeralda*, incorporated into a Romberg musical, *Hands Up*, in 1915. Another song, *Two Big Eyes* (words not by Porter but by John Golden in this case) was put into a Jerome Kern musical, *Miss Information*, at the George Cohan Theatre in October 1915. As a writer for Broadway, Cole had set foot on the first rungs of the ladder.

Cole was now sufficiently confident to let his successes as a songwriter be communicated to J.O., and wrote to his mother, "Tell Grandad that Lew Fields gave me $50 for each song I sold him and 4 cents on each copy" and, in December 1915, "Tell Grandad that unless something extra-ordinary happens this show will go into rehearsal in a few weeks' time." The show in question was *See America First*, produced by his friend Bessie Marbury. It used a number of Porter songs. But, like all the other Porter shows of the period, it was too much like a college show. As a college show it was fine, but in Broadway terms it was a flop, running for only 15 performances. Nevertheless, Cole was on the up and up, and in 1916 Schirmer

The Melody Lingers On

published 13 of the show's songs. One of them, *I've a Shooting Box in Scotland*, was recorded by Victor in 1916 with the Joseph C. Smith Orchestra, the first commercial recording of a Cole Porter song. Needless to say Cole never graduated from Harvard. He had gradually drifted away from the College and was now a fully-fledged professional songwriter.

Cole's lifestyle was now established in the way it was to continue; a songwriter and man-about-town, wearing loud suits and flashy ties. A vain man, he continued to pretend he was two years younger than he was. In December 1916 J.O. set up a trust for Cole from J.O.'s half-interest in real-estate holdings in Virginia and Kentucky which he had purchased with a partner, Clinton Crane. This provided for Cole to receive a substantial income from J.O.'s holdings after the death of both partners, which in the opinion of Cole could not be long delayed as both were then in their 80s.

As a songwriter now getting his work performed on Broadway, Cole had moved to New York, where his apartment on East 19th Street became the scene of numerous glittering parties. When the Great War finally caught up with the United States in 1917 he sailed for France, but not as part of the U.S. Armed Forces, for he somehow managed to escape the draft. He never enlisted but associated himself with an organisation that helped distribute food in the parts of France that were occupied. Later he spread stories around that he had served in the French Foreign Legion during the war and had been awarded the Croix de Guerre. This was pure invention; there is no reference to it whatever in any official French records. Much of his wartime 'service' was in fact spent in Paris, which never fell to the Germans during the First World War, and in Paris he was able to maintain the same kind of social life as he had done in New York. He even managed to have some of his songs included in London musicals in 1918.

In 1918 Cole met Linda Lee Thomas, an American divorcee, in Paris. Seven years older than Cole, she had married Edward Russell Thomas, a member of a prominent publishing family, in 1901 but the marriage ended in 1912. Under the terms of the divorce settlement she had acquired a fortune, over $1,000,000 in stocks and shares. She enjoyed a life of luxury, and was a leading socialite. Cole and Linda's friendship quickly developed but Cole felt he did not have enough money to propose marriage to such a rich woman. So he returned to the USA to ask for an advance from J.O. on the trust fund. On the liner he met Raymond Hitchcock, an impresario, then planning his third Hitchy-Koo revue for Broadway. Hitchcock commissioned Cole to write the music and lyrics for the Hitchy-Koo revue for 1919, and also introduced him to Max Dreyfus, the song publisher. The show was a great success and made a lot of money for Cole - enough for him to go back to Paris and propose to Linda. She and Cole were married on 18th December 1919, in the presence of a few friends at a non-religious civil ceremony. She knew about and accepted his homosexuality. She saw in him the seeds of greatness as a popular composer and was deeply ambitious for him to succeed; he saw in her financial security and stability. They accepted each other as they were. Though many would regard the marriage as one of convenience there is no doubt there was a genuine mutual affection.

The money from Hitchy-Koo and the royalties from his songs that Dreyfus published compensated for J.O.'s refusal to give Cole the advance he had sought. The old man showed no sign of dying, and Cole's mode of living required vast sums of money; after his marriage to Linda he had no need to rely on J.O., for his wife was a source of wealth, which she was happy to lavish on Cole.

After their wedding they bought a large house at 13, rue Monsieur, which was to remain their Paris home for many years. Linda led the way in fashion, and her bright yellow Rolls Royce phaeton was a well-known sight in Paris. Because of Linda's wealth, Cole was able to do as he pleased. She was devoted to him and indulged him like a mother. Moreover, her social contacts were a great help to him, for through them many doors were opened.

The Paris home was only one of the Porter residences. In 1921 the couple rented a large villa at Cap d'Antibes on the French Riviera, and they stayed in sumptuous apartments in the best hotels wherever they went. All the while Cole was getting his songs published and inserted into shows on both sides of the Atlantic. He was moderately successful; his work brought him a good income, though it was as nothing compared with the largesse handed out by Linda. But none of his songs from this period were real hits. A few of them enjoyed transient popularity at the time but all are forgotten today. Critics used to say that the tunes were too tricky and the lyrics too sophisticated.

In 1923 J.O. finally died at the age of 94. He had outlived his business partner Clinton Crane, so after his death Cole became the recipient of even greater riches than before. It showed in his lifestyle. In the summer seasons from 1923 he and Linda rented a 4-storey palazzo fronting the Grand Canal in Venice. There he worked, and the location became the scene of the most riotous parties Venice had ever seen, usually when Linda was away. At these events Cole and his guests indulged not only in heavy drinking but also drugs, including opium, cocaine and hashish. Finally, in 1927, Cole was forced to leave Venice after police raided the Porters' palazzo when a party was in full swing. They found a crowd of Italian boys dressed in Linda's fancy clothes cavorting for the delectation of Cole and his cronies. It turned out that one of the boys happened to be the son of the police chief in charge of the raid. Consequently, to protect his own interests, the officer hushed the matter up, but insisted Cole should leave Venice forthwith.

From time to time Cole had aspired to write 'serious' music and in the mid 1920s he wrote the music for a ballet, *Within the Quota* (orchestrated by Charles Koechlin, a renowned French music teacher), which was presented along with a ballet by Darius Milhaud and performed by the Ballets Suédois Company which was then in Paris. Later the ballet was taken to New York. In Paris it was marginally successful but in the USA it failed. After that Cole gave up any ambitions he might have had as a 'serious' composer and devoted himself to what he was best at, writing popular music, much to the world's benefit.

Cole's father, Sam Porter, died in 1927 after a prolonged nervous breakdown, at a time when Cole's shows, including *Greenwich Village Follies*, were keeping the theatres going for relatively brief periods. In 1928 Cole was put in touch with Raymond Goetz, producer and playwright (whose sister Dorothy was Irving Berlin's first wife) with a view to putting on a new show. It was *Paris*, which had trial runs in the hinterlands before appearing at the Music Box Theatre on 8th October 1928. Five Porter songs were in the show. One of them, *Let's Do It, Let's Fall in Love*, was the great hit of the show, and lives to this day. It was Cole's first really big hit song - and he was then 37 years old. As a top Broadway songwriter, he had finally made the grade.

Let's Do It was a typical Porter song. A catchy melody combined with inventive, slightly risqué, lyrics were the standard Porter formula. The song was the prelude to a tremendously productive period that was to last for more than 20 years. Cole seemed to have suddenly found the secret of how to write a good song. He once said that he decided about then to write 'Jewish type music', having noticed that the best songwriters of the day (Berlin, Kern and Gershwin) were Jewish, and there does seem to be evidence in his songs of Jewish rhythm and melodies, with oft-repeated phrases that became a kind of Porter trademark. Whatever the secret was, Cole had certainly found it. The next few years brought a string of Broadway shows and Hollywood films featuring Porter scores. Hit songs of the next few years, after *Let's Do It* in 1928 included *What Is This Thing Called Love* (1929), *You Do Something To Me* (1929), *Night and Day* (1932), *The Physician (He Never Said He Loved Me)* (1933), *Solomon* (1933), *I Get a Kick Out of You* (1934), *Miss Otis Regrets* (1934), *Anything Goes* (1934), *You're the Top* (1934), *Why Shouldn't I?* (1935), *Begin the Beguine* (1935), *Just One of Those Things* (1935), *I've Got You Under My Skin* (1936), *It's De-Lovely* (1936), *In the Still of the Night* (1937) and *My Heart Belongs To Daddy* (1938). Such a brilliant 10-year creative period is probably unsurpassed amongst songwriters. It was Porter at his best.

Porter's songs earned the praise of his peers. Irving Berlin, after seeing the show *Fifty Million Frenchmen* on Broadway said the score was "One of the best collection of song numbers I have ever listened to", and added that it was worth the price of admission just to hear Cole Porter's lyrics. A few years later he was also most complimentary about *Night and Day*.

In the 1930s Cole's Broadway shows were so successful that he was much sought after by Hollywood, for in the years of the Depression America was cheered up only by the celluloid fantasy emanating from California. Thus, many of the Broadway successes were made into films. His first film, *The Battle of Paris* (Paramount, 1929) was not a success but the later ones fared better. One of the first of his movie hits was *The Gay Divorcee* (RKO, 1934), a development of the show *Gay Divorce* which opened at the Ethel Barrymore Theatre in 1932. Fred

Astaire appeared in both versions, whilst in the film Ginger Rogers was cast as Fred's partner. The hit song of both show and film, *Night and Day*, was written by Cole specifically for Fred Astaire and was in fact the only song to appear in both the stage and film versions. Fred had recently lost his dancing partner, his sister Adele, who had retired after marrying a rich Englishman. Keen to make good on his own, he was undeterred by the famous judgment of a recent screen test: "Balding; can't sing; can't act; can dance a little." So Cole's invitation to Fred was timely, for the song suited him down to the ground. Cole was very keen to acquire Fred for the stage show, and had invited him to his home to hear the tunes.

Not all Cole's songs were hits by any means. As with the other major songwriters, one hit per show was thought to be very good going indeed. An inspection of the complete list of Cole Porter songs indicates hundreds that have remained under dust covers since they were created. They were just not good enough. It was the same with Berlin, Kern and Gershwin. But the really good songs stood out. Many of Cole's songs were sexually orientated and he often had trouble with the censors. His first big hit, *Let's Do It*, was saved through the mollifying sentiment of its last line, 'Let's fall in love'. *My Heart Belongs To Daddy* is not just a tale of a little girl's affection for her father. *Love for Sale* (from *The New Yorkers*, 1933), a sad and plaintive song, was to be sung by a white girl acting the part of a prostitute, but its planned inclusion caused such a furore that the casting was changed so that it was sung by a black girl in Harlem; by the mores of the day this was more acceptable to the white audiences. Several Porter songs were banned altogether from Broadway and the radio as too sexually suggestive.

In 1935 Cole, with his wife and Moss Hart (a scriptwriter) set off on a world cruise on the liner *Franconia*, the intention being that Cole and Moss should write a new musical, *Jubilee*. Linda, as usual, saw to it that he worked, though in fairness to Cole he always exercised his own discipline, and kept his work and play very firmly apart. The resulting show (in 1935) contained no less than four hit songs, *Begin the Beguine, A Picture of Me Without You, Why Shouldn't I?* and *Just One of Those Things*. *Begin the Beguine* was the longest tune he ever wrote, containing 198 bars. It got off to a slow start but Artie Shaw's orchestral version of it in 1938 popularised the song and made Shaw's name. Many of Cole's shows were presented in London after they had established themselves on Broadway. *Anything Goes*, for instance, ran for 261 performances at the Palace Theatre, London, after opening there in June 1935.

From the mid 1930s Cole's Hollywood commitments had become such a major part of his work that he used to spend four to six months a year there. This was to continue for the rest of his active life. The RKO film *The Gay Divorcee* has already been mentioned. It was followed by other films. They were *Born To Dance* (1936) with Eleanor Powell and James Stewart; Paramount's *Anything Goes* (1936) with Bing Crosby, Ethel Merman and Ida Lupino; MGM's *Rosalie* (1937) with Nelson Eddy and Eleanor Powell; and Monogram Pictures' *Break the News* (a British film) released in Britain in 1938 and in the USA in 1941, with Maurice Chevalier and Jack Buchanan.

Cole described his method of writing songs as follows:

"First I think of an idea for a song and then I fit it to a title. Then I go to work on a melody. Then I write the lyric - the end first - that way it has a strong finish. It's terribly important for a song to have a strong finish. I do the lyrics the way I'd do a crossword puzzle. I try to give myself a metre which will make the lyric as easy as possible to write, but without being banal . . . I try to pick for my rhyme words of which there is a long list with the same ending."

He didn't doodle at the piano, which was the method used by many writers. He had a reasonable musical background and created most of his tunes away from the piano, using a notebook and manuscript paper. Only when he had thought out the basic lyrics and melody would he try the song out at the piano. The finishing touches were applied by his musical aides - men who had a very sound knowledge of music but did not possess Cole's creative flair. Several times a week he would meet Dr. Albert Sirmay (Cole's musical editor, first at Harms' music publishers, then at Chappell's), or Alexander Steinert, or any of several other helpers. He would play his tunes for them at the piano but without harmony or rhythmic patterns for the accompaniment. Then he would make comments, such as "Make the bass line stand out." He was precise in his instructions, and his aides would carry them out to the letter. The manuscript would then be annotated to reflect his wishes. His aides commuted between Broadway and Hollywood to help him when required; he paid them $20/hour, and more if they had to travel.

In 1936, at the peak of his career, Cole was 45 and looked 35. Linda, on the other hand, at 52 was looking older than her age. The victim of chronic bronchial and asthmatic problems, she could almost be mistaken for his mother. Though she had always accepted his homosexuality within reason, by 1937 she felt she had had more than she could stand. Hollywood, with its large homosexual population, provided him with more than sufficient sexual encounters. Cole, possessor of vast wealth, had no problems in paying procurers. Even so, he and his friends were not averse to 'kerb crawling' in order to seek the he-man types they favoured. Not only did Linda disapprove of all this, she felt his career would suffer if word of his escapades became public knowledge. Eventually she packed her bags and left for Paris.

None of this affected Cole's creative output. When he was engaged to write songs for MGM's *Rosalie* (the 1937 film version of the 1928 Broadway musical by George Gershwin and Sigmund Romberg), the star of the film, Nelson Eddy, didn't like Cole's song *In the Still of the Night*, and requested that it be dropped. Cole played it through to MGM's boss, L.B. Mayer. The hard-boiled old tycoon was so overcome by Cole's banal lyrics that he started to weep. Cole had won and the song went into the film. But he had great difficulty in writing a good title song for *Rosalie*. Just as Beethoven wrote three versions of the *Leonora* overture before coming up with *Fidelio*, so did Cole get as far as 'Rosalie No. 6' before he was satisfied. But Mayer didn't like the song, and insisted Cole should write yet another version. Cole did not have a very high opinion of the result, Rosalie No. 7; in fact he said it was a terrible song. He had written it overnight and some said he deliberately wrote a bad song to try to get his own back on Mayer. But the song took off and became a hit. Afterwards Irving Berlin, on hearing how Cole disliked it, said to him: "Listen, kid. Never hate a song that sold half a million copies."

In 1937 Cole went to Paris to see Linda, but relations remained cool. Soon he was back in America, where an event occurred that was to have a profound effect on his life. He was invited for a weekend's holiday to the home of Countess di Zoppola, one of the Porters' society friends, in Oyster Bay, Long Island. They belonged to the equine fraternity and the weekend's events included horse-riding. Against the advice of the groom (Cole was never very good at taking advice) he selected a particularly high-spirited horse. As the party rode along, Cole's horse was suddenly frightened by a noise. It reared up and fell, taking Cole with it, for he wasn't able to extricate himself from the stirrups. It fell on one of Cole's legs, shattering it. Terrified, the animal tried to right itself but fell again, this time on its opposite side, shattering Cole's other leg. When the horse finally freed itself of its rider Cole lay on the ground dazed, conscious, but very severely injured. No hospital ambulances were available and Cole was eventually taken to the local hospital in the Fire Department's ambulance. For a couple of days he alternated between delirium and unconsciousness. After he finally came to he showed he hadn't lost his wit, remarking, "Now I know why fifty million Frenchmen can't be wrong. They eat their horses instead of riding them."

Cole's dutiful wife, Linda, came hurrying back from Paris as soon as she heard of the accident. Re-united after their brief separation, she pleaded with the surgeons not to amputate one of Cole's legs, which was what they were proposing to do. She knew how carefully he had always looked after himself, applying skin treatments to make himself look younger, and so on, and she realised that amputation would finish him off psychologically. By a strange quirk of fate, Linda's first husband had also faced the prospect of amputation, and she had dissuaded the surgeons from that course of action, a decision that had proved medically correct. So Cole kept both legs, but his convalescence was to be long and painful. He was transferred to a hospital in Manhattan and remained there for months. In fact he was never free of pain for the rest of his life and could only walk with difficulty. He was to undergo over 30 operations on his legs over the years.

As the months of recovery slowly passed, Cole regained something of his old spirits. He was a model patient, doing all that the doctors asked of him, and he never complained. Linda and the doctors realised that for Cole the best form of therapy would be a return to his writing. In 1938, still in a wheelchair, he resumed work on the show *You Never Know* that had been interrupted by his accident. He had his piano put on blocks in his Waldorf apartment so that it was at the right height for his wheelchair, and with Linda now back with him life returned to something like normality. *You Never Know* opened on Broadway on

21st September 1938. It was not prime Porter, and the critics were unenthusiastic. It ran for only 78 performances, but it had served a useful purpose in getting Cole back into harness again. *Leave It To Me* in 1938, starring Sophie Tucker, fared better. It ran for 309 performances at the Imperial Theatre on Broadway before going on tour. It contained the Porter hit, *My Heart Belongs to Daddy.*

By the end of 1938 Cole was as fully occupied in his profession as before, and five very successful shows with Porter scores appeared between December 1939 and January 1944. They ran for over 400 performances each, with two of them topping 500; some were also presented in London. The first show, *DuBarry Was a Lady* (1939) had a cast including Ethel Merman and Betty Grable. The chief songs of the show were *Do I Love You?* and *Well, Did You Evah!* *Panama Hattie* (1941) had Danny Kaye in the cast and *Something for the Boys* (1943) featured Ethel Merman and contained *Hey, Good Lookin'*. The last show of the five, *Mexican Hayride* (1944) included the song *Count Your Blessings.* Many versions of this song have subsequently been recorded.

During this period of Broadway success Cole had not ignored his Hollywood commitments. MGM's *Broadway Melody of 1940*, starring Fred Astaire and Eleanor Powell, was followed in 1941 by Columbia Pictures' *You'll Never Get Rich*, also starring Fred Astaire but this time with Rita Hayworth. A 1942 film version of *Panama Hattie* (MGM) contained songs from the original stage musical, but Columbia Pictures' *Something To Shout About* found room for a new Cole Porter song, *You'd Be So Nice To Come Home To.* MGM's film of *DuBarry Was a Lady* contained no original numbers but was enlivened by the presence of Lucille Ball, Red Skelton, Gene Kelly and the Tommy Dorsey Band.

Financially successful as Cole Porter's shows of the 1940s were, his rate of achieving hits was less than in the 1930s and some critics complained about the 'double entendres' in his lyrics. One writer referred to the song *But in the Morning, No* (from *DuBarry Was a Lady)* as "Dirt without wit." Another critic said: "Mr. Porter is not the composer he once was." However, none of these remarks bothered Cole.

After Cole's accident Linda had removed the best furniture, silver and other valuables from their Paris house and brought it to the USA.

In 1939 when war in Europe seemed imminent they had closed their Paris home and never lived there again. In 1940 he and Linda bought a mansion on a 200-acre country estate at Buxton Hill in Williamstown, Massachusetts, and filled it with their best treasures. They lived there for part of the year only, spending several months each year in Hollywood and New York, At Buxton Hill there was a small guest house in the grounds which Cole converted into a work cottage.

In the mid 1940s a film about Cole Porter's life was made at Irving Berlin's suggestion. A Warner Brothers production, it starred Cary Grant as Porter and the cast included Mary Martin. As might be imagined, the film was packed with Cole Porter hit songs. But it conformed to the usual Hollywood formula of "Only the facts have been changed." The account of Cole's life was highly fictional, with songs appearing at points in his life story years before they had been written. Events such as Cole's minimal contribution to the Allied cause in World War I were glossed over. Cole found the whole thing very amusing. Publicly he lauded the film; privately he laughed at it. But of course, it made a lot of money for him.

In 1944 Cole contributed to *Seven Lively Arts*, a series of writings and compositions by Moss Hart and others. Cole's big song for this production was *Ev'ry Time We Say Goodbye.* For this same production Billy Rose, the producer, commissioned Igor Stravinsky to write a 15-minute ballet to be performed by the dancers Alicia Markova and Anton Dolin, He duly obliged, and after the show's big try-out in Philadelphia, Rose telegraphed Stravinsky as follows:

YOUR MUSIC GREAT SUCCESS STOP COULD BE SENSATIONAL SUCCESS IF YOU WOULD AUTHORIZE ROBERT RUSSELL BENNETT RETOUCH ORCHESTRATION STOP BENNETT ORCHESTRATES EVEN THE WORKS OF COLE PORTER

Stravinsky promptly wired back:

SATISFIED WITH GREAT SUCCESS

In the late 1940s Cole suffered a period of depression. His legs were playing him up more than ever and he was starting to feel the critics might be right when they suggested he was well over the hill as a songwriter. But *Kiss Me, Kate*, which opened on Broadway in 1948, changed all that. Based on Shakespeare's *The Taming of the Shrew*, Cole didn't want to write the score for the show, but once he had agreed to do it he entered into the work with enthusiasm. The result was a string of hit songs, including *Another Op'nin', Another Show, Wunderbar* (actually written, with different words, in 1933), *So in Love, Always True To You in My Fashion*, and *I Hate Men*. It ran for a record-breaking 1077 performances on Broadway, more than any other Porter show, and to this day it is often revived in professional and amateur productions. It was voted the best musical of the 1948-49 season and won several Tony awards. A movie version starring Kathryn Grayson and Howard Keel was made by MGM in 1953.

Cole and Linda's travels continued but their pre-war Paris home was now a girls' school, so when in Paris they stayed in a luxury suite at the Ritz. In the early 1950s Cole's depression returned, to the extent that he required psychiatric treatment, which included electro-convulsive therapy. In 1952 his mother, Kate, died of a stroke at the age of 90 and Linda, beset by bronchial problems and now looking old and stooped, was in very poor health. After his depressive problems, Cole still managed to produce a good score for *Can Can* (1953) which contained *I Love Paris*. 20th Century Fox made a film of the show in 1960 with Shirley MacLaine, Frank Sinatra and Maurice Chevalier in the cast. *Silk Stockings* opened on Broadway in 1955 and a film of the show was released by MGM in 1957. But the film highlight of the 1950s for Cole was *High Society* (MGM, 1956), with Bing Crosby, Grace Kelly, Frank Sinatra and Louis Armstrong in a star-studded cast. It included the duet *True Love*, sung by Bing Crosby and Grace Kelly, which was to be the last of Cole Porter's hit songs. He was now 65, enormously wealthy, and had done well still to be as successful as he was at an age which, for a songwriter, was relatively advanced.

After a long battle against ill health, Linda Porter died on 20th May 1954, aged 70. Her body was taken to Cole's birthplace of Peru and interred in the family plot. She had devoted much of her life to her often errant husband. Her headstone bore the simple legend, "Linda Lee, wife of Cole Porter". After inheriting a fortune following the death of his mother, who left the bulk of her estate to him, Cole now inherited nearly $2 million from Linda. His pattern of life was so settled that it barely changed after Linda's death, but he had his home in Williamstown bulldozed to the ground, and his working cottage in the grounds moved to the site of the house. There he resided, looked after by his valet and a number of other staff; he still gave parties, for he loved to be the centre of attention.

In 1956 he was operated on for a stomach ulcer; also, the condition of his legs, which had been a constant source of trouble since his riding accident of 1937, was rapidly deteriorating. In 1958 he entered hospital because of chronic osteomyelitis of the right upper tibia. Amputation had been staved off in 1937, but this time his leg was in such a diseased state that the surgeons had no option but to insist on amputation. So, on 3rd April, 1958, his right leg was removed close to the hip. The irony of the situation was that if he had had it amputated in 1937 after the accident, it would apparently not now have needed to be removed so close to the hip.

The loss of his leg was, to Cole, virtually the end. Always proud of his physical appearance and anxious to look younger than he was, he never really accepted his condition. An artificial leg was fitted, but he was never really reconciled to it, and between 1958 and 1964 he had spells in hospital each year, necessitated by kidney problems, pneumonia, bladder infections, malnutrition and depression. He drank too much and became morose, moody and rude to his guests, so that eventually it was difficult for him to persuade anyone to come to his once-glittering social evenings. The situation degenerated to such an extent that on occasions his sole companion in the evenings would be his valet, doubling uneasily in the roles of guest and employee. After the amputation of his leg Cole wrote no more songs. But he had done enough to deserve immortality as one of the world's great songwriters.

In Cole's final years he tried to maintain a semblance of his former lifestyle, and there was one highlight, in June 1960, when a deputation from his old University, Yale, arrived at Cole's Waldorf apartment to confer on him the degree of Doctor of Humane Studies, an honour he felt he should have received years earlier. In 1962 a party of 300 guests was held in New York to celebrate his 70th birthday, but he didn't attend. Even then he was still pretending to be a year younger than he was, which explains why the party was held a year later than it should have been. Most of his time was now spent in California or New York, with occasional weekends at his home in Williamstown. But his physical decline continued, and was accentuated by excessive consumption of alcohol. Eventually he gave up caring about his appearance, and no longer bothered to wear his artificial leg. Spells of incoherence were the prelude to his final days, and he died in St. John's Hospital, Santa Monica, on 15th October 1964, aged 73.

Cole's body was buried between that of Linda and his father (to whom he had never been close in life) in Peru, Indiana. He left nearly $6 million, carefully allocated according to the wishes expressed in his 29-page will, with many bequests to friends. But the bulk of his estate went to his cousin who bore the same name, James Omar Cole, as his grandfather. In the last year of his life he had earned more than $500,000 in royalties, though he hadn't written a song for years.

When Cole's career was ending in the 1950s, a new age of popular music was beginning, characterised by 'rock and roll' and pop groups. His songs represent the best of an earlier age, for no song writer better epitomises the 1930s and 1940s than Cole Porter.

A list of Cole Porter's shows, films and songs is given in Appendix 8.

The Melody Lingers On

George Gershwin

9. George Gershwin

In the early years of the present century few musicians bridged the gap between the 'popular' and 'serious' sides of their art so successfully as did George Gershwin. He lived in an era when great songwriters abounded - Irving Berlin, Jerome Kern, Cole Porter and others - yet his popular tunes were as good as any produced by his prolific fellow-writers. But Gershwin was different from the others, for his orchestral compositions were taken seriously by the musical establishment of his day, and some have stood the test of time. It was said in his lifetime that he had one foot in Tin Pan Alley and the other in Carnegie Hall. Gershwin's was an unusual talent; his life was brief but his inspiration was at the highest level, and his music brought pleasure to millions.

George Gershwin, like so many great musicians of his era, was of Russian Jewish extraction. Both parents came from St. Petersburg. His father, Morris Gershovitz, was in business in Russia; his mother, Rose (née Bruskin) was the daughter of a wealthy furrier. The couple had met in St. Petersburg but Rose's family and Morris emigrated (separately) to the USA in the early 1890s, at about the same time as many other of their compatriots including Irving Berlin's family, and settled in New York, where Morris used the name Gershvin, which had been allocated to him by the immigration authorities. It was there that Morris and Rose met again, and were married in 1895 when he was 22 and she 19. They settled in the east side of the city and, though not rich, earned enough to make life comfortable. Morris originally earned his living by designing fancy uppers for women's shoes, but at heart he was a minor entrepreneur and many different business interests followed, some of which were moderately successful.

The couple's first child to be born, on 6th December 1896, was Ira, always called Isidore by his parents until early manhood though the name on his birth certificate was Israel. About a year later the family moved to Brooklyn and it was there that George was born on 26th September 1898. His real name was Jacob but he was never known as anything other than George, either by his parents or anyone else. Throughout his childhood and adolescence the family name remained Gershvin; it was only when George started to earn his living from music that he changed his name to Gershwin, and other members of the family then followed suit. Another brother, Arthur, was born on 14th March 1900, and finally came a sister, Frances, who had the same birthday as Ira (6th December), but was ten years younger than him. She was to show a modest talent for singing and dancing, and later married Leopold Godowsky jr., son of the great concert pianist.

The Gershvins were something of a nomadic family in New York, for Morris liked to live near his place of work, the nature of which changed often, though for one relatively lengthy period he was in the restaurant business. In spite of his enterprising character, Morris was essentially gentle, unambitious and easy-going and lacked the single-minded drive necessary to become really successful as a businessman. Rose was strong, and possessed a driving ambition for her children. It soon became evident that Ira had inherited his father's personality; he was quiet, even-tempered, withdrawn, and an avid reader. George on the other hand was like his mother - headstrong, assertive, dominating and dynamic. Ira did well at school; he was solid, reliable, dependable and paid careful attention to his work. George, though clever, was inattentive and mischievous. He was not a great reader; he preferred street games and roller skating.

As Ira grew older he was paid by his mother to work in one of his father's restaurants. He continued to do well at school. At his Bar Mitzvar ceremony in 1909 the family arranged a dinner for 200 guests. The family cannot have been strongly 'orthodox' because they didn't bother with a celebration when it was George's turn! Music played no part in the children's upbringing; most of George's spare time was spent in playing in the street and by the mores of the street anyone interested in music was a "cissy". But one day George heard Rubinstein's *Melody in F* played on a player piano and this immediately sparked off an interest. The music held him spellbound. Then he heard a jazz band playing negro rags and similar items, all of which fascinated him. At 10, George struck up a friendship with Maxie Rosenzweig (later Rosen), an eight-year-old violin prodigy who was to become a concert violinist. It was Maxie who introduced George to good music, and George instantly absorbed all he heard. About this time the Gershvins bought a piano so that Ira, the eldest of the family, could learn to play. But George started to play it too, playing pieces he had heard at

Maxie's, and showed a natural aptitude that amazed his family. In the face of such competition Ira soon gave up - and from then on the piano was George's!

Naturally enough, lessons were arranged for George. His teacher, Charles Hambitzer, provided the necessary direction and purpose to George's efforts and introduced him to the great literature of the piano; Bach, Beethoven, Chopin, Debussy, Liszt and (remarkably for those days) Ravel. George learned musical theory too. Hambitzer was impressed by the boy's ability and wrote in a letter to a sister: "I have a new pupil who will make his mark in music if anybody will." George was now, as a young teenager, mad about music and kept a scrapbook in which he put concert programmes and pictures of the great composers. By 1912/1913 he was an avid concert-goer, attending concerts of the New York Symphony Orchestra and the New York Philharmonic Orchestra, and he heard the great recitalists of the day such as Paderewski and Hofmann. After the concerts he would go home and repeat the musical themes on his piano from memory.

During the summer of 1913, when George was still only 14, he found a job as a pianist at a New York State resort in the Catskill Mountains, earning $5/week. For a while he had been composing as well as playing, and his job enabled him to perform his music publicly, though at that time none of it was published. His compositions included his first song, *Since I Found You*. George's musical tastes were wide ranging; he still liked the music of the great masters but was equally enthralled by the popular songs then current, including Irving Berlin's *Alexander's Ragtime Band* which had taken America by storm. George's teacher wrote:

"He wants to go in for all this modern stuff, jazz and what not. But I'm not going to let him for a while. I'll see that he gets a firm foundation in the standard music first."

George at 15 was an excellent pianist and could play popular music effortlessly and brilliantly. His ambition at that time was to get a job on 'Tin Pan Alley' (28th Street, home of New York's numerous music publishers) and this he duly achieved in May 1914. George's mother wanted him to be an accountant but he would have none of it. He was determined to be a musician, and at last his mother gave up the struggle. George was introduced to Mose Gumble, ace song plugger with the firm of Jerome H. Remick. He liked the way George played and offered him a job as a staff pianist at $15/week. Not yet 16, George was the youngest demonstrator in the song industry, and the first inexperienced employee that Remick had ever hired for the job. George was employed as a demonstration pianist - a song plugger. His duties were to demonstrate songs that were published by his company for the benefit of would-be purchasers. Each pianist occupied his own cubicle and was a virtual prisoner at the keyboard for eight to ten hours a day, pounding out the latest Remick song releases for visiting performers in search of new numbers. As George wrote later: "Some of the customers treated me like dirt; some were charming." Amongst the latter group were the youthful duo of Fred Astaire and his sister Adele, then travelling in vaudeville in a song and dance routine. George struck up an immediate friendship and rapport with the Astaires which was to last throughout his life.

In the course of his work George became a very accomplished pianist and made many useful contacts. In his spare time he wrote songs, but his firm discouraged this for his job was to sell their songs, of which there was no shortage. But in 1916 the first Gershwin song was published by one of Remick's competitors, Harry von Tilzer. It gloried under the title *When You Want 'Em You Can Get 'Em*. Another song was published soon afterwards, *My Runaway Girl*, and was the first Gershwin song to reach the musical comedy stage, for in 1916 it was used in the Sigmund Romberg show, *Making of a Girl*. So George was taking his first steps as a successful songwriter. In 1917 an instrumental number, *Rialto Ripples*, appeared and was published.

George was an admirer of many of his fellow musicians, Irving Berlin and Jerome Kern in particular, and also Felix Arndt, who had a studio in the Aeolian Company building and was employed by that Company. Through Arndt, Gershwin started to record piano rolls in 1916 under the 'Perfection' and later 'Universal' labels. Initially he was paid $25 to record six rolls, and later in the same year he recorded about 30 popular numbers of the day. Some of them were recorded in his own name and for others he used various pseudonyms (Bert Wynn, Fred Murtha and James Baker), possibly to dispel any impression that the piano-roll market was monopolised by one performer. Between 1916 and 1926 Gershwin recorded over 100 rolls for the player piano, on labels that included Universal hand-played, Metro-Art, Melodee,

George Gershwin

Perfection, Angelus and Duo-Art, and the music included a number of his own compositions.

During his period of employment with Remick, George continued to study the piano under his teacher, Mr. Hambitzer, until Hambitzer's untimely death in 1918. He also studied harmony and theory with another music teacher, Edward Kilenyi. George was by now establishing himself as a professional musician, and his brother, Ira, was becoming known as a writer. Ira had had a few items published, and in 1917 he became Vaudeville Critic of *The Clipper*, a small newspaper. In the same year George left Remick's. He had had enough of song plugging, and got a job as the rehearsal pianist for the show *Miss 1917*, for which Jerome Kern and Victor Herbert composed the music and P.G. Wodehouse and Guy Bolton wrote the script. Kern, a frequent visitor to the rehearsals, soon formed a high opinion of George's playing and remarked, "This young man is surely going to go places." George's songs were now being published more frequently, some of them now by his old employer, Remick, and his lyric writer at this period was Irving Caesar. George's life was a whirl of activity. Songs were being turned out, he was a member of a brilliant circle of songwriters and performers, and his zest for parties, night life and the like, coupled with his burning ambition to emulate Kern and Berlin, left no time for other leisure.

In 1918 Irving Berlin offered George $100 a week to act as his arranger, but told him, "I hope you don't take it." He knew that Gershwin had greater things to offer. Wisely, George declined, but in 1918 accepted the publisher Max Dreyfus's offer to write songs for him at $35/week + 3 cents/copy on any sold. George promptly came up with *The Real American Folksong*, the lyric of which was by his brother Ira, who had turned his literary talent to supplying material for George. More of George's songs were being used in shows, some in Broadway productions and in 1919 he wrote the complete score for a Broadway musical, *La, La, Lucille*, which opened in May 1919 and contained 12 Gershwin songs, six old and six written specially for the show. But George's big breakthrough in 1919 was one song, *Swanee*, with words by Irving Caesar. It was a sensation. George wrote it for a stage show preceding the opening of a new theatre, and it did not arouse much immediate interest. But then Al Jolson heard it and was interested; he

The Melody Lingers On

used it in a Sunday evening concert and then introduced it, slightly modified according to his own requirements, into his current stage show, *Sinbad*, with music by Sigmund Romberg. Jolson's magnetic personality and inimitable style brought out the best in the song and it spread within weeks through the USA, Caesar and Gershwin drawing $100,000 each in royalties during the song's first year of publication.

George was now firmly on the songwriting map. Moreover, his talent in the field of popular music had attracted the attention of eminent musicians. The concert pianist Beryl Rubinstein, a member of the Faculty of the Cleveland Institute of Music, said of Gershwin in a newspaper interview:

"This young fellow has the spark of musical genius which is definite in his serious moods . . . With Gershwin's style and seriousness he is not definitely from the popular music school, but one of the really outstanding figures in the country's musical efforts . . . . I really believe that America will at no distant date honour him for his talent . . . . and that when we speak of American composers George Gershwin's name will be prominent on our list."

It is clear from Mr. Rubinstein's assessment that although Gershwin had become famous by virtue of composing popular songs, classical musicians were beginning to note the originality of his style. George had not lost his love of the classics and his training in that field had stood him in good stead.

About the same time as *Swanee* appeared, George wrote a string quartet, but his songs continued to form the dominant and more important sector of his work until 1924, when *Rhapsody in Blue* appeared. The classically-trained conductor Paul Whiteman had planned a jazz concert for that year and had asked George to contribute to it. George visualised a concert rhapsody and, once he started writing, soon completed the piece, but there remained the problem of finding a title. He was going to call it *American Rhapsody*, but Ira had recently been to an art exhibition where he had seen a number of paintings by James Whistler; 'Nocturne in Blue and Green', 'Harmony in Grey and Green', etc. "Why not call it *Rhapsody in Blue?*" Ira suggested. And so the piece was named as Ira had proposed. It was written for piano and orchestra, but George subsequently produced other versions, for orchestra alone, two pianos and orchestra, piano alone, and so on.

The composition received its first public performance on 12th February (Abraham Lincoln's birthday) 1924, an event described as

'The emancipation proclamation of jazz', with George Gershwin as piano soloist with the Paul Whiteman Orchestra. The venue was The Aeolian Hall, New York. Whiteman financed the performance at a cost of $11,000 and it was reckoned that the concert made a deficit of $7,000. However, in view of the subsequent popularity of the composition, the money received in royalties on recordings and sheet music sales, and the glory reflected on both Whiteman and Gershwin, the concert was deemed to have been a success. Many celebrities were present at this first performance, including John Philip Sousa, Walter Damrosch (conductor of the New York Symphony Orchestra), Leopold Godowsky, Jascha Heifetz, Fritz Kreisler, John McCormack, Sergei Rachmaninov, Leopold Stokowski, Moriz Rosenthal, Mischa Elman, and Victor Herbert, apart from many from the field of popular music. The composition received an ovation of several minutes at its conclusion. George Gershwin was only 25 years old at the time. The piece has retained its place in the concert repertoire. It has been criticised on the grounds that it lacks shape and form and consists of a number of themes linked together in a rather haphazard and disjointed way. But these themes are themselves good and worth listening to, and it is that fact which has made the composition an enduring success. In the first decade of its existence it earned more than $250,000 in royalties.

The *Rhapsody in Blue* was Gershwin's most successful venture for the concert platform to that date but its triumph was really no surprise to discerning musicians, for its appearance had been preceded in 1923 by concert performances of a number of Gershwin songs by operatic artists, which had been favourably received by the critics. Nor was *Rhapsody in Blue* to be Gershwin's last major concert composition, for he followed it in 1925 with his *Piano Concerto in F*. He began work on this piece in July of that year and spent the whole of the summer on it, during which time he studied the structure of several major concertos. It received its première on 3rd December 1925, to a mixed reception from the critics. It is perhaps a better-structured piece than *Rhapsody in Blue*, being less rambling, but on the other hand it has less of the *Rhapsody*'s eerie charm. However, it has endured well and a number of recordings of it are currently available. Following its American first performance it was also presented in various major cities in Europe.

The Melody Lingers On

These concert works of Gershwin, successful as they were, never stood in the way of his main vocation, that of songwriter. After the brilliant success of *Swanee* in 1919, the lyrics of which were by Irving Caesar, the words of nearly all his subsequent songs were by his brother Ira, and his part in the success of the Gershwin songs should not be underestimated. Initially Ira wrote his lyrics under the name Arthur Francis (adapted from the names of his brother and sister), not wanting to capitalise on the name of Gershwin that George had already made famous. Ira had become a thoughtful and competent writer, who would work on a line, even a phrase, for hours until he was satisfied it had the necessary sparkle. A well-read and erudite man, Ira was a craftsman in words, and the wit and apparent spontaneity of his lyrics is a tribute to his painstaking skill. It was Ira who wrote the lyrics for the first of the great Gershwin musicals - *Lady, Be Good!* - produced in New York in December 1924, and starring Fred and Adele Astaire. Apart from the title number, *Oh, Lady Be Good,* memorably performed by Fred and Adele, the show also featured *Fascinating Rhythm, The Man I Love* and *The Half of It, Dearie, Blues.* At George's insistence the two-piano team of Phil Ohman and Victor Arden were hired to play in the pit, sometimes unaccompanied and sometimes with the orchestra. Their playing proved so novel to the audiences that many of those present would linger in the theatre after the final curtain to listen to the pianists play the exit music for them. Occasionally, when the audience refused to leave, Ohman and Arden would do an impromptu two-piano concert. Later, *Lady, Be Good!* was presented in London after a two-week try-out in Liverpool. Again Fred and Adele Astaire were the stars.

After *Lady, Be Good!* several other stage shows with music by George Gershwin and lyrics by Ira were to follow. In addition, numerous 'one-off' songs were written, many of which were interpolated into musicals or films where the main music was written by someone else. The successful run of Gershwin popular compositions continued unabated throughout the twenties. Big Gershwin hit songs of the decade, other than those already mentioned, included *Somebody Loves Me* (1924), *Looking for a Boy* (1925), *That Certain Feeling* (1925), *Clap Yo' Hands* (1926), *Do, Do, Do* (1926), *Funny Face* (1927) from the show of the same name, again with Fred and Adele Astaire, *'S Wonderful* (1927), *How Long Has This Been Going On* (from the show *Rosalie* (1928)), and *Liza* (1929). Ira Gershwin wrote the words of all of these except the first, *Somebody Loves Me*, which were by Buddy deSylva and Ballard MacDonald.

The best Gershwin songs won the admiration of many well-known musicians. When the composer John Ireland acquired a recording of *The Man I Love* in 1924 his action is recorded in the biography by Kenneth Wright:

"When the record had finished, Ireland put the needle back to the beginning, and whilst it played he kept walking back and forth, his hands behind his back, pausing now and again to sip whisky. The music was haunting in its nostalgic way; logical in its melodic and harmonic sequences. I liked it, but still could not divine whether Ireland was about to conduct a case of plagiarism, censorship, or what. Three times we heard the record. Then he stopped the machine and turned to me. "Well?" he said, in a fierce query. "What about *that?*" He stopped in front of the little stove and wagged a finger at me. "That, my boy, is a masterpiece. This man Gershwin beats the lot of us. He sits down and composes one of the most original, most perfect, songs of our century. Symphonies? Concertos? Bah! Who wants a symphony if he can write a song like that? Perfect, my boy, perfect. This is the music of America, it will live as long as a Schubert Lied, a Brahms Waltz. Listen to it again, and tell me I am right!" So we had it again - and yet again. He *was* right. And I for one have never tired of it."

Ireland's reaction is instructive, for it verifies that there was no dichotomy between the two facets of Gershwin's art. His works were all written in similar vein, but inclined towards the 'popular' or 'concert' audience as necessary.

In 1923 Gershwin had visited London for the first time. Whilst in Britain his frenzied social life continued and he was lionised just as he had been in New York. He became a friend of royalty and the Mountbattens. He came to England again in 1928 for the London production of *Oh, Kay*, starring Gertrude Lawrence, which included *Clap Yo' Hands, Do, Do, Do* and *Someone To Watch Over Me*. Whilst in Britain he gave concerts, raised money for charities, and visited stately homes. There was never a quiet moment in the life of the dynamic young composer.

At George's parties could be found such international celebrities as Douglas Fairbanks, Jack Dempsey, Charles Chaplin, Lord and Lady Mountbatten, Noël Coward, Jascha Heifetz, Maurice Chevalier, Gertrude Lawrence, and Fred and Adele Astaire. The parties would go on well into the night and would always centre around George at the piano. He loved the spotlight; Ira preferred to stay in the background. Not only would George play and sing at the parties, he would also do passable imitations of some of his friend Fred Astaire's dances, even emulating the latter's more intricate steps. George was a human dynamo; he had more vitality when ill than most people when healthy; his zest for living was tremendous. His 17th floor penthouse apartment in New York was like a railway station, with people coming and going all the time. George was a brilliantly skilled pianist, particularly as an exponent of his own music, and good musicians liked to listen to him for hours on end. Kreisler, Zimbalist, Godowsky, Hofmann, Heifetz and Ravel all paid tribute to his virtuosity.

A trip to France followed Gershwin's London visit of the late 1920s, and from it Gershwin drew the inspiration to compose *An American in Paris* (1928), another enduringly popular work which still figures regularly in concert programmes. This composition, described as a 'tone poem', was first performed by the New York Symphony Orchestra, conducted by Walter Damrosch.

During the 1920s the pattern of George's life had become established; he was one of America's best songwriters; his successes in this field were interspersed with a number of excellent concert compositions; he lived a whirlwind social life; he was immensely rich, and he was the friend and confidant of many of the world's best known people. This pattern continued as the 1930s opened with the production on Broadway of *Strike Up the Band* with its theme song of the same title, followed very soon afterwards by the equally successful *Girl Crazy*. It was in the latter production that the ear-splitting tones of the 21-year old Ethel Merman were first heard in an important show, in the number *I Got Rhythm*, in which she held a high C for 16 bars. The clarion-voiced Merman caused a sensation. Gershwin had picked her out for the show at an audition, having recognised the unique nature of her voice. "Don't ever go near a singing teacher", he told her, "he'll ruin you". Other hit songs in the show were *Embraceable You* and *But Not for Me*, both sung with much panache by another talented youngster, 19-year-old Ginger Rogers, appearing in only her second Broadway show.

As the years went by Gershwin's creative flow was maintained, seemingly undiminished, with songs, musical shows, and concert works. Some of George and Ira Gershwin's musical comedies followed W.S. Gilbert's example in satirising current events. *Of Thee I Sing* (1931), parodied the presidential election campaign, and won the Pullizer book prize, Ira being the first song lyricist to win the award. In 1931 George's *Second Rhapsody* was written, but it has never been as popular or as commercially successful as *Rhapsody in Blue.* Its European première was in 1933 when the London Symphony Orchestra, conducted by Sir Hamilton Harty, performed the work. In 1932 George visited Cuba for a holiday and on his return wrote *Rhumba*, later renamed *Cuban Overture.* It is a brash and jolly work. He also made a number of concert arrangements of many of his best songs.

But perhaps the best known of all Gershwin works was to come in 1935 when *Porgy and Bess* appeared. George had been fascinated with the idea of writing a negro opera for years, and had toyed with the notion since the 1920s of setting to music Dubose and Dorothy Heyward's book, *Porgy.* There were always other things to do, but eventually the three-act opera was written and there is no doubt that George was more proud of this work than of any other. It took him 20 months to compose the music, and Ira wrote the lyrics. The opera opened in New York on 10th October 1935. Initial reviews were mixed; the drama critics liked it, but the response of the music critics was half-hearted. Some critics said that the show was more like a musical than an opera.

Nevertheless *Porgy and Bess* gradually took hold as a serious composition. The opera had an all-negro cast, and helped to shape American social history, for racial barriers were dropped at the National Theatre when negroes were given their right as American citizens to attend performances without the indignity of segregation. The opera even went on tour to Stalinist Russia; the authorities there were glad to welcome it on the grounds that, in their view, it portrayed the downtrodden status of the natives in the USA. The opera's three best known songs, *Summertime, It Ain't Necessarily So,* and *I Got Plenty o' Nuttin'* are very familiar and much-recorded pieces.

In the mid 1930s George's interests widened still further when he inaugurated a radio programme, *Music by Gershwin*, with *The Man I Love* as theme song. Rather unromantically it was sponsored by 'Feen-a-Mint', a laxative. For a period of several months the programme went out every Monday and Friday evening from 7.30 to 7.45 and George appeared in the varied role of genial master of ceremonies, conductor, composer and pianist, at a fee of $2,000/week.

In 1936, George and Ira Gershwin signed a contract to write songs for an RKO film starring Fred Astaire and Ginger Rogers, at a fee of $55,000 for 16 weeks, with an option on a second picture at $70,000 for 16 weeks if the first was successful. Though high, this fee was not unduly so for songwriters of their status. The company thought George's music was a bit highbrow for films and in consequence was somewhat cautious in the terms offered in its contract. Astaire and Rogers had recently had big successes in two other RKO films, *Top Hat* (music by Irving Berlin) and *Swing Time* (music by Jerome Kern). Both had done very well so RKO and the Gershwin brothers knew they would be hard acts to follow. But they need not have worried. *Shall We Dance?* (1937) with Astaire, Rogers, and music and words by the Gershwins was a great success and contained some of their best songs, including *Let's Call the Whole Thing Off, They All Laughed, Slap That Bass* and *They Can't Take That Away From Me*, all enhanced by Astaire's and Rogers' dancing, and Fred's supreme skill in putting the songs across.

Whilst in Beverly Hills the Gershwins rented a palatial home, and the interminable round of evening parties and dinners continued, attended by the leading Hollywood stars of the day. After *Shall We Dance?* there were no problems about extending the Gershwins' contract to write songs for their second film, *A Damsel in Distress*, which followed in the same year. It starred Fred Astaire again, but this time with Joan Fontaine as his partner. The best songs in the film were *Nice Work if You Can Get It* and *A Foggy Day*. After this success the Gershwins stayed in California to write songs for their next film, *The Goldwyn Follies*. This Goldwyn production lacked the big stars of the RKO films but even so did reasonably well. The best songs in the film were *Love Walked In* and *Love Is Here To Stay*.

George Gershwin always lived life to the full, but deep down he remained essentially rather a lonely person. He never married. Somewhat egocentric, he had many girl friends but when matrimony loomed he always found some excuse to put off the event. It is probable that he was too committed to music and to his lifestyle for marriage to have worked out successfully. His most passionate affair was in the late 1930s when he fell in love with the actress Paulette Goddard, whom he wanted to marry. She refused him, partly no doubt because she happened to be married to Charles Chaplin at the time. Gershwin's main interest when not writing music or engaging in his social whirl, was painting, and in particular painting portraits of his friends. He had taken this up in the late 1920s and both he and Ira showed useful artistic talent. Several well-known visitors to the Gershwin household were the subjects of George's portraits, including Jerome Kern and Arnold Schoenberg. The pictures were somewhat impressionistic in style.

It seemed that George Gershwin was set for a lifetime of achievement and prosperity, for his songs written for the Hollywood films of the later 1930s showed no diminution of his creative talent. But fate was to decree otherwise. On 10th and 11th February 1937, George took part in two concerts with the Los Angeles Philharmonic Orchestra at their home auditorium, as soloist in his own *Rhapsody in Blue* and *Piano Concerto in F*. During the second of these concerts his mind went blank for a few seconds, something that had never happened before. The same thing happened in April of the same year, and moreover he was feeling listless, confused and washed out. By June he was getting severe headaches. George refused to have a thorough check-up but a superficial hospital examination failed to reveal any disorders. But by the end of the month he was rapidly losing co-ordination. On 9th July George could barely be awakened from a deep sleep, and by the end of the day he had lapsed into a coma. He was rushed into hospital; the tragic fact was now unmistakeable - George was the victim of a brain tumour. There were frenzied medical consultations, but the doctors knew the outlook was grim. Early next morning an operation was performed but it was clear that nothing could be done to save George's life. He died at 10.35a.m. the next day, 11th July 1937, without regaining consciousness. He was 38.

The world of music was shocked by George's death, as was his family. His sister Frances (Godowsky) had to be contacted by cable in Vienna, where she was on holiday. Until she received the message she had not even known that George was ill. George's body was taken by train from Los Angeles to New York and his funeral, on 15th July, was an emotional affair. *Rhapsody in Blue* was played, and apart from George's family, many celebrities were present. A simultaneous service was held in Hollywood. He left no will, and by New York law his estate of $350,000 plus his paintings went to his mother.

Following George's death, Ira Gershwin continued his work as a lyric writer and librettist, and collaborated over the years with many musicians. He died in 1983, aged 86, having outlived his younger brother George by 46 years.

A film based on George Gershwin's life was released by Warner Brothers in 1945. Entitled *Rhapsody in Blue*, it followed the usual Hollywood formula of paying little attention to factual accuracy. Even so, it was packed with Gershwin's songs, and as it really amounted to a two-hour concert of music by Gershwin it could hardly fail to be entertaining and worth watching. With Robert Alda playing the part of George, those taking part included such famous artists as Oscar Levant, Al Jolson and Paul Whiteman.

Now, nearly 60 years after George Gershwin's death, he is recalled as one of the major figures in music of the 1920s and 1930s. Many of his songs have become classics and have retained their popularity in an era when the lifetime of a popular song is extremely short. His concert works (including the concert arrangement of some of his songs) have increased in popularity in recent years, and if we measure 'classical' popularity by the volume of recorded works on offer, he occupies a position about equal with Frederick Delius and John Ireland. His was a remarkable talent. Possibly, with the passage of time, his popular songs will recede into the mists of history but, in the words of one of them, It Ain't Necessarily So!

A list of George Gershwin's concert works, shows, films and songs is given in Appendix 9.

The Melody Lingers On

'Fats' Waller

10. Thomas 'Fats' Waller

Amongst the giants of the jazz era there was none bigger, in any sense of the word, than 'Fats' Waller. A huge man, weighing more than 20 stones (most estimates put him at 300lb) he lived a frenzied and dissipated lifestyle which undoubtedly contributed to his early death. But he was a true giant of jazz; his contribution to it was enormous. As a jazz pianist and organist he became a household name, achieving fame through his personal appearances, piano rolls, radio broadcasts and above all his gramophone records, of which he made hundreds. He developed a unique style and on many of his records he sang as well as played. His vocal records, irrespective of whether the songs were his own or the work of others, were always enlivened by his own brand of relaxed humour which set his work apart from others.

Edward Waller, the father of 'Fats', was born around the year 1870 in a district known as Bermuda Hundred in Virginia. Tall and thin, he was a very reserved man. As a teenager he became engaged to Adeline Lockett, but was reluctant to marry until he could forsee some sort of financial security. He thought this could be achieved in New York where, he believed, his knowledge of horses would stand him in good stead. In this he was correct; moving to New York he soon found work in a stable and went home to fetch Adeline. They were married in Bermuda Hundred when he was 18 and she 17. They then set out for New York and found rented accommodation in a tenement block in Waverley Place, Greenwich Village, which was then a negro district.

Edward and his wife came from a deeply religious background and were keen churchgoers. They joined the local Abyssinia Baptist Church and Edward soon became one of the church's leading members. He was prevailed upon to give sermons on street corners and continued to do so for many years. Eventually he became superintendent of the Sunday School.

In common with the custom of the time the Wallers had a large family. Children were born at intervals for many years, but of the eleven born only five survived childhood. The children were Charles A. Waller (September 1890, died as an infant), Edward Lawrence(1892), William Robert (1893), Alfred Winslow (1895, died 1905), Ruth Adeline (1902, died 1905), May Naomi (1903), Thomas Wright (1904),

Esther and Samuel (both 1907, died in infancy), an unnamed boy (1909, died in childbirth) and Edith Salome (1910). Some of the five who survived into adulthood were called by their middle names; thus the surviving children, excluding Alfred who died soon after his 10th birthday, were Lawrence, Robert, Naomi, Thomas and Edith. It is Thomas (born 21st May 1904) who is the subject of our story.

At the time Thomas was born there were five older children. Times were hard and money difficult to come by but Edward was a hard worker and had by then set up his own trucking business. The family had moved into 63rd Street, Harlem and later went to live at 107, West 134th Street. It was then predominantly a white area, but negro entrepreneurs were buying property there and moving into the district in large numbers, the Wallers included, and the general movement of people helped Edward's business.

The years of childbearing had taken a heavy toll on Adeline Waller's health and her big family was really more than she could cope with. When the final child, Edith, was born, Adeline was not at all well and the child was sent off to Virginia to live with an aunt. She used to visit her family in New York from time to time. Naomi was the nearest in age to Thomas and they became inseparable playmates. The children received a very religious upbringing. They went to church, knew their Bible, and any wrongdoing brought swift retribution. But Thomas had an engaging personality and knew how to wheedle forgiveness from his mother. He had a discerning eye and knew his mother's strengths and weaknesses. He realised that religion was a chink in her armour and he could quote at will relevant passages from the Bible for reasons why punishment should not be administered.

Needless to say, music formed a major part of the church services, within the church and in the outside meetings, so from his earliest years Thomas knew all the old hymns. His mother played the piano and organ, but finances did not allow a piano in the Waller home. One day Thomas, then aged six, had the chance to tinker on the keys of a neighbour's piano and immediately he was hooked. His brother Robert came home one day and found Thomas kneeling on the floor in front of two upright chairs placed side by side, his hands gliding back and forth as he 'played' on the seats. When Robert asked him if he would like to play the piano, Tom answered, "I sure would. I played on one upstairs

- the lady let me". A series of family conferences concluded that a piano could not be afforded, but eventually, with the help of Adeline's half-brother, a new Waters upright was bought, much to Tom's joy.

No lessons could be afforded for the time being with the last baby on the way, so at first Thomas had to learn by his own efforts. The piano didn't occupy all his time and there was plenty of scope for mischief. After the new baby (Edith) arrived, Tom and Naomi were playing with the piano stool one rainy afternoon. It was the type that spun round on a screw thread to raise and lower the seat. After spinning it round for a while they decided it would be a good idea to give the baby a ride. Naomi sat on the stool with the baby in her arms, as Thomas revolved them, slowly at first but then faster and faster as they rose higher and higher. Suddenly the top of the stool flew off the end of the screw and Naomi was sent crashing to the floor. Fortunately the baby was still clutched safely in her arms and wasn't hurt. Hearing the commotion their mother rushed in and was confronted by the sight of the top of the piano stool on the floor with Naomi and the baby beside it. Seizing a strap she turned her attention to tanning Naomi's bottom. But Thomas sat in a corner softly singing "Everything that's not of Jesus shall go down" and with a sad expression on his round face said, "Momma, I don't know what got into me, I really don't - that naughty old devil, he told me to do it. Don't you think we ought to pray?" So with Naomi still smarting, Tom and his mother knelt on the floor and prayed for forgiveness. He knew his mother's weakness for a penitent approach and exploited it unscrupulously, often escaping the punishment inflicted on his brothers and sisters.

The Wallers were very active in the Abyssinia Baptist Church where Edward was now Sunday School Superintendent and Chairman of the Board of Deacons. But the nearby pentecostal church acquired a new minister who preached the doctrine of sanctification, and on hearing him, Edward and Adeline were so impressed they transferred their membership. The whole family, having been baptised at their previous church, were now baptised again at the Refuge Temple at 56 West 133rd Street. Thomas had evidently become competent at the piano entirely by self-teaching, for he started to play hymns for outdoor services on the portable harmonium. His mother led the singing and his father preached.

The Melody Lingers On

Thomas's obvious desire to learn to play the piano properly impressed his family and eventually lessons were arranged, and given by an elderly lady, Miss Perry. He didn't like her rigid régime which involved learning scales and doing routine exercises. But when he persuaded her to play some "proper music" for him he watched her fingers intently. His family found, to their astonishment, that he could sit down and play at home what he had just watched his teacher play. From then on, and for some time to come, he learned entirely by ear. He did not learn to sight read until much later.

One day there was a knock at the Waller door. His mother answered and there was a small boy there. "Is Fats home?" he asked. "Who?" she replied. The boy repeated it. "No-one of that name here!" she said. Naomi, half hearing the conversation, asked who it was. "Some little boy wanting Fats. I guess he got the wrong house." Naomi said, "Momma, I think he wanted Thomas." Mrs. Waller called the boy back. "His name is Thomas, not Fats!" But he *was* "Fats" to his friends, and remained so to everyone for the rest of his life. He had been putting on weight for a long time and with the candour and frankness of schoolboys he had been aptly named. His brother, Robert, was called "Zip" by his friends and his mother rebelled at that too. "Tell them your name's Robert, not Zip", she said. Robert replied, "They know my name's Robert, Momma, but they just want to call me Zip."

Thomas's childhood was entirely normal; he had his circle of friends and engaged in all the usual pastimes at school and church. At Christmas 1912 all the children were in the church nativity play. Thomas was the innkeeper and on being told who the homeless couple and baby really were, had to deliver the immortal line, "Gosh, if I had only known!"

He was invited to join the school orchestra and started string bass lessons. But soon he was back to his first love, the piano, and at last learned to read music. He played at school assemblies, was good at it, and started to achieve kudos amongst his school-mates as a result. He learned to play 'off-beat', and discovered that he could raise a laugh by clowning or making a face over his shoulder. He could get the kids tapping their feet and rocking to and fro to his music and could achieve wild applause. The Fats Waller of later years was beginning to take shape.

Edward Waller was proud of his son's achievements at the piano and as a spur he took him to hear Paderewski at Carnegie Hall, hoping it might inspire an interest in classical music. In that he was only partly successful, for although Thomas was very impressed by the performance, he was not attracted to that type of music. He preferred ragtime which, to his father, was "music from the devil's workshop".

When he was about 12 Thomas started a part-time job, doing home deliveries for local stores. One day he was set upon and stabbed by a gang of white youths but fortunately the wound was only superficial. Shortly afterwards the family moved again, this time to East 134th Street. There was a piano in the apartment already, so Edward presented the Waters instrument to their pentecostal church.

In 1917, when Thomas was 12, America entered the war and Lawrence went off to fight in Europe. There was much anguish in the family when Lawrence was reported missing, but fortunately he turned up unharmed several weeks later and returned home unscathed at the end of the war. In 1918 Thomas and Naomi each got a job in the same jewel-box factory in Manhattan, he polishing the outside of the boxes, she assembling the soft decorative material for the inside. At lunch times he used to play the piano in a nearby church, having made friends with the verger. But the job didn't last long. As he said, "It's not music". So, back he went to Harlem. Music was now his great ambition.

Harlem had by then become predominantly a negro area and theatres, clubs and cinemas had sprung up everywhere. Thomas was attracted to the nearby Lincoln Theatre, which operated mainly as a cinema. It boasted not only a piano to accompany the films but also a small pipe organ. The resident pianist, Maizie Mullins, used to let him sit in the pit near her and watch her play. After she had listened to him play he was able to persuade her to let him take over at the piano for a few minutes whilst she went off for short breaks. Later he played as relief organist when the resident organist was ill. Encouraged by his school friends at the back of the theatre he started to play jazzy numbers which were immediately popular. When the resident organist left soon afterwards Fats got his job at $23/week. His professional career had begun. It was then 1919 and he was 15. His playing improved rapidly and as well as playing the organ he played the piano more and more as

Maizie took longer breaks. His own style was developing and he was becoming a local celebrity.

Tom was now meeting a lot of other musicians. One of them was a drummer, Reuben Harris, who invited Tom to join a small band for an open-air party, the first of many such engagements. He also acquired a girl friend, Edith Hackett, who came from a good Christian home. Adeline and Edward approved of her and she became a frequent visitor to the Waller home. Unfortunately by then Tom's mother was a very sick woman. She had suffered from diabetes (then virtually untreatable) for several years, childbearing had taken its toll, and her health was rapidly failing. She told Tom she would not be around much longer; a shattering blow as he had had no idea how ill she was. Her prediction, sadly, was correct. On 8th November 1920 she suffered a stroke and died two days later. Tom was devastated. He had always been close to his mother. He had enjoyed playing hymns on the piano at home whilst she sang; it is said that he never touched the family piano again.

Thomas had never been very close to his father, and after his mother died he decided to leave home. For a time he lived with a friend, Wilson Brooks, and his parents, a decision which Edward Waller accepted without argument. It so happened that there was a pianola at the Brooks' home with a large supply of rolls, including some QRS ones cut by the famous black pianist and composer James P. Johnson. By playing them through slowly and placing his hands on the depressed keys Thomas soon learned to play the tunes proficiently. Russell Brooks was a friend of James P. Johnson and Fats sought an introduction. Johnson didn't want to take any pupils but Russell was persuasive and Johnson eventually agreed to meet Thomas.

On the appointed day Russell took Thomas round to Johnson's home. Johnson, then in his late 20s, was most unimpressed at the sight of the untidy-looking obese 16-year old, but he dispatched Russell Brooks and sat down to listen to what Fats could do; he soon realised that the young pianist had potential, and in fact kept him at his home for several hours whilst he listened, made suggestions, demonstrated, and so on. The next day Fats started to incorporate what he had learned when he played at the Lincoln. A friendship developed and Fats became a Johnson protégé, absorbing all he could from the master. It is an interesting fact that Johnson, who had had a formal musical training, impressed on Fats the importance of scales and technical exercises, the very things Fats had scorned when Miss Perry had insisted on them.

In those days the 'parlour social' or 'rent party' was a feature of Harlem life; late evening get-togethers where the drink flowed and pianists tried to out-do each other at the keyboard to provide the entertainment. Rags, stomps, blues; all the pianists had an established repertoire. James P. Johnson was the master pianist; others not far behind were Jack 'The Bear', Luckey Roberts and Willie 'The Lion' Smith, so named because of his exploits of bravery in France in 1917-18. Eubie Blake, another such pianist, had moved on to musical comedy and vaudeville. Smith, like Johnson, had received a formal musical education. Most of the big rent parties were on Saturday nights but smaller ones took place nearly every night. One night 'James P' took Fats to one of these and not surprisingly it was an eye-opener to the young pianist. Willie 'The Lion' was playing when they arrived and wasn't impressed by the sight of the "fat kid" that his friend had brought. But when Willie went off for a drink James P. edged Fats onto the piano stool and urged him to show what he could do. Under James P's recent tutelage Fats was now quite accomplished and duly showed off his skills. Willie 'The Lion' had to reluctantly admit, "That was pretty good, kid." Thus Fats was launched on the rent party circuit as a pianist in his own right.

Soon afterwards, when he was still only 18, Fats and Edith Hackett were married and went to live with Edith's parents. But he wasn't at home for long; the Lincoln Theatre sent a vaudeville show on tour and Fats went as accompanist to an act called 'Liza and her Shufflin' Six'. In Boston he renewed acquaintance with a pianist friend from New Jersey, Bill Basie (to be known later as 'Count'). Fats had just written a piece which he played for Bill, and back in New York he played it again to his mentor, James P. Johnson.

Edith was already pregnant, which prompted in Fats a minor sense of family responsibility - but not much. Already involved in the whirl of rent parties and touring, he drank a lot and his lifestyle often involved absence from home. Even when touring he was usually out until the small hours of the morning as he worked and drank with his piano-playing friends. Nevertheless he was getting regular work and meeting the major musicians in his own field. Before 1920 was out he had met and knew Irving Berlin, Paul Whiteman and George Gershwin.

About this time Willie 'The Lion' Smith had had enough of Leroy's club where he was currently working as resident pianist and decided to move on. Fats was hired in his place. Willie 'The Lion' had noticed, and remarked to Johnson, that Fats was no longer just an imitator of James P, he was introducing his own style, musical features unique to himself.

Soon after Willie 'The Lion' departed, James P. Johnson set out 'on the road' for various engagements. Before he left he introduced Fats to the QRS Piano Roll Company so that he could record for them whilst he himself was away. So it came about that between 1922 and 1927 Fats recorded about 22 piano rolls for QRS at a fee of $50 per roll. His first roll was *Got To Cool My Doggies Now* by Clarence Williams and Spencer Thompson, with both of whom he was to collaborate later in writing songs. One of the later rolls, *If I Could Be With You*, was a duet with James P. Johnson. These 22 rolls are the only piano rolls Waller cut.

For a time Fats doubled as pianist at Leroy's Club and the Lincoln Theatre. Life was a hectic round of work, parties and drinking. Whilst he was playing there was always a bottle at hand. The birth of Thomas junior didn't change his lifestyle. Edith saw little of him and it was becoming rapidly clear that his marriage was taking a back seat to his musical life. She was a keyboard widow.

The next step on the musical ladder was a job at Scotty's Bar and Cabaret in New York and then he followed Willie 'The Lion' into the Capitol, a large club, where he played the piano in the band and was also featured as soloist. All the time his playing improved. Soon he moved from the Lincoln to the Lafayette, a movie house which put on occasional stage performances. The move increased his salary from $25-odd dollars a week to $50 initially, and eventually to over a hundred. One of the main attractions of the place to Fats, apart from the money, was that it had a large pipe organ which enabled him to become a skilled practitioner of the instrument.

In October 1922, when still only 18, Fats' career as a gramophone recording artist began, for the Okay Record Company. The company ran a series of what they called their 'Race' records, featuring the work of negro artists. Mamie Smith was already a popular singing contributor and the company wished to extend the series. His first record for them was *Muscle Shoals Blues*, coupled with *Birmingham Blues* on the reverse side, with the name Thomas Waller on the label. Later in the year he recorded *'Tain't Nobody's Biz-ness If I Do* for them with *Last Go-Round Blues* on the other side. They were the first of hundreds of Fats Waller gramophone records; in fact he made records every year, except 1932, for the rest of his life.

In 1923 James P. Johnson, Fats' teacher, had his greatest song hit published. It was *The Charleston*, (words by Cecil Mack) from the show *Runnin' Wild*, and it came to epitomise the 1920s. Possibly this acted as a spur to Fats for he started to get his own songs published, starting with *Wildcat Blues*, which preceded *Squeeze Me*, often said to have been the first Fats Waller published number, by some months. At this period he was helped a lot by his friend Clarence Williams, a proficient musician himself, who acted as a sort of unofficial manager. He certainly needed one for Fats was totally disorganised, he had no business sense, and would often fail to turn up for engagements unless someone made it their business to get him there. He was earning a lot of money; over a five-year period he sold over 70 songs to the Clarence Williams Music Company, but as soon as he got it he spent it.

The next major event in his career was his first broadcast, which was from the stage of the Fox Terminal Theatre, over a local New Newark station. Then he won a piano contest at the Roosevelt Theatre, though he was the youngest contestant. He played *Carolina Shout* and had the advantage over his rivals in that he had been taught the piece by its composer, James P. Johnson. It was there at the competition that he met the young lyricist Andy Razaf, then 28, who was destined to become a major collaborator by writing the words to many of Waller's tunes practically to the day of Fats' death. Andy's full name was Andrea Menentania Razafinkeriefo, which he wisely abbreviated as no-one in the USA could pronounce it. He was born in Washington D.C. and his mother was the daughter of the United States' consul in Madagascar, then a monarchy. When France invaded the island the consul escaped to the United States with his daughter. Andy and Fats were to become good friends and their professional association was very profitable to them both. When they wrote songs together they used to take them to publishers to demonstrate them and Fats played whilst Andy sang. But Andy decided that they would do better if Fats did the singing as well as the playing, and so it proved. They sold more songs!

By 1923 it was clear that Thomas's and Edith's marriage was a failure; it existed only in name. She wasn't interested in his party-going and he hardly ever came home. Later that year they were divorced. He was still only 19. Naturally he was instructed to make alimony payments to help towards the upbringing of his son, and the sum agreed in court was $35/week. But money was extracted from him only with the greatest of difficulty. Payments were invariably late or non-existent and they became a bone of contention between the former partners for the rest of his life. He was always running away from the 'process servers' as the debt-collectors were called. Many court appearances over non-payment followed.

Fats already knew everyone who was anyone in the jazz business. Louis Armstrong, Duke Ellington and many others were friends and he had already worked with some of them. Soon he played with Duke Ellington and his orchestra on Broadway and more gramophone recording sessions followed, this time for Vocalion for whom he recorded with Perry Bradford and his Jazz Phools and featuring Fats and James P. Johnson on twin pianos.

Life was now an endless whirl of activity. Every night he was out playing and partying into the small hours, a bottle always at hand. Exercise was non-existent, and his large bulk got even larger. But undeniably he was a brilliant pianist. In addition he was writing a lot of commercially successful piano pieces as well as music for songs and stage shows.

In the mid 1920s Fats met Anita Rutherford, a local well brought-up girl who was then 16. It wasn't long before he asked her to marry him but she and her family knew of the failure of his previous marriage and wanted to be as sure as possible that the same thing wouldn't happen again. After a lot of talking and the mediation of a family friend who assured her that this time Fats was sincere and wanted the marriage to work, Thomas and Anita were married in 1926 when she was 17 and he 22. The marriage did in fact straighten out Fats to some extent. He still partied and stayed out late but he was anxious to do well for Anita's sake as well as his own and he applied himself to his projects with renewed vigour.

Fats was anxious to improve his playing still further and embarked on a series of regular lessons with no less a figure than Leopold Godowsky, a pianist with his own outstandingly brilliant technique in the classical field. Godowsky introduced Fats to the classical repertoire and taught him advanced harmony. It must have brought obvious benefits for soon afterwards James P. Johnson also went for lessons with Godowsky. Whilst this was happening Fats continued to sell songs, including *St. Louis Shuffle, Whiteman Stomp, Keep a Song in Your Soul, Crazy 'Bout My Baby,* and *Stealin' Apples*.

On 17th November 1926 Fats made his first record for Victor, America's premier record company (HMV was, and is, one of its associated companies). They too had a 'Race' label and Fats soon became one of its mainstays, along with Fletcher Henderson, McKinney's Cotton Pickers, and 'Jelly Roll' Morton. His first Victor recording, *St. Louis Blues*, was backed by his own *Lenox Avenue Blues*. The recording studio was an old church in Camden, New Jersey, complete with grand piano and a large pipe organ. Fats recorded there not only as a pianist but also as an organist. In fact he was recognised as the best jazz organist of the day.

In 1927 Fats played at Princeton and Yale Universities, thereby gaining many new youthful fans. Anita was then pregnant and in May Fats took her with him to Chicago where he performed with Louis Armstrong in a band led by Erskine Tate. His life on the rent party circuit was over for good; he was one of the big stars of the day.

On 10th September 1927 Maurice Thomas Waller was born. Anita was still only 17. Fats' work prospered but something of a crisis occurred when the alimony problem caught up with him. He was unceremoniously arrested and bundled off to New York to face a family court whilst Anita and the baby were left stranded in Chicago. Fortunately for him he was let off with a stern lecture but it impressed on him the need to maintain regular work and income. It had already been agreed that, should Fats end up in jail, his father would look after Anita and the baby until he was released. It was a relief to them all when a jail sentence wasn't imposed.

In the same year his *Alligator Crawl* was published - a perenially popular piano piece. Fats then wrote some of the music for *Keep*

The Melody Lingers On

Shufflin', a revue at Daly's Theatre on 63rd Street. James P. Johnson wrote music for it too, and both pianists played selections in the intermissions between the acts. The programme said: "On the white keys, Fats Waller. On the black keys, James P. Johnson." He also played at the Carnegie Hall for the first time in a gala night to mark the 25th anniversary of the writing of *Memphis Blues*. W.C. Handy, the famous "Father of the Blues", presented a programme of blues, jazz and negro spirituals, in which Fats played the piano part of an ambitious rhapsody, *Yamekraw*, recently written by James P. Johnson. Johnson couldn't be there to play it himself so he nominated Fats instead.

After the Carnegie Hall concert Fats left the Daly's Theatre show to take on a job as organist at the Royal Grand Theatre in Philadelphia. But once again he conveniently 'forgot' his alimony payments and this time the judge was less sympathetic. Fats was sent to jail and sadly, whilst he was locked up, his father died. The prison authorities granted him permission to attend the funeral but he declined the offer on the grounds that his appearance at the funeral under police guard would not be appropriate, in view of his father's position as a leading figure in the church. Fats spent several weeks in jail whilst the money owed was found. Shortly after his release Anita gave birth to a second son, Ronald. He was to be the last of the Waller children.

Fats' pattern of life and work was now firmly established. Much of his time was spent 'on the road' doing one-night engagements. When not touring, engagements at theatres were interspersed with recording, song writing and radio broadcasting, all accompanied by much drinking of gin, party-going and days of sleeping.

In 1929 Fats and Andy Razaf wrote a new floor show for Connie's Inn, next door to the Lafayette Theatre in New York. It was called *Load of Coals* and featured one of his best compositions, *Honeysuckle Rose*, which was immediately broadcast by the Paul Whiteman Orchestra. In the same year Fats and Andy wrote one of their biggest hits, *Ain't Misbehavin'*, for another revue, *Hot Chocolate*. It was performed by many artists but it was Louis Armstrong who made it famous. Another big hit came in 1929, *I've Got a Feelin' I'm Fallin'*.

Fats' lack of business sense was demonstrated in that same year. As usual he was short of money and on 17th July he sold all rights to 21 of his songs including *Ain't Misbehavin'* for $500 for the lot. It was an identical act to that of Stephen Foster 70 years earlier. Fats felt he could always get more money just when he needed it simply by writing more songs. And he knew he could get easy money for short theatre engagements. The Paramount Theatre for instance employed him for a while as an organist at $750 a week.

Louis Armstrong had been a cast member of *Hot Chocolate* in New York but when the show went on tour he left the cast and Fats took over, performing his hit song *Ain't Misbehavin'* himself. Anita often travelled with him on tour whilst the children stayed behind with her mother.

At the end of 1930 Fats secured a spot on Columbia Radio in the 'Paramount on Parade' programme and his broadcasts extended to the middle of 1931. It was in this period that he started to sing his songs, on radio and on record. Previously he had just been a pianist or leader of a jazz group. Columbia recorded *I'm Crazy 'Bout My Baby* and *Draggin' My Heart Around*, entitling his record, "Thomas (Fats) Waller (singing to his Hot Piano)."

In 1932 Fats' friend Spencer Williams invited Fats to visit Paris with him. New songs were needed and Fats and Spencer set about the task with such gusto that 27 songs were written in three days and all of them were sold. In August they sailed to France on the *Ile de France* and, not surprisingly, Fats was invited by the ship's orchestra to play. He was immediately the star turn. Once in Paris Fats took to the night life like a fish to water; there was no prohibition, and here, unlike the USA, black and white people could mix freely. A number of engagements had been arranged for Fats and they were very successful but the visit to Paris was brief and before long he was back in the USA. Soon afterwards he at last took on an official manager, Bill Ponce. This was a long overdue move, for if anyone needed a manager Fats did. Acting as manager to Fats must have tested the patience of the strongest individual. Getting him to the right place at the right time in a sober state was a full-time job and Fats had to be constantly prevented from selling the rights of his best songs just to get ready cash.

Late in 1932 Fats' new manager negotiated a 2-year radio contract in Cincinnati. Fats was a 'natural' for radio and his humorous asides on the song lyrics had by now become part of his act. Anita and the boys went with him to Cincinnati. His programme was called 'Fats Waller's

The Melody Lingers On

Rhythm Club' and he also played in the 'Moon River' late-night programme, devoted to sentimental music played on the organ.

In 1934 Fats and the family were back in New York where he played in the Harlem nightspots. Then, at a party given by an impresario for George Gershwin and Paul Whiteman, Fats was heard (and seen) by William Paley, head of the Columbia Broadcasting System. He immediately offered him a lucrative radio engagement. Afterwards Paley called his programme director and asked him, "Where are we going to put Fats Waller?" "Mr. Paley, we haven't got any room for him just now," replied the man. "Then make room!" said the boss. So once again Fats was on the air.

During the run of the broadcast show Fats continued all his other work. "Fats Waller and His Rhythm" began to appear on record labels and a new Victor recording contract was negotiated which paid him 3% royalty on all sales and an advance of $100 per selection. He appeared in a stage show at the Academy of Music Picture House in Manhattan and early in 1935 once more embarked on a strenuous tour. He also did one day's work for RKO in Hollywood for the film *Hooray for Love* in which he sang *I've Got My Fingers Crossed* and did a speciality number, *Livin' in a Great Big Way* with 'Bojangles' Robinson, the dancer. Fats was paid $500 for his day's work. He was also promised a part in another film, *King of Burlesque*, this time for 20th Century Fox.

In 1935 he recorded *I'm Gonna Sit Right Down and Write Myself a Letter* (not one of his own songs). It was a huge success and sold more records than any of his other recordings. In the same year he bought himself a Hammond Organ and installed it in his Morningside Avenue apartment. The following year he bought a brand new custom-built Lincoln convertable for $7,200. His records alone were now bringing in a large income. His style was completely his own, not only as a pianist but also the way he sang the lyrics - always with humour. His records are unfailingly cheerful - guaranteed to lift the spirits. Fats' popularity was such that he was prevailed upon to record many of the standard hits of the day, even songs he hated, and if the lyrics were particularly syrupy he would 'send them up' mercilessly. All his vocal records ended with a little remark by Fats.

For the whole of Fats' working life he sustained himself by a liberal imbibement of gin, and 48-hour sleeping bouts would be interspersed with compulsive work and roistering. His dependence on the bottle was known to everyone. When his son Ronald, at six, was asked at school the routine question. "What does your father do?" he replied innocently, "Drinks gin!"

In 1938 Bill Ponce gave up his job as Fats' manager owing to ill health. Bill was then a very sick man and in fact died of emphysema in 1940. The challenge of replacing him was taken up by Ed Kirkeby, a veteran of the band and recording business. At that time Fats was getting tired of 'one-nighters' and his new manager, seeing the possibility of a lucrative tour of Britain (where Fats' fame was already assured through his records) arranged for him to appear at the Moss Empire Theatres in the UK at $2,500 a week. This was for Fats alone, without his band. He was to follow the Mills Brothers, currently touring the Moss Empires. Fats and Anita sailed on the *Transylvania* and disembarked in Greenock after Fats had once again entertained the passengers on the voyage with the help of the ship's orchestra. After a sight-seeing tour of Loch Lomond Fats gave his first British performance at the Glasgow Empire, dressed in a kilt, which must have been a sight to see. It was a triumphal performance and he took 10 curtain calls. The success was repeated in Edinburgh.

Fats and Anita then travelled to London where they were met by his old friend and collaborator Spencer Williams who took them to his cottage in Sudbury-on-Thames. The weather was wet which prompted Fats to write the music for the song *A Cottage in the Rain* to which Spencer Williams added the words. Fats then gave his first performance at the London Palladium where his name was up in lights as "Fats Waller. World's Greatest Rhythm Pianist." Below his name were those of Max Miller and Florence Desmond. Fats went through his usual part comic, part serious, jazz act. As he lowered himself gently onto the small piano stool, he said, "Is you all there, Fatsy Watsy - Yes, I sees you is!" as he prodded his huge posterior with his finger. This was a standard part of his routine which never failed to get a laugh.

Whilst in London he made some records for HMV with a hurriedly-collected jazz group that included George Chisholm (trombone) and Edmundo Ross on drums. They were issued under the title "Fats Waller and his Continental Rhythm". A few days later he recorded some organ solos and negro spirituals. It is said that when he attempted to record

Sometimes I Feel Like a Motherless Child he broke down in tears part way through and couldn't complete it. He refused to do another 'take'. Later he appeared at the Holborn Empire and the Finsbury Park Empire and took part in a BBC radio broadcast with Adelaide Hall.

After London, Fats made a brief tour of Denmark, Norway and Sweden and was then back in Britain for his first TV appearance from Alexandra Palace. After three more dance hall engagements he and Anita returned to the USA on the *Ile de France*.

As soon as he was back in America Fats opened in a new show at the Yacht Club in New York, and he bought a large new home on Long Island. But the British tour had been such a big success that Fats' manager wanted to cash in again, so on 10th March 1939 Fats once more sailed for Britain, this time on the *Queen Mary*. On this occasion he toured with the Mills Brothers (Ted Ray was in the supporting cast) and also appeared in a Sunday evening benefit with band leaders Ambrose, Carroll Gibbons, Nat Gonella, Jack Jackson, Joe Loss and Lew Stone. The tour of Britain (again playing at the Moss Empires) that Fats embarked on was a major one taking in all the big cities. Fats was never one to go to bed early and to him the evening performances were just a prelude to the drinking and partying that followed. After his performance in Sheffield he went out for a meal as usual but then discovered that night life in the steel city was non-existent. So there was nothing else to do but go back to his hotel room, like it or not, and he then whiled away the small hours writing the music for a new song, to which his manager Ed Kirkeby later added words. It was published and recorded as *Honey Hush*. On their return to London after the tour Fats wrote a *London Suite*, probably the nearest he ever got to writing any 'classical' music, though he had grown to know and respect the classical field.

Fats and his manager sailed from Britain to New York on 14th June 1939 on the *Ile de France*, never to return. He was soon back to his hectic whirl, but did find a little more time now to be with his wife and two boys. He still read his Bible and could quote long passages by heart, and insisted his children went to Sunday School regularly. When asked why he didn't go to church himself he simply said he didn't think the life he led qualified him to go to church. It was curious logic but everyone knew he was sincere.

After some engagements in New York Fats embarked on another exhausting tour of 'one-nighters', interspersed with more radio, and recording sessions for Victor. On 14th January 1942 he gave a concert in Carnegie Hall, the first time a solo jazz artist had played there. He received a tremendous ovation from the audience of 2,800 people and wonderful reviews in the papers. In Milwaukee he heard Dimitri Mitropoulos conduct the Minneapolis Symphony Orchestra in a performance of Prokoviev's Third Piano Concerto in which Mitropoulos also played the piano part. Fats was very impressed; later he met Mitropoulos at the conductor's home and they talked jazz and classics and played the piano for each other. America had now entered the war and there were lots of charity concerts in aid of various war funds, and the friendship of the two pianists led to their joint appearance in one of these events. Mitropoulos conducted a cast of 122 swing musicians and Fats played the piano in *Anchors Away* and *The Star-Spangled Banner*.

In January 1943 Fats was back in Hollywood for another film in which, this time, he had a bigger part. It was the 20th Century Fox film *Stormy Weather* with an all-black star cast. After that he was busy writing the music for a new Broadway show, *Early to Bed*, for which George Marion wrote the lyrics. Fats wasn't in it himself but he and Anita went to the opening performance before embarking on another tour, this time to Canada.

These were busy days for Fats because of the many concerts in aid of the war effort, with additional special charity shows in hospitals and for the troops, and so on. In September 1943 he recorded some of the music from *Early to Bed* for Victor, thirteen sides in all, vocals with piano and Hammond organ. They were completed on the 13th of the month and on the 30th he recorded a vocal refrain for a special Victor record. The song, *That's What the Well Dressed Man in Harlem Will Wear*, was from the all-soldier show *This is the Army* by Irving Berlin. It was the last of his recordings.

In October Fats set off on what was to be his final tour. Ed Kirkeby had arranged a series of engagements in Hollywood - a journey of over 2,700 miles from New York. Fats was tired before they even set out so Ed arranged a 2-week break in Omaha en route. But it didn't turn out to be much of a rest, for Omaha was a big army town and Fats did his bit unstintingly, as always, for the war effort by entertaining the troops at

The Melody Lingers On

several benefit shows. The train they had to catch for Los Angeles, the LA Streamliner, normally passed though Omaha without stopping but in recognition of the extra concerts Fats had given, the army generously arranged for it to stop to pick up Ed and Fats, so they duly arrived in Los Angeles without further problems. In the first week there Fats gave a show in the Zanzibar room of the Knickerbocker Hotel in Hollywood, which could seat and dine a thousand guests. Several more shows at the Zanzibar were scheduled and he also gave a broadcast for the RCA-Victor 'What's New?' programme.

Unfortunately, although Fats' solo spot at the Zanzibar was a great success, the air-conditioning was primitive and Fats' Steinway was blasted throughout his performances by cold air from the ventilators. The next week he went down with 'flu. He wouldn't go to hospital but ten days in bed appeared to have cured him and he was pronounced fit. The doctors urged him to "take it easy", but Fats didn't know how to. As soon as he was on his feet, but still weak, he appeared at another benefit concert, postponed through his illness, for 'Coloured USA'. Next day came a Command Performance with Dinah Shore and Abbott and Costello, followed by another show for NBC. To round off the week he insisted on doing a 'Hollywood Canteen' show for the armed forces. All these shows were 'extras', on top of his Zanzibar Room engagements - and he was only just out of bed.

Fats still had three more nights at the Zanzibar. After the final performance on the Saturday night a happy boss paid Fats a bonus and presented him with a case of Scotch whisky and half a dozen bottles of champagne. Ed tried to persuade Fats to take it all home to New York for Christmas but most of it had disappeared before they left Los Angeles.

After the concluding performance at the Zanzibar there was a big Press party with all the usual drinking, and next morning Fats was shattered. There was still one more engagement, that night at the Florentine Gardens, which Fats somehow got through but was virtually 'out on his feet' when it ended.

Next morning Ed Kirkeby and Fats set off on the Santa Fé Chief train for the long journey across America, back home to New York, via Santa Fé and Kansas City. The next morning Fats was exhausted and said he was going to sleep. He slept all day - not unusual for him, whilst Ed pottered around the train and looked in on Fats now and again to make sure he wasn't being disturbed. At 2 a.m. the next morning Ed looked in on Fats and was met by an icy blast of cold air. Fats was awake and Ed commented on the cold. "Yeah, Hawkins is sure blowing out there", Fats replied. (The train was speeding through the Kansas plains in a howling blizzard which reminded Fats of the stormy sax playing of his friend Coleman Hawkins). At 5 o'clock in the morning Ed found Fats lying down, trembling all over and making choking sounds. Ed couldn't wake him so fetched the bar steward and asked him to get a doctor. Luckily one appeared very quickly for the train had stopped, as it happened, in Kansas City and a doctor had already been called to attend another passenger. The doctor examined the now-motionless Fats for some time and then looked up and said, "This man is dead." The date was 13th December 1943 and Fats was 39.

No-one knew what Fats had died of but an autopsy showed the cause to be influenzal bronchial pneumonia. He had evidently had the condition for some days and no one, including Fats himself, had realised. By an ironic chance another train travelling in the opposite direction was also in Kansas City station waiting for Fats' train to pull out. On it was Louis Armstrong. It is said that when he was told of Fats' death he cried all day.

Anita had not accompanied Fats on this tour so Ed had to phone her with the sad news and then, after the appropriate arrangements had been made, make the long, dismal journey back to New York with Fats' body.

The funeral service was held at the Abyssinia Church in Harlem and many of Fats' friends and colleagues were there including James P. Johnson and Clarence Williams who had both helped him in his early days. The cast of *Early to Bed* filled several pews. Fats' and Anita's sons, Maurice and Ronald, were then 16 and 15 respectively. At the funeral they noticed a well-dressed woman and a young man in an army corporal's uniform being conducted to a prominent place at the front of the church. Maurice asked who they were. "That's your father's first wife and your half-brother Tom." The boys were astonished. They had no idea until then that their father had had a previous marriage.

Fats' early death when he was still at the peak of his career saddened the world of jazz. He had a unique personal style and touch, a natural flair as an entertainer, and an amiable nature. His recordings were rich

The Melody Lingers On

in jazz as well as comedy. Now, more than half a century after his death, he is still remembered with affection as one of the great names in jazz. He lived life at a cracking pace. If he had lived a more temperate life, drunk less, and looked after himself he may well have lived a lot longer. But then, he wouldn't have been Fats Waller.

Fats Waller's best compositions are listed in Appendix 10.

Bibliography

a) General

The New Grove Dictionary of Music and Musicians, Ed. Stanley Sadie. Macmillan, London, 1980.
The New Grove Dictionary of Women Composers, Ed. Julie Anne Sadie and Rhian Samuel. Macmillan, London, 1984.
The New Grove Dictionary of Jazz, Ed. Barry Kernfeld. Macmillan, London, 1994.
The Concise Baker's Biographical Dictionary of Composers and Musicians, Comp. Nicolas Slonimsky. Simon & Schuster, London, 1988.
The Faber Companion to 20th Century Popular Music, by Phil Hardy and Dave Laing. Faber & Faber, London, 1990.
The Oxford Companion To Popular Music, by Peter Gammond. Oxford University Press, Oxford & New York, 1993.
The Great Song Thesaurus, by Roger Lax and Frederick Smith. Oxford University Press, New York, 1989.
The BBC Music Library Song Catalogue. British Broadcasting Corporation, London, 1966.
American Popular Song, by Alec Wilder. Oxford University Press, New York, 1972.
A History of Popular Music in America, by Sigmund Spaeth. Phoenix House, London, 1960. (First published in the USA in 1948).
They All Played Ragtime, by Rudi Blesh and Harriet Janis. Borzoi Books, Alfred A. Knopf, New York, 1950. Re-published by The Jazz Book Club by arrangement with Sidgwick & Jackson, London, 1960.
Who's Who and Who Was Who, various years. Adam & Charles Black, London.

Bibliography

b) Publications relevant to particular chapters

1. Stephen Foster

Stephen Foster, America's Troubadour, by J.T. Howard.   Tudor Publishing Company, New York, 1935.
Biography, Songs and Musical Compositions of Stephen C. Foster, by Morrison Foster.   Percy F. Smith, Pittsburgh, 1896.
Stephen Collins Foster, a Biography of America's Folk Song Composer, by H.V. Milligan.   G. Schirmer, New York, 1920.
The Stephen Foster Song Book, Ed. R. Jackson.   Dover Publications, New York, 1974.

2. Cécile Chaminade

Scarf Dance, The Story of Cécile Chaminade, by Laura Kerr.   Abelard Press, New York, 1953.
French Piano Music, by Norman Demuth.   Museum Press Ltd., London, 1959.
How to Play My Best-known Pieces, by Cécile Chaminade.   Étude, xxvi, p. 759, 1908.
Recollections Of My Musical Childhood, by Cécile Chaminade.   Étude, xxix, p.805, 1911.

3. Leslie Stuart

Numerous books on the theatre by W. Macqueen-Pope.
Sixty Years of the Theatre, by Ernest Short.   Eyre & Spottiswoode, London, 1951.
A Guide to Popular Music, by Peter Gammond and Peter Clayton.   Phoenix House, London, 1960.
The Songwriters, by A. Staveacre.   BBC Publications, London, 1980.
First and Second Albums of Leslie Stuart's Most Famous Songs.   Francis, Day & Hunter Ltd., London, c. 1929.

4. Scott Joplin

Scott Joplin and the Ragtime Era, by Peter Gammond. Sphere Books Ltd., London, 1975.

Scott Joplin: The Man Who Made Ragtime, by James Haskins, with Kathleen Benson. Doubleday & Co. Inc., New York, 1978.

5. Jerome Kern

The World of Jerome Kern, by David Ewen. Holt, Rinehart & Winston, New York, 1960.

Jerome Kern, by Michael Freedland. Robson Books, London, 1978.

Jerome Kern - His Life and Music, by Gerald Bordman. Oxford University Press, Oxford, 1980.

6. Irving Berlin

The Story of Irving Berlin, by David Ewen. Holt, New York, 1950.

A Salute To Irving Berlin, by Michael Freedland. W.H. Allen, London, 1986.

As Thousands Cheer: The Life of Irving Berlin, by Laurence Bergreen. Hodder & Stoughton, London, 1990.

7. Jelly Roll Morton

Mister Jelly Roll, by Alan Lomax. Cassell & Co., London, 1952. (re-printed 1973).

The Making of Jazz, by James L. Collier. Houghton Mifflin Co., Boston, USA, 1978.

A Pictorial History of Jazz, by O. Keepnews and W. Grauer, jr. Crown Publishers, Inc., New York, 1955.

Bibliography

8. Cole Porter

The Cole Porter Story, by David Ewen. Holt, Rinehart & Winston, New York, 1965.
The Life That He Led: a Biography of Cole Porter, by George Eells. Putnam, New York, 1967.
Cole, by R. Kimball and B. Gill. Holt, Rinehart & Winston, New York, 1971.
Cole Porter - a Biography, by Charles Schwartz. The Dial Press, New York, 1977.
The Cole Porter Song Book (Foreword by Moss Hart). Simon & Schuster, New York, 1959.

9. George Gershwin

George Gershwin - His Journey To Greatness, by David Ewen. Prentice Hall Inc., Eaglewood Cliffs, New Jersey, 1956. (revised 1970).
Gershwin - His Life and Music, by Charles Schwartz. The Bobbs-Merrill Co. Inc., Indianapolis & New York, 1973.

10. Fats Waller

Ain't Misbehavin' - The Story of Fats Waller, by Ed. Kirkeby, with D. Scheidt and S. Trail. Dodd, Mead & Co., New York, 1966. (re-published by Da Capo Press, New York, 1975, 1978, 1985).
Fats Waller, by Maurice Waller and Anthony Calabrese. Cassell Ltd., London, 1977.

The Melody Lingers On

Recordings on Compact Disc and Cassette

Some readers, having followed the story of these musicians, may wish to be reminded of their music. The recordings listed below illustrate their art. They are not the only records available but are selected purely as a representative sample. All the recordings quoted here are currently available (summer 1995).

Those marked * are cassettes; the others are compact discs. The cassettes are quite cheap and may be purchased at prices ranging from £2.50 to £5.00. Most of the compact discs are in the mid-price region though some are full-price.

1. Stephen Foster

RCA Victor 'Living Stereo' Series. 9026-61253 2 *The Stephen Foster Song Book.* A good selection of 16 of Foster's songs, sung by the Robert Shaw Chorale.

2. Cécile Chaminade

Hyperion CDA 66584 *Piano Music by Cécile Chaminade - 1.* A selection of 19 pieces
Hyperion CDA 66706 *Piano Music by Cécile Chaminade - 2.* Another 19 pieces.
    All played by Peter Jacobs, piano.
Recordings of Chaminade's *Concerto for Flute and Orchestra*, Op. 107 and her *Concertino for Flute and Piano* are also available. (There is a choice of these recordings on compact disc).

3. Leslie Stuart

Opal CD 9835 *Floradora.* Historic recording with the original cast. Supplied with an informative booklet.
    No collection of Leslie Stuart's songs appears to be available on one compact disc or cassette, but individual Stuart songs appear on miscellaneous song collections.

4. Scott Joplin

Nonesuch 7559-79159-2 *Scott Joplin's Piano Rags.* Played by Joshua Rifkin, piano. 17 of the 24 Joplin rags which Rifkin recorded for Nonesuch in the early 1970s.
RCA Victor GD 60842 and GD 87993 *Scott Joplin's Piano Works.* Played by Dick Hyman and James Levine.

5. Jerome Kern

PAST CD 9767 *A Jerome Kern Showcase.* Selections from *Show Boat, Blue Eyes, Swing Time, Cabaret Girl, Sally* and *Sunny* sung by the artists who created the shows (Evelyn Laye, Elsie Randolph, etc.)
    * WESTend - WEM 307 (Avid Records). *Jerome Kern Song Book.* A selection of 21 songs. Singers include Fred Astaire, Jessie Mathews, Billie Holliday, Elsie Randolph, Paul Robeson, and George Gershwin at the piano in *Whose Baby Are You?*

6. Irving Berlin

PAST CD 9733 *An Irving Berlin Showcase.* Highlights of his heyday.

Recordings

* Parade PAR 6020 *Irving Berlin - Let's Face the Music and Dance.* A selection of 20 Berlin songs. Singers include Al Jolson, Al Bowlly and Fred Astaire.
* WESTend - WEM 306 (Avid Records). *Irving Berlin Song Book.* A selection of 21 songs. Singers include Alice Faye, Fred Astaire, Ruth Etting, Ethel Waters, Billie Holliday, Bing Crosby and Al Bowlly.
* 'Happy Days' Series (Conifer records). MCHD 166. *Irving Berlin.* 22 songs. Singers include Fred Astaire, Ginger Rogers, Eddie Cantor, Bing Crosby, Dick Powell, Al Jolson, Alice Faye and Gracie Fields.

7. Jelly Roll Morton

TOPAZ TPZ 1003 *Jelly Roll Morton - Sweet and Hot.* 21 pieces played by Jelly Roll Morton with various groups. He sings on some; many of the pieces are his own compositions.
* Giants of Jazz MCJT 23 *Jelly Roll Morton.* 16 pieces played by Jelly Roll Morton with various groups, some with vocals by himself. Several of the pieces are his own compositions.

8. Cole Porter

PAST CD 9751 *The Centenary Tribute to Cole Porter.* A selection of his music, mostly by original cast artists such as Ethel Merman and Fred Astaire.
* WESTend - WEM 304 (Avid Records). *Cole Porter Song Book.* A selection of 21 Porter songs. Singers include Billie Holliday, Bing Crosby, Josephine Baker, Gertrude Lawrence, Fred Astaire, and Cole Porter himself.
* Polygram 'Venue' series 847 202-4. *Night and Day - The Cole Porter Song Book.* 17 Porter songs sung by a number of artists including Fred Astaire, Dinah Washington, Billie Holiday and Ella Fitzgerald. (The songs on this cassette are modern arrangements; not to everyone's taste.)

9. George Gershwin

PAST CD 9777 *'S Wonderful - The Music of George Gershwin.* Sung by Fred Astaire, Gertrude Lawrence, Al Jolson, Bing Crosby, etc.
GEMM CDS 9483 2-CD set. *George Gershwin plays George Gershwin.* Includes *Rhapsody in Blue, An American in Paris, 3rd Movement of the Piano Concerto in F, Selections from Porgy and Bess,* and four items with Fred and Adele Astaire singing. (George at the piano).
* WESTend WEM 305 (Avid Records). *George and Ira Gershwin Song Book.* A selection of 21 songs sung by a variety of artists including Al Jolson, Judy Garland and Fred Astaire.

A lot of recordings are available of *An American in Paris, Concerto in F for Piano and Orchestra, Cuban Overture, Rhapsody in Blue, Second Rhapsody, Variations on 'I Got Rhythm', Preludes for Piano, Porgy and Bess,* and *Catfish Row* (arrangements from Porgy and Bess).

10. Fats Waller

PAST CD 9742 *The Cream of Fats Waller - I.* A selection of 24 pieces performed by Fats.
PAST CD 7020 *The Cream of Fats Waller - II.* A further selection, of 17 pieces.
* ASV Living Era ZC AJA 5040 *Fats Waller - You Rascal You.* A selection of 18 pieces played by Fats Waller and his groups.

N.B. In addition to the above recordings, many of the films mentioned in the text are available for purchase in video-cassette form.

The Melody Lingers On

Appendices - Compositions of the Ten Musicians

All the musicians in this book wrote hundreds of compositions. The following lists are selective, quoting their best-known music.

The appendices in which the compositions are listed are in the same order as the chapters.

Appendix 1 - Stephen Foster's Songs

Open Thy Lattice Love	(1844)	The Village Maiden	(1855)
There's a Good Time Coming	(1846)	Gentle Annie	(1856)
Lou'siana Belle	(1847)	Thou Art the Queen of My Song	(1859)
Oh! Susanna	(1848)	Down Among the Cane-Brakes	(1860)
Old Uncle Ned	(1848)	The Glendy Burk	(1860)
Nelly Was a Lady	(1849)	Old Black Joe	(1860)
Ah! May the Red Rose Live Alway!	(1850)	Don't Bet Our Money	(1861)
Camptown Races	(1850)	Better Times Are Coming	(1862)
Nelly Bly	(1850)	Gentle Lena Clare	(1862)
Way Down in Ca-i-ro	(1850)	That's What's the Matter	(1862)
Old Folks At Home	(1851)	There Are Plenty of Fish in the Sea	(1862)
Ring de Banjo	(1851)	We Are Coming, Father Abraham	(1862)
Wilt thou Be Gone, Love?	(1851)	300,000 More	(1862)
Maggie By My Side	(1852)	My Wife Is a Most Knowing Woman	(1863)
Massa's in de Cold Ground	(1852)	Nothing But a Plain Old Soldier	(1863)
My Old Kentucky Home	(1853)	The Song Of All Songs	(1863)
Old Dog Tray	(1853)	When This Dreadful War Is Ended	(1863)
Jeanie With the Light Brown Hair	(1854)	Willie Has Gone To the War	(1863)
Come Where My Love Lies Dreaming	(1855)	Beautiful Dreamer	(1864)
Hard Times Come Again No More	(1855)	If You've Only Got a Moustache	(1864)
Some Folks Do	(1855)	The Voices That Are Gone	(1865)

Appendix 2

Appendix 2 - Cécile Chaminade's Compositions

Instrumental:

Suite d'Orchestre, Op. 20 (1881)
Les Amazons, Symphonie Dramatique (1888)
Callirhoë (Ballet Symphonique), Op. 37, (c. 1888); as Orchestral Suite (c. 1890)
Concertstück, Op. 40, Pianoforte and Orchestra (c. 1893)
Concertino, Op. 107, for Flute and Orchestra (c. 1902)
Concertino for Flute and Pianoforte (date unknown)
Chamber works: Two Pianoforte Trios, Op. 11 (1881); Op. 34 (1887); Three Morceaux, Op. 31, for Violin and Pianoforte (c. 1885).
Chanson (Sérénade) Espagnole, Op. 150, for Violin and Pianoforte (1903); melody transcribed by Fritz Kreisler (1925).

Songs for Voice and Piano:

L'Heure du Mystère	(1878)	Nuit d'Été	(1896)
Ritournelle	(1886)	Au Pays Bleu	(1898)
L'Anneau d'Argent	(1891)	Reste	(1899)
Tu Me Dirais	(1891)	Écrin	(1902)
Si J'Étais Jardinier	(1893)	Amour Invisible	(1905)
Viatique	(1895)	L'Heureuses	(1909)
Fleur du Matin	(1896)	Le Village	(1915)
Mon Cœur Chante	(1896)	L'Anneau du Soldat	(1916)

Cécile Chaminade's compositions continued on next page . . . .

Cécile Chaminade's compositions (contd.)

Works for Solo Piano:

As there are a very large number of compositions in this category this list is very selective. Except for those marked * they are the compositions which were recorded on piano roll, which can be taken as a rough measure of their popularity. The dates of the compositions shown without dates is unknown but may be determined, approximately, by comparing the opus numbers with those of the dated compositions.

* Two Mazurkas, Op. 1	(1869)	Valse Carnavalasque, Op. 73	(1894)
Pièce Romantique, Op. 9, No. 1		Six Romances sans Paroles, Op. 76	
Gavotte, Op. 9, No. 2		(Only No. 2, Élevation, on piano roll)	
* Sonata, Op. 21	(1895)	Valse No. 2, Op. 77	
Orientale, Op. 22		Valse Brillante, Op. 80, No. 3	
Minuette, Op. 23		Ritournelle (transcription), Op. 83	
Libellules, Op. 24	(1881)	Six Pièces Humoresques, Op. 87:	
Humoresque, Op. 25, No. 2		No. 1, Réveil	
Étude Symphonique, Op. 28	(1881-90)	No. 2, Sous Bois	
Sérénade Espagnole, Op. 29	(1884)	No. 3, Inquiétude	
Airs de Ballet, Op. 30		Valse Brillante, Op. 91, No. 4	
Guitare, Op. 32		Danse Créole, Op. 94,	
Valse Caprice, Op. 33		Trois Danses Anciènnes, Op.95	(1899)
Six Airs de Concert, Op. 35	(1882-86)	Six Feuilles d'Album, Op. 98	
No. 1, Scherzo		No. 1, Promenade	
No. 2, Automne	(1882)	No. 2, Scherzetto	
No. 3, La Fileuse		No. 4, Valse Arabesque	
No. 5, Impromptu		L'Ondine, Op. 101	
Airs de Ballet, Op. 37		Souvenirs Lointaines, Op. 111	
No. 1, Pas de Amphores		Caprice Humoresque, Op.113	(1904)
No. 2, Pas des Écharpes		Sous le Masque, Op. 116	
No. 3, Callirhoë (variations)		Valse Tendre, Op. 119	
No. 4, Unnamed		Contes Bleus, Op. 122	(1906)
No. 5, Unnamed		Nos. 1, 2, 3.	
Marine, Op. 38		Marche Americaine, Op. 131	
Sérénade and Air de Ballet, Op. 41		Étude Romantique, Op. 132	
(Pierrette)		Le Retour, Op. 134	
Les Willis, Op. 42		* Étude Humoresque, Op. 138	(1910)
La Lisonjera, Op. 50	(1890)	Feuilles d'Automne, Op. 146	
La Livry, Op. 51		Berceuse du Petit Soldat Blessé	
Arlequine, Op. 5		Op.156	(1919)
Lolita (Caprice Espagnole), Op. 54		Gavotte, Op. 162	
Scaramouche, Op. 56			
Mazurka Suédoise, Op. 58		*Unknown Opus Number:*	
Les Silvains, Op. 60		Étude Pathetique	
Arabesque, Op. 61		Valse Caprice in D major	
Studio, Op. 66		Berceuse (Wiegenlied)	
La Morena, Op. 67		Madrigal No. 1 in D major	
Arabesque, Op. 71		Partout No. 1 in C major	

Appendix 3

Appendix 3 - Leslie Stuart's Compositions

Score for Musical Plays:

Floradora	(1899)	Captain Kidd	(1910)
The Silver Slipper	(1901)	The Slim Princess	(1910)
The School Girl	(1903)	Peggy	(1911)
The Belle of Mayfair	(1905)	The Midnight Frolic	(1917)
Havana	(1908)		

Songs:

The Girl On the Ran Tan Dan	(1893)	The Shade of the Palm	(1900)
Lou'siana Lou	(1894)	I Want To Be a Military Man	(1900)
Sweetheart May	(1894)	Class	(1901)
The Bandolero	(1895)	The Detrimental Man	(1901)
The Soldiers of the Queen	(1895)	A Happy Day	(1901)
The Little Mad'moiselle	(1895)	Two Eyes of Blue	(1901)
Rip van Winkle	(1896)	I May Be Crazy But I Love You	(1902)
The Willow Pattern Plate	(1896)	Belinda On the Line	(1903)
Is Yer Mammie Always With Ye?	(1897)	Looking for a Needle in a Haystack	(1903)
Little Dolly Daydream	(1897)	My Little Canoe	(1903)
She's an English Girl	(1897)	My Little Black Pearl	(1904)
The Dandy Fifth	(1898)	Hello People	(1908)
The Cake Walk	(1898)	The Yacht Zara	(1908)
Lily of Laguna	(1898)	I'm a Cuban Girl	(1908)
The Coon Drum Major	(1899)	Don't Forget You're a Lady	(1911)
My Little Octoroon	(1899)	Ladies, Beware	(1911)
The Banshee	(1900)	Whistle and the Girls Come Round	(1911)
The Silver Star of Love	(1900)	You're the Only Girl	(1911)
Tell Me, Pretty Maiden	(1900)	I Beg Your Pardon	(1917)

The Melody Lingers On

Appendix 4 - Scott Joplin's Compositions

Operas:

A Guest of Honor - A Ragtime Opera (Completed 1903, unpublished)
Treemonisha - Opera in Three Acts   (1911)

Piano Rags:

Original Rags	(1898)	Gladiolus Rag	(1907)
Maple Leaf Rag	(1899)	Search Light Rag	(1907)
Peacherine Rag	(1901)	Rose Leaf Rag	(1907)
The Easy Winners	(1901)	Fig Leaf Rag	(1908)
A Breeze from Alabama	(1902)	Pineapple Rag	(1908)
Élite Syncopations	(1902)	Sugar Cane	(1908)
The Strenuous Life	(1902)	Paragon Rag	(1909)
The Entertainer	(1902)	Wall Street Rag	(1909)
Weeping Willow	(1903)	Country Club	(1909)
Palm Leaf Rag - A Slow Drag	(1903)	Solace - A Mexican Serenade	(1909)
The Favorite	(1904)	Euphonic Sounds	(1909)
The Chrysanthemum	(1904)	Stoptime Rag	(1910)
The Sycamore - A Concert Rag	(1904)	Scott Joplin's New Rag	(1912)
The Cascades	(1904)	Magnetic Rag	(1914)
Eugenia	(1906)	Reflection Rag - Syncopated	
The Ragtime Dance - Two Step	(1906)	Musings	(1917)
The Nonpareil	(1907)		

Syncopated Waltzes:

Bethena - A Concert Waltz   (1905)   Pleasant Moments   (1909)

Piano Rags written in collaboration with others:

Swipesey Cake Walk	(with Arthur Marshall)	(1900)
Sunflower Slow Drag	(with Scott Hayden)	(1901)
Something Doing	(with Scott Hayden)	(1903)
Heliotrope Bouquet	(with Louis Chauvin)	(1907)
Lily Queen	(with Arthur Marshall)	(1907)
Felicity Rag	(with Scott Hayden)	(1911)
Kismet Rag	(with Scott Hayden)	(1913)

Other Compositions:

A Picture of Her Face - Waltz Song	(1895)	March Majestic - 6/8 March	(1902)
Please Say You Will - Waltz Song	(1895)	Cleopha Two-Step - Piano Solo	(1902)
The Great Collision Crush March -Piano	(1896)	Rosebud March - 6/8 Piano Solo	(1905)
Combination March - Piano Solo	(1896)	Binks Waltz - Piano Solo	(1905)
Harmony Club Waltz - Piano Solo	(1896)	Antoinette - 6/8 March Piano Solo	(1906)
Augustan Club Waltzes - Piano Solo	(1901)		

Appendix 5

Appendix 5 - Jerome Kern's Compositions

Instrumental:

String quartet versions of several of his songs, in collaboration with Charles Miller. Scenario (1941), and Portrait of Mark Twain (1942), both for Orchestra.

Stage Shows with Jerome Kern's Music:

Miss Information	(1915)	Stepping Stones	(1923)
Cousin Lucy	(1915)	Sitting Pretty	(1924)
Very Good, Eddie	(1915)	Dear Sir	(1924)
Have a Heart	(1917)	Sunny	(1925)
Love o' Mike	(1917)	The City Chap	(1925)
Oh, Boy!	(1917)	Criss-Cross	(1926)
Leave It To Jane	(1917)	Lucky	(1927)
Oh, Lady! Lady!!	(1918)	Show Boat	(1927)
Toot-Toot!	(1918)	Blue Eyes	(1928)
Head over Heels	(1918)	Sweet Adeline	(1929)
Rock-a-Bye Baby	(1918)	The Cat and the Fiddle	(1931)
Hitchy-Koo	(1920)	Music in the Air	(1932)
Sally	(1920)	Roberta	(1932)
Good Morning, Dearie	(1921)	Three Sisters	(1934)
The Bunch and Judy	(1922)	Gentleman Unafraid	(1938)
The Cabaret Girl	(1922)	Very Warm for May	(1939)
The Beauty Prize	(1922)		

Films with Jerome Kern's Music

Sally	(1929)	Goldwyn Follies of 1938	(1938)
Sunny	(1930)	One Night in the Tropics	(1940)
The Cat and the Fiddle	(1934)	Sunny (re-make)	(1941)
Music in the Air	(1934)	You were Never Lovelier	(1942)
I Dream Too Much	(1934)	Can't Help Singing	(1944)
Reckless	(1935)	Cover Girl	(1944)
Roberta	(1935)	Song of Russia	(1944)
Sweet Adeline	(1935)	Centennial Summer	(1946)
Show Boat	(1936)	Till the Clouds Roll By	
Swing Time	(1936)	(biography featuring Kern's songs)	(1946)
High, Wide and Handsome	(1937)	Look for the Silver Lining	(1949)
When You're In Love	(1937)	Show Boat (re-make)	(1951)
Joy of Living	(1938)	Lovely To Look At	(1952)

In addition to the two film versions of *Show Boat* listed above, a primitive talkie version, now lost, was made in 1929.

Jerome Kern's compositions continued on next page....

Jerome Kern's compositions (contd.)

Songs:

How'd You like To Spoon with Me?	(1905)	Smoke Gets In Your Eyes	(1933)
They Didn't Believe Me	(1914)	I Won't Dance	(1935)
Till the Clouds Roll By	(1917)	Lovely To Look At	(1935)
Ain't It a Grand and Glorious Feeling?	(1917)	I Still Suits Me	(1935)
Bill	(1917)	A Fine Romance	(1936)
Look For the Silver Lining	(1920)	Never Gonna Dance	(1936)
Sally *	(1921)	Pick Yourself Up	(1936)
Who?	(1925)	The Way You Look Tonight	(1936)
Sunny	(1925)	Can I Forget You?	(1937)
Why Do I Love You?	(1927)	The Folks Who Live On the Hill	(1937)
Ol' Man River	(1927)	All the Things You Are	(1939)
Can't Help Lovin' dat Man	(1927)	The Last Time I Saw Paris	(1940)
Only Make Believe	(1927)	Dearly Beloved	(1942)
She Didn't Say Yes	(1931)	Long Ago and Far Away	(1944)
Music in the Air	(1932)	Can't Help Singing	(1944)
I've Told Ev'ry Little Star	(1932)		

*Not the *Sally* which was the theme song of Gracie Fields. That was a British song written ten years later.

Appendix 6 - Irving Berlin's Compositions

Stage Shows with Irving Berlin's Music:

Ziegfeld Follies of 1910	(1910)	Dance and Grow Thin	(1918)
He Came from Milwaukee	(1910)	Yip, Yip, Yaphank	(1918)
The Jolly Bachelors	(1910)	Ziegfeld Follies of 1919	(1919)
Up and Down Broadway	(1910)	The Music Box Revue	(1921)
Temptations	(1911)	The Cocoanuts	(1925)
Ziegfeld Follies of 1911	(1911)	Ziegfeld Follies of 1927	(1927)
Everybody's Doin' It	(1912)	Face the Music	(1932)
The Whirls of Society	(1912)	As Thousands Cheer	(1933)
The Sun Dodgers	(1913)	Louisiana Purchase	(1940)
All Aboard	(1913)	This Is the Army	(1942)
Watch Your Step	(1914)	Annie Get Your Gun	(1946)
Stop! Look! Listen!	(1915)	Miss Liberty	(1949)
The Century Girl		Call Me Madam	(1950)
(with Victor Herbert)	(1916)	Mr. President	(1962)
Cohan Revue of 1918	(1918)		

Films with Irving Berlin's Music:

Hallelujah!	(1929)	Second Fiddle	(1939)
Puttin' On the Ritz	(1929)	Holiday Inn	(1942)
Mammy	(1929)	Blue Skies	(1946)
Ready for the Moon	(1931)	Easter Parade	(1948)
Top Hat	(1935)	Annie Get Your Gun	(1950)
Follow the Fleet	(1936)	Call Me Madam	(1953)
On the Avenue	(1937)	White Christmas	(1954)
Carefree	(1938)	There's No Business Like	
Alexander's Ragtime Band	(1938)	Show Business	(1954)

Irving Berlin's compositions continued on next page . . . .

Irving Berlin's compositions (contd.)

Songs:

Alexander's Ragtime Band	(1911)	Isn't This a Lovely Day To Be Caught in the Rain	(1935)
Everybody's Doin' It	(1911)	I'm Putting All My Eggs in One Basket	(1935)
I Want To Be in Dixie	(1913)	Let's Face the Music and Dance	(1936)
When the Midnight Choo-Choo Leaves for Alabam'	(1913)	Let Yourself Go	(1936)
Play a Simple Melody	(1914)	We Saw the Sea	(1936)
Easter Parade (as 'Smile and Show Your Dimple')	(1916)	I've Got My Love To Keep Me Warm	(1937)
I Love a Piano	(1916)	It's A Lovely Day Tomorrow	(1940)
Oh, How I Hate To Get Up in the Morning	(1918)	White Christmas	(1942)
I've Got My Captain Working for Me Now	(1919)	This Is the Army, Mr. Jones	(1942)
A Pretty Girl Is Like a Melody	(1919)	A Couple of Song and Dance Men	(1946)
God Bless America (published 1939)	(1919)	You Keep Coming Back Like a Song	(1946)
Say It With Music	(1921)	They Say It's Wonderful	(1946)
All Alone	(1924)	You Can't Get a Man With a Gun	(1946)
What'll I Do?	(1924)	Anything You Can Do I Can Do Better	(1946)
Remember	(1924)	The Girl That I Marry	(1946)
Always	(1926)	I'm an Indian Too	(1946)
Shaking the Blues Away	(1927)	My Defenses Are Down	(1946)
Blue Skies	(1927)	Doin' What comes Natur'lly	(1946)
The Song Is Ended	(1927)	I Got the Sun in the Morning	(1946)
Puttin' On the Ritz	(1929)	There's No Business Like Show Business (written earlier)	(1946)
Let Me Sing and I'm Happy	(1929)	Steppin' Out With My Baby	(1948)
Say It Isn't So	(1932)	We're a Couple of Swells	(1948)
How Deep Is the Ocean?	(1932)	It's a Lovely Day Today	(1950)
Let's Have Another Cup of Coffee	(1932)	You're Just In Love (alternatively known as 'I Wonder Why?')	(1950)
Heat Wave	(1933)		
Top Hat, White Tie and Tails	(1935)	Something To Dance About	(1950)
Cheek To Cheek	(1935)		

Appendix 7 - 'Jelly Roll' Morton's Compositions

Many of Jelly Roll Morton's compositions were unpublished. For those that were published, the dates given are those of publication. They were often written years earlier.   U = Unpublished

Piano Rags:

Alabama Bound (U)	(c. 1905)	Seattle Hunch (U)	(1929)
Superior Rag (U)	(1915)	Turtle Twist (U)	(1930)
Cadillac Rag	(1917)	Ponchartrain (U)	(1931)
Someday, Sweetheart	(1917)	Fickle Fay Creep (U)	(1931)
The Pearls	(1923)	Fat Frances (U)	(1931)
Grandpa's Spells	(1923)	Pep (U)	(1931)
Kansas City Stomp	(1923)	Gambling Jack (U)	(1932)
King Porter Stomp (written earlier)	(1924)	Crazy Chords (U)	(1932)
Milenberg Joys (jointly with others)	(1925)	Sweet Peter (U)	(1933)
Shreveport Stomps	(1925)	Mister Joe (U)	(1939)
Midnight Mama	(1925)	The Naked Dance (arrangement of	
Chicago Breakdown	(1926)	a Tony Jackson rag) (U)	(1939)
Black Bottom stomp	(1926)	The Finger Breaker (U)	(1942)
Ham and Eggs	(1928)	*Dates unknown of* Bert Williams; Albert	
Boogaboo	(1928)	Carroll's Blues; Crazy Chord Rag; Buddy	
Freakish (U)	(1929)	Carter's Rag; The Perfect Rag. (all unpubl.)	

Instrumental Blues:

The Original Jelly Roll Blues	(1915)	Sidewalk Blues	(1926)
Wolverine Blues	(1923)	Cannonball Blues	(1926)
London Blues	(1923)	Deep Creek Blues (U)	(1930)
New Orleans Blues	(1925)		

Instrumental Tangos:

The Crave (U)	(1939)	Spanish Swat (U)	(date unknown)
Creepy Feeling (U)	(date unknown)	Mama 'mita (U)	(date unknown)

Vocal Blues:

The Winin' Boy (U)	(1939)	Don't You Leave Me Here (U)	(date unknn.)
Buddy Bolden's Blues (U)	(1939)	Mamie's Blues (U)	(date unknown)

Songs:

Mr. Jelly Lord	(1923)	Jazz Jamboree (U)	(1938)
My Home is in a Southern Town	(1923)	Anamule Dance (U)	(1939)

The Melody Lingers On

Appendix 8 - Cole Porter's Compositions

Stage Shows with Cole Porter's Music:

A Night Out	(1920)	You Never Know	(1938)
Mayfair and Montmartre	(1922)	Leave It to Me	(1938)
Hitchy-Koo of 1922	(1922)	DuBarry Was a Lady	(1939)
Greenwich Village Follies	(1924)	Panama Hattie	(1941)
Paris	(1928)	Let's Face It	(1941)
Fifty Million Frenchmen	(1929)	Something for the Boys	(1943)
Wake Up and Dream	(1929)	Mexican Hayride	(1944)
The New Yorkers	(1930)	Seven Lively Arts	(1944)
Gay Divorce	(1932)	Around the World in Eighty Days	(1946)
Nymph Errant	(1933)	Kiss Me Kate	(1948)
Hey, Diddle Diddle	(1934)	Out of this World	(1950)
Anything Goes	(1934)	Can-Can	(1953)
Jubilee	(1935)	Silk Stockings	(1955)

Films with Cole Porter's Music:

The Battle of Paris	(1929)	Hollywood Canteen	(1944)
The Gay Divorcee	(1934)	Night and Day	
Anything Goes	(1936)	(fictitious biog. of Cole Porter)	(1946)
Born To Dance	(1936)	The Pirate	(1948)
Rosalie	(1937)	Stage Fright	(1950)
Break the News	(1938)	Kiss Me, Kate	(1953)
Broadway Melody of 1940	(1940)	Anything Goes (re-make)	(1956)
You'll Never Get Rich	(1941)	High Society	(1956)
Panama Hattie	(1942)	Silk Stockings	(1957)
DuBarry Was a Lady	(1943)	Les Girls	(1957)
Let's Face It	(1943)	Can-Can	(1960)
Something To Shout About	(1943)		

Cole Porter's compositions continued on next page . . . .

Appendix 8

Cole Porter's compositions (contd.)

Songs:

Let's Do It, Let's Fall In Love	(1928)	Friendship	(1939)
What Is This Thing Called Love?	(1929)	Do I Love You?	(1939)
You Do Something To Me	(1929)	Well, Did You Evah?	(1939)
Love for Sale	(1930)	You'd Be So Nice To Come Home To	(1942)
Let's Fly Away	(1930)	Hey, Good Lookin'	(1943)
Night and Day	(1932)	Ev'ry Time We Say Goodbye	(1944)
The Physician (He Never Said He Loved Me)	(1933)	Count Your Blessings	(1944)
Solomon	(1933)	Don't Fence Me In	(1944)
I Get a Kick Out of You	(1934)	Another Op'nin', Another Show	(1948)
Miss Otis Regrets	(1934)	Wunderbar (written earlier)	(1948)
Anything Goes	(1934)	So In Love	(1948)
You're the Top	(1934)	Always True To You In My Fashion	(1948)
Why Shouldn't I?	(1935)	Be a Clown	(1948)
Begin the Beguine	(1935)	I Hate Men	(1948)
Just One of Those Things	(1935)	I Love Paris	(1953)
I've Got You Under My Skin	(1936)	True Love	(1956)
It's De- Lovely	(1936)	Who Wants To Be a Millionnaire?	(1956)
In the Still of the Night	(1937)	You're Sensational	(1956)
My Heart Belongs To Daddy	(1938)		

Appendix 9 - George Gershwin's Compositions

Opera:

Porgy and Bess: Opera in Three Acts. Libretto by Dorothy Heyward and Ira Gershwin. (1935)

Instrumental:

Piano: Rialto Ripples; Rag. (In collaboration with Walter Donaldson).	(1917)
Lullaby for String Quartet.	(1919)
Rhapsody in Blue, for Jazz Band and Pianoforte. Orchestrated by F. Grofé.	(1924)
Novellettes, arranged as a short story by S. Dushkin.	(1925)
Concerto in F for Pianoforte and Orchestra.	(1925)
Preludes.	(1926)
An American in Paris. Tone Poem for Orchestra.	(1928)
Second Rhapsody, for Pianoforte and Orchestra.	(1931)
George Gershwin Song Book (arrangement of 18 songs).	(1932)
Two Waltzes.	(1933)
Cuban Overture (Rhumba) for Orchestra.	(1934)
Catfish Row, Suite. Arrangement for Orchestra of themes from *Porgy and Bess*.	(1936)

Various fragments, e.g. *Three Quarter Blues*.

Stage Shows with George Gershwin's Music:

La-La Lucille	(1919)	Oh, Kay!	(1926)
Morris Gest's Midnight Whirl	(1919)	Strike Up the Band	(1927)
George White's Scandals (1920, 21, 22, 23, 24)		Funny Face	(1927)
Dangerous Maid	(1921)	Rosalie (with Sigmund Romberg)	(1927)
Our Nell	(1922)	Treasure Girl	(1928)
The Rainbow	(1923)	Show Girl	(1929)
Sweet Little Devil	(1924)	Girl Crazy	(1930)
Primrose	(1924)	Of Thee I Sing	(1931)
Lady, Be Good!	(1924)	Pardon My English	(1932)
Tell Me More	(1925)	Let 'Em Eat Cake	(1933)
Tip-Toes	(1925)	Porgy and Bess (Opera)	(1935)
Song of the Flame	(1925)		

Films with George Gershwin's Music:

The Sunshine Trail *	(1923)	Goldwyn Follies	(1938)
Delicious	(1931)	Rhapsody in Blue (biography of	
Shall We Dance?	(1937)	George Gershwin's life)	(1945)
A Damsel in Distress	(1937)	An American in Paris	(1951)

* Theme song and interludes, including *Walking the Dog*, later published as *Promenade*.

George Gershwin's compositions continued on next page . . . .

Appendix 9

George Gershwin's compositions (contd.)

Songs:

The Real American Folk Song	(1918)	Embraceable You	(1930)
Swanee	(1919)	Summertime	(1935)
The Half of It, Dearie, Blues	(1924)	It Ain't Necessarily So	(1935)
The Man I Love (not used until later)	(1924)	I Got Plenty o' Nuttin'	(1935)
Oh, Lady Be Good	(1924)	Bess, You Is My Woman Now	(1935)
Somebody Loves Me	(1924)	Let's Call the Whole Thing Off	(1937)
That Certain Feeling	(1925)	They All Laughed	(1937)
Looking for a Boy	(1925)	They Can't Take That Away From Me	(1937)
Clap Yo' Hands	(1926)	Nice Work if You Can Get It	(1937)
Do, Do, Do	(1926)	A Foggy Day	(1937)
Someone To Watch Over Me	(1926)	Shall We Dance?	(1937)
Strike Up the Band	(1927)	Slap That Bass	(1937)
'S Wonderful	(1927)	Love Walked In	(1938)
How Long Has This Been Going On?	(1928)	Our Love Is Here To Stay	(1938)
Liza	(1929)		
I Got Rhythm	(1930)		

Appendix 10 - 'Fats' Waller's Compositions

Concert pieces:

London Suite: Whitechapel, Limehouse, Soho, Piccadilly, Chelsea, Bond Street.
Boogie Woogie Suite (for piano): Boogie-Woogie Blues; Boogie-Woogie Stomp; Boogie-Woogie Rag; Boogie-Woogie Jump.

Other compositions: These are in many cases available as piano pieces or songs. Sometimes the words of the songs are by Fats Waller himself and sometimes with various collaborators.

Wildcat Blues	(1923)	Handful of Keys	(1932)
Squeeze Me	(1925)	Vipers Drag	(1934)
Chinese Blues	(1926)	Numb Fumblin'	(1935)
Fats Waller Stomp	(1927)	Stealin' Apples	(1936)
St. Louis Shuffle	(1927)	Fractious Fingering	(1938)
Darkies' Lament	(1927)	Bach Up To Me	(1938)
Alligator Crawl	(1927)	Black Raspberry Jam	(1938)
Come On and Stomp, Stomp, Stomp	(1927)	Latch On	(1938)
My Fate Is in Your Hands	(1928)	Cottage in the Rain	(1938)
Sweet Savannah Sue	(1928)	The Joint Is Jumpin'	(1938)
Valentine Stomp	(1929)	Paswonky	(1938)
What Did I Do To Be So Black and Blue?	(1929)	Honey Hush	(1939)
Blue, Turning Grey Over You	(1929)	Happy Feeling	(1940)
I've Got a Feeling I'm Falling	(1929)	China Jumps	(1941)
Ain't Misbehavin'	(1929)	Sneakin' Home	(1941)
Honeysuckle Rose	(1929)	Palm Garden	(1941)
Smashing Thirds	(1931)	Wandrin' Aroun'	(1941)
I'm Crazy 'Bout My Baby	(1931)	Falling Castle	(1941)
Keepin' Out of Mischief Now	(1932)		

Organ solos:

The Rusty Pail	(1927)
Lenox Avenue Blues	(1927)
Hog Maw Stomp	(1928)
I Got Rhythm	(1930)

Index

Abbott, Bud, 162.
Abercrombie, Dr., 111.
Adams, John, 2.
Alda, Robert, 142.
Ambrose, Bert, 160.
Andrews Sisters, The, 29.
Arden, Victor, 136.
Arlen, Harold, 67.
Armstrong, Louis, 104, 124, 154, 155, 156, 157, 163.
Astaire, Adele, 80, 118, 132, 136, 137.
Astaire, Fred, 33, 64, 65, 66, 67, 68, 80, 85, 86, 87, 117-118, 122, 132, 136, 137, 138, 140.

Bach, Johann Sebastian, 30, 131.
Baker, James (pseudonym of George Gershwin), 132.
Baline, Israel (Izzy), 73-76; see Berlin, Irving.
Baline, Leah, 73, 77, 78, 79, 82.
Baline, Moses, 73, 74.
Ball, Ernest, 55.
Ball, Lucille, 122.
Barrett, Kitty (Mrs. Thomas Barrett), 32, 37.
Barrett, May, 32, 37.
Barrett, Mr. (Thomas's father), 29.
Barrett, Steve, 30.
Barrett, Thomas Augustine;
see Stuart, Leslie, 29 - 32, 39.
Basie, William 'Count', 104, 151.
Battenburg, Prince Louis of, 75.
Beatles, The, 29.
Beethoven, Ludvig van, 21, 27, 30, 46, 120, 131.
Bennett, Robert Russell, 67, 123.
Berlin, Elizabeth Iris, 84.
Berlin, Irving (b. Israel Baline), 53, 56, 59, 65, 70, 73-90, 109, 112, 116, 117, 118, 120, 123, 129, 131, 132, 133, 140, 152.
Berlin, Irving, Inc., Music Publishers, 81.
Berlin, Irving jr., 84.
Berlin, Linda Louise, 84.
Berlin, Mary Ellin, 84.
Berlin, Mrs. Irving:
  I: Dorothy (née Goetz), 79.
  II: Ellin (née Mackay), 83, 84, 85, 89, 90.
Bernstein, Leonard, 31.
Bertrand, Mabel (Mrs. Ferdinand Morton), 103.
Bishop, Sir Henry, 12.
Bizet, Georges, 15, 17.
Blake, Eubie, 151.
Bledsoe, Jules, 63.
'Blind Sol', 75.
Bolger, Ray, 67.
Bolton, Guy, 58, 60, 61, 69, 133.
Bradford, Perry, 154.
Brookfield, Charles, 35.
Brooks, Wilson, 150.
Bruskin, Rose (Mrs. Morris Gershovitz), 129, 130, 131.
Buchanan, Jack, 62, 119.

Caesar, Irving, 133, 134, 136.
Cantor, Eddie, 78, 81.
Carbonel, Louis-Mathieu (Cécile Chaminade's husband), 21, 22.
Carey, 'Papa' Mutt, 107.
Carus, Emma, 78.
Caryll, Ivan, 31.
Castle, Vernon and Irene, 100.
Chabrier, Emmanuel, 15, 18.
Chamberlain, Neville, 85.
Chaminade, Camille, 15, 17.
Chaminade, Cécile Louise Stéphanie, 15 - 27.
Chaminade, Henri, 16, 17.
Chaminade, Madame (Cécile's mother), 15, 16, 17, 18, 20, 21, 22.
Chaminade, Monsieur (Cécile's father), 15, 16, 17, 19.
Chappell Music Co. Ltd., 119.
Chaplin, Charles, 137, 141.
Chauvin, Louis, 100.
Chevalier, Maurice, 119, 124, 137.
Chisholm, George, 159.
Chopin, Frédéric, 20, 26, 27, 131.
Christy, E. P., 8.
Churchill, Winston, 86.
Clooney, Rosemary, 89.
Cole, Kate (Mrs. Samuel Porter), 110.

187

The Melody Lingers On

Cole, James Omar, 109, 110, 111, 112, 113, 114, 115, 116, 126.
Cole, James Omar jr., 126.
Cole, Louis, 110.
Cole, Rachel (née Henton), 110.
Collins, Lottie, 31.
Costello, Lou, 162.
Coward, Noël, 137.
Crane, Clinton, 114, 116.
Crosby, Bing, 11, 83, 84, 86, 87, 119, 124.

Dale, Alan, 57.
Damrosch, Walter, 135, 138.
Davis, James ('Owen Hall'), 34.
Debussy, Claude, 131.
de Groot (violinist), 36.
Delius, Frederick, 142.
Dempsey, Jack, 137.
Desmond, Florence, 159.
deSylva, Buddy, 137.
Dickens, Charles, 5, 7.
Dickson, Dorothy, 60.
Dillingham, Charles, 62.
Dolin, Anton, 123.
Donaldson, Walter, 81.
Dorsey, Tommy, 122.
Dreyfus, Max, 56, 57, 115, 133.
Dvorak, Antonin, 12, 13.

Echo, Eulalie, 93, 95, 96, 106.
Eddy, Nelson, 119, 120.
Edward VII, HRH King, 34.
Edward (above), when Prince of Wales, 35.
Elgar, Sir Edward, 32, 34.
Elizabeth, HRH Princess, 86.
Elizabeth II, HRH Queen, 33.
Elizabeth, Queen (now the Queen Mother), 86.
Ellington, Duke, 104, 154.
Elliott, G. H., 38, 39.
Elman, Mischa, 135.
Etting, Ruth, 84.

Fairbanks, Douglas, 137.
Ferdinand of Spain, King, 93.
Fields, Dorothy, 69.
Fields, Lew, 113.
Firth, Pond & Co., New York, 7, 10.
Fontaine, Joan, 140.

Formby, George, 60.
Foster, Ann Eliza, 1, 2, 13.
Foster, Charlotte, 1, 2.
Foster, Dunning, 1, 2, 6, 9, 10.
Foster, Eliza, 1, 2, 4, 10.
Foster, Henrietta, 1, 13.
Foster, Henry Baldwin, 1, 7, 10, 12, 13.
Foster, James, 1.
Foster, Jane, (Mrs. Stephen Foster; née McDowell), 7, 8, 9, 10, 12, 13.
Foster, Marion, 7, 8, 10, 13.
Foster, Morrison, 1, 2, 3, 5, 7, 8, 10, 12, 13.
Foster, Stephen Collins, 1 - 13, 39, 41, 157.
Foster, William (adopted brother), 2, 4, 10, 11.
Foster, William Barclay, 1, 3, 4, 5, 6, 10.
Foster, William Barclay jr., 1.
Foster Welsh, Marion; see Foster, Marion, 13.
Francis, Arthur (pseudonym of Ira Gershwin), 136.
Franck, César, 17.
Frohman, Charles, 57, 59.
Furber, Edna, 62.

Garland, Ed, 107.
Garland, Judy, 87, 88.
George V, HRH King, 75.
George VI, HRH King, 86.
Gershovitz, Morris, 129, 130.
Gershovitz, Rose (née Bruskin), 129, 130, 131, 142.
Gershwin, Arthur (b. Gershvin), 130, 136.
Gershwin, Frances (b. Gershvin), 130, 136, 141.
Gershwin, George (b. Jacob Gershvin), 53, 56, 60, 64, 66, 67, 78, 80, 85, 109, 117, 118, 120, 129 - 142, 152, 158.
Gershwin, Ira (b. Israel Gershvin), 56, 64, 68, 129, 130, 131, 133, 134, 136, 138, 139, 140, 142.
Gibbons, Carroll, 160.
Gilbert, W.S., 139.
Godard, Benjamin, 18.
Goddard, Paulette, 141.
Godowsky, Frances (née Gershvin), 141.
Godowsky, Leopold, 130, 135, 138, 155.
Godowsky, Leopold, jr., 130.

Index

Goetz, Dorothy (Mrs. Irving Berlin I), 79, 116.
Goetz, Raymond, 79, 116.
Golden, John, 113.
Gonella, Nat, 160.
Gonzales, Anita, 101, 107.
Goodman, Benny, 98.
Grable, Betty, 122.
Grainger, Percy, 27, 50.
Grant, Cary, 123.
Grayson, Kathryn, 124.
Green, John, 67.
Green, Richard (Dick), 67, 68.
Grossmith, George jr., 36, 57.
Gumble, Mose, 131.

Hackett, Edith (Mrs. Thomas Waller I), 150, 151.
Hale, Binnie, 62, 64.
Hall, Adelaide, 160.
Hall, Owen (pseudonym of James Davis), 34, 35.
Hambitzer, Charles, 131, 133.
Hamilton, Cosmo, 36.
Hamilton, Henry, 35.
Hammerstein, Oscar II, 62, 63, 66, 67, 68, 69, 70, 87.
Hammerstein, William, 67.
Handy, W. C., 156.
Harbach, Otto, 62, 64.
Harms, T. B. & Co., 56, 119.
Harris, Reuben, 150.
Harris, Sam H., 82.
Hart, Lorenz, 68.
Hart, Moss, 118, 123.
Harty, Sir Hamilton, 139.
Hawkins, Coleman, 163,
Hawthawne Sisters, The, 32.
Hayworth, Rita, 68, 122.
Heifetz, Jascha, 135, 137, 138.
Henderson, Fletcher, 155.
Henton, Rachel (Mrs. J. O. Cole), 110.
Herbert, Victor, 82, 133, 135.
Hewitt, John, 9.
Heyden, Belle (Mrs. Scott Joplin I), 45.
Heyden, Scott, 45.
Heyward, Dorothy, 139.
Heyward, Dubose, 139.
Hicks, Sir Seymour, 57.
Hitchcock, Raymond, 115.

Hitler, Adolf, 67.
Hoffman, Carl, 44.
Hoffman, Josef, 131, 138.
Hope, Bob, 64.
Humiston, William Henry, 26.
Hunter, Thomas, 3.
Hutton, Betty, 88.

Ireland, John, 137, 142.
Isabella of Spain, Queen, 93.

Jack 'The Bear', 151.
Jackson, Jack, 160.
Jackson, Tony, 96.
Jefferson, Thomas, 2.
Joachim, Joseph, 20.
Johnson, James P., 150, 151, 152, 153, 154, 155, 156, 163.
Jolson, Al, 78, 79, 80, 81, 83, 84, 133, 134, 142.
Joplin, Florence Givens, 41.
Joplin, Jiles (or Giles), 41.
Joplin, Scott, 41 - 51, 100.
Joplin, Mrs. Scott:
  I: Belle (née Heyden), 45, 47.
  II: Lottie (née Stokes), 47, 49, 50, 51.
Joplin, Scott, Music Publishing Co., New York City, 48.

Kakeles, Fannie, 53.
Kaye, Danny, 122.
Keel, Howard, 124.
Keeton, Buster and parents, 75.
Kelly, Edie, 57.
Kelly, Gene, 68, 87, 122.
Kelly, Grace, 124.
Kern, Bertram, 53.
Kern, Charles, 53.
Kern, Edwin, 53, 55, 57.
Kern, Elizabeth Jane (Betty), 59, 61, 64, 65, 67, 68, 69, 70.
Kern, Eva (Mrs. Jerome Kern), 58, 59, 61, 63, 64, 65, 66, 69, 70.
Kern, Fannie (née Kakeles), 53, 57.
Kern, Henry, 53, 55, 57.
Kern, Irving, 53.
Kern, Jerome David, 35, 53 - 70, 85, 87, 109, 112, 113, 117, 118, 129, 132, 133, 140, 141.
Kern, Joseph, 53, 55, 57.

Kern, Milton, 53.
Kilenyi, Edward, 133.
King, Porter, 98.
Kirkeby, Ed, 159, 160, 161, 162, 163.
Kleber, Henry, 5.
Koechlin, Charles, 116.
Korda, Alexander, 86.
Kreisler, Fritz, 135, 138.
Krell, William H., 43.

Lamb, Joseph, 47.
La Menthe, F. P., 93, 94.
La Menthe, Ferdinand Joseph; see Morton, Ferdinand 'Jelly Roll', 93 - 98.
La Menthe, Mrs. F. P., (née Monette, Louise), 93, 95.
Lamour, Dorothy, 66.
Lamoureux, Charles, 18.
Laska, Edward, 57.
Lawrence, Gertrude, 137.
Le Couppey, Félix, 16, 19.
Lehár, Franz, 36.
Levant, Oscar, 142.
Lincoln, Abraham, 134.
Liszt, Franz, 27, 131.
Liza and her Shufflin' Six, 151.
Lockett, Adeline (Mrs. Edward Waller), 145.
Lomax, Alan, 105.
Lorel, Antoinette, 25.
Loss, Joe, 160.
Low, Joshua, 83.
Lupino, Ida, 119.
Lyceum Music Co., New York, 55, 56.

McCormack, John, 135.
MacDonald, Ballard, 137.
McDowell, Dr. A. N., 7, 10.
MacDowell, Edward, 20.
McDowell, Jane (Mrs. Stephen Foster), 7.
Mack, Cecil, 153.
Mackay, Clarence, 82, 83, 84.
Mackay, Ellin (Mrs. Irving Berlin II), 82 - 83.
McKinney's Cotton Pickers, 155.
MacLaine, Shirley, 124.
Macqueen-Pope, W., 32, 34, 38.
Marbury, Elizabeth, 113.
Margaret Rose, HRH Princess, 86.
Marion, George, 161.

Markova, Alicia, 123.
Marks, Edward B., 55.
Marshall, Arthur, 43.
Martin, Mary, 123.
Matthews, Jessie, 68.
Mayer, Louis B., 120.
Melba, Dame Nellie, 23.
Melrose, Lester and brother, 102.
Mercer, Johnny, 67.
Merman, Ethel, 88, 89, 119, 122, 138.
Milhaud, Darius, 116.
Miller, Marilyn, 60, 62.
Miller, Max, 159.
Millet & Co., New York, 6.
Mills Brothers, The, 159, 160.
Mitropoulos, Dimitri, 161.
Monette, Gus, 93.
Monette, Henri, 93.
Monette, Laura (née Pechet), 93, 95.
Monette, Louise, (Mrs. F. P. La Menthe), 93.
Monette, Margaret, 93.
Monette, Nelusco, 93.
Monette, Neville, 93.
Monette, Viola, 93.
Monckton, Lionel, 31, 36.
Monroe, Marilyn, 81.
Morris, George P., 5.
Morton, Amède, 95.
Morton, Ferdinand Joseph ('Jelly Roll'), 93 - 107, 155.
Morton, Mimi, 95.
Morton, Mr. (Ferdinand's step-father), 95, 98.
Morton, Mrs. Ferdinand (née Bertrand, Mabel), 103, 104, 105, 106, 107.
Mountbatten, Lady Edwina, 86, 137.
Mountbatten, Lord Louis, 137.
Mozart, Wolfgang Amadeus, 51.
Mullins, Maizie, 149, 150.
Murtha, Fred (pseudonym of George Gershwin), 132.

Neagle, Anna, 67.
Nicholson, Nick, 76.
Nickerson, Professor, 94.
Nilsson, Christine (Kristina), 12.

Ohman, Phil, 136.
Ory, 'Kid', 107.

Index

Paderewski, Ignace, 32, 131, 149.
Paley, William, 158.
Patti, Adelina, 12, 32.
Pechet, Felicie, 93.
Pechet, Laura, 93.
Pechet, Pierre, 93.
Pentland, Susan, 5, 9.
Perry, A. W., 44, 46.
Perry, Edward, 21.
Perry, Miss, 148, 151.
Peters & Co., Pittsburgh, 6.
Pine, Olivia, 3.
Ponce, William, 157, 159.
Porter, Cole, 53, 85, 109 - 126, 129.
Porter, Kate (Mrs. Samuel Porter, née Cole), 110, 111, 113, 124.
Porter, Mrs. Cole (née Thomas, Linda Lee), 114, 115, 116, 118, 120, 121, 123, 124, 126.
Porter, Samuel Fenwick, 110, 116, 126.
Potter, Paul, 35.
Powell, Eleanor, 67, 119, 122.
Previn, André, 31.

Rachmaninov, Sergei, 135.
Ravel, Maurice, 131, 138.
Ray, Ted, 160.
Razaf, Andy, 153, 154, 156.
Remick, Jerome H., Music Corporation, New York, 80, 112, 131, 132, 133.
Rifkin, Joshua, 51.
Roberts, Luckey, 151.
Robeson, Paul, 63, 65.
Robinson, Bill 'Bojangles', 158.
Rodgers, Richard, 68, 69, 87.
Rogers, Ginger, 64, 65, 67, 85, 118, 138, 140.
Romberg, Sigmund, 113, 120, 132, 134.
Rose, Billy, 123.
Rosenthal, Moriz, 135.
Rosenzweig, (Rosen), Maxie, 130, 131.
Ross, Edmundo, 159.
Rubinstein, Anton, 130.
Rubinstein, Beryl, 134.
Rutherford, Anita (Mrs. Thomas Waller II), 154.

Salter, Mike, 75.
Savard, Emmanuel, 17, 18.
Schirmer, G., Inc., New York, 113.

Schoenberg, Arnold, 141.
Schumann, Clara Wieck, 23.
Schwartz, Arthur, 68.
Schwartz, Jean, 55.
Scott, Bud, 94.
Scott, James, 47, 100.
Shaw, Artie, 68, 118.
Shaw, Steven Kern, 68.
Shore, Dinah, 162.
Short, Edward, 31.
Simeon, Omer, 103.
Sinatra, Frank, 69, 124.
Sirmay, Dr. Albert, 119.
Skelton, Red, 122.
Smith, Kate, 85, 86.
Smith, Mamie, 153.
Smith, Willie 'The Lion', 151, 152.
Snyder, Ted, 76, 77.
Sousa, John Philip, 23, 82, 135.
Stark, John, 44, 45, 46, 48, 50, 51.
Steinert, Alexander, 119.
Stephens, Ward, 24.
Stewart, James, 119.
Stokes, Lottie (Mrs. Scott Joplin II), 47.
Stone, Lew, 160.
Story, Alderman Sidney, 95.
Stratton, Eugene, 33, 34, 35, 36, 38.
Strauss, Richard, 20.
Stravinsky, Igor, 123.
Struthers, John, 3.
Stuart, Dave, 107.
Stuart, Leslie (b. Thomas A. Barrett), 29 - 39.
Sullivan, Sir Arthur, 30.
Swope, Herbert Bayard, 75.

Tate, Erskine, 155.
Terriss, Ellaline, 31.
Thomas, Ambroise, 18.
Thomas, Edward Russell, 114.
Thomas, Lester, (pseudonym of Thomas A. Barrett), 30.
Thomas, Linda Lee; see Mrs. Cole Porter, 114, 115.
Thompson, Spencer, 152.
Tilley, Vesta, 32.
Tilzer, Harry von, 75, 132.
Tucker, Sophie, 122.
Turkey, Sultan of, 20.

Valentino, Rudolph, 37.
Vallee, Rudy, 84.
Victoria, HRH Queen, 20, 32, 33, 34.

Waller, Adeline (née Lockett), 145, 146, 147, 148, 150.
Waller, Alfred Winslow, 145, 146.
Waller, Anita; see Mrs. Thomas Waller II.
Waller, Charles A., 145.
Waller, Edith; see Mrs. Thomas Waller I.
Waller, Edith Salome, 146, 147.
Waller, Edward, 145, 146, 147, 149, 150, 156.
Waller, Edward Lawrence, 145, 146, 149.
Waller, Esther, 146.
Waller, Maurice Thomas, 155, 157, 163.
Waller, May Naomi, 145, 146, 147, 148, 149.
Waller, Ronald, 156, 157, 159, 163.
Waller, Ruth Adeline, 145.
Waller, Samuel, 146.
Waller, Thomas Wright ('Fats'), 145 - 164.
Waller, Mrs. Thomas Wright,
  I: Edith (née Hackett), 150, 151, 152, 154, 163.
  II: Anita (née Rutherford), 154, 155, 156, 157, 159, 161, 163.
Waller, Thomas jr., 152, 154, 163.
Waller, William Robert, 145, 146, 148.
Wanamaker's Music Store, 55.
Washington, Fred, 107.
Waterson, Henry, 77.
Waterson, Berlin & Snyder Co., New York, 77, 80.
Whistler, James, 134.
Whiteman, Paul, 134, 135, 142, 152, 156, 158.
Wiley, Mrs; see Foster, Mrs. Jane, 12, 13.
Williams, Clarence, 152, 153, 163.
Williams, John, 31.
Williams, Spencer, 157, 159.
Williams, Zack, 101.
Willig Music Co., Philadelphia, 5.
Wodehouse, P.G., 57, 59, 60, 61, 62, 133.
Wolff, D. & Co., New York, 54, 55.
Wright, Kenneth, 137.
Wynn, Bert (pseudonym of George Gershwin), 132.

Youmans, Vincent, 60.

Young, Robert, 67.

Ziegfeld, Florenz, 60, 62.
Zimbalist, Efrem, 138.
Zoppola, Countesse di, 120.